From Eden
to the
New Jerusalem

From Eden to the New Jerusalem

AN INTRODUCTION
TO BIBLICAL THEOLOGY

T. DESMOND ALEXANDER

Kregel
Academic & Professional

From Eden to the New Jerusalem

© 2008 by T. Desmond Alexander

T. Desmond Alexander has asserted his right under the Copyright, Designs and Patent Act, 1988, to be identified as the Author of this work.

Published in the United States of America in 2009 by Kregel Publications, a division of Kregel, Inc., P.O. Box 2607, Grand Rapids, MI 49501, by permission of Inter-Varsity Press, Leicester, England.

British Library Cataloguing in Publication Data
A catalogue record for this book is available from the British Library.

ISBN 978-0-8254-2015-3

Printed in the United States of America

09 10 11 12 13 / 5 4 3 2 1

CONTENTS

Preface 7

1. Introduction 9

2. From sacred garden to holy city: experiencing the
   presence of God 13
   Overview 15
   The motif of temple 19
   The temple-garden of Eden 20
   The tabernacle 31
   The Jerusalem temple 42
   The church as temple 60

3. Thrown from the throne: re-establishing the
   sovereignty of God 74
   The throne of God 75
   Adam and Eve as God's viceroys 76
   The theocracy of Israel 80
   The church and the kingdom of God 89

4. Dealing with the devil: destroying the source of evil 98
   The dragon who is the devil and Satan 99
   Ruler of this world 100
   The ancient serpent 102
   The kings of the earth 109
   Satan defeated 111
   Satan's reign ended 117
   Resisting the devil 118

5. **The slaughter of the Lamb: accomplishing the**
   redemption of creation   121
   The Lamb   121
   Christ, our Passover Lamb   125
   The Passover in Exodus   127
   Atonement   130
   Purification   132
   Sanctification   134

6. **Feasting from the tree of life: reinvigorating the**
   lives of people from every nation   138
   Holy people in the New Jerusalem   139
   Holiness and wholeness   151
   The tree of life   155
   Ecological transformation   157
   Social transformation   163

7. **Strong foundations and solid walls: living securely**
   among the people of God   171
   Old and New Testaments united   172
   Genuine hope   174
   A tale of two cities   175

8. **Conclusion**   188

   Select bibliography   193
   Index of Biblical References   202

PREFACE

This study began life as a short course exploring what Revelation 20 – 22 reveals about life after death. In unpacking this, two things became evident: (1) the biblical description of our future existence has more in common with our present life than most people assume; (2) the concluding chapters of Revelation offer a window through which the main themes of the biblical meta-story may be studied. I hope both of these observations will be demonstrated in the chapters that follow.

It goes without saying that no one is an island. The ideas contained in this study have been shaped and coloured by many others. If their present formulation proves instructive and enables others to see further, it is due only to the author being lifted as a child upon the shoulders of giants. The footnotes that accompany the main text go some way towards acknowledging my indebtedness to many scholars, even when on occasions I have differed in my interpretation of the evidence. My involvement in two projects, both linked to the Tyndale Fellowship Biblical Theology Study Group, has significantly shaped my own understanding of the Bible. These resulted in the publication of the *New Dictionary of Biblical Theology* (IVP, 2000) and *Heaven on Earth* (Paternoster, 2004). I am indebted to all who contributed to these two volumes, and especially my co-editors: Don Carson, Simon Gathercole, Graeme Goldsworthy and Brian Rosner.

By way of expressing thanks to those who have supported me in the long process by which this book evolved, I would like to mention the following. For many years I have benefited from the excellent administrative support of my secretary within the Institute for Christian Training, Miss Renée McCracken. She has contributed much to the programme of courses run by the Institute and her efficient approach has been of great help to me. I am indebted to Dr Ian Hart for his insightful comments on an initial draft of chapters 2 and 3, and to the staff of IVP, especially Dr Philip Duce, for overseeing the whole process of turning a manuscript into a book. Naturally, however, I alone bear the responsibility for the shortcomings that remain. Words cannot adequately express my appreciation for the support and encouragement I have received from my wife, Anne, and children, Jane and David; their constant love has enriched my life beyond measure. Finally, I wish to dedicate this book to Mrs Catherine Leach as a token of thanks for all the loving care and support she, as a family friend, has graciously lavished upon us.

SOLI DEO GLORIA

T. Desmond Alexander

1. INTRODUCTION

Why does the earth exist? What is the purpose of human life? Arrogant as it may seem, this short book attempts to answer both of these questions. It does so by exploring a unique story.

One of the distinctive features of modern Western culture is the particular emphasis now given to telling one's story. Everyone has a story to tell, although some may be more interesting than others. Undoubtedly, this is a product of a society that has imbibed the postmodern ideology that all truth is relative. In such a world, every story merits a hearing. Yet, no matter how many stories we hear, we may still be left with a sense of emptiness, for few stories address the fundamental questions of life.

Yet, one story stands apart from all the rest. It claims for itself an authority not derived from human beings but from God. As divine revelation it presents us with a meta-story that claims to communicate absolute truth that cannot be discovered by any other means. While the story itself acknowledges that it does not contain all truth, for much truth may be discovered outside it, it claims to answer particular questions that lie beyond scientific investigation.

This unparalleled meta-story comes from an anthology of literature, the Bible, linked by common themes, centred on a unique deity. Produced over many centuries, the differing texts that comprise this library are amazingly diverse in terms of genre, authorship and even language. Nonetheless, they produce a remarkably unified story that addresses two of life's most fundamental questions: (1) Why was the earth created? (2) What is the reason for human existence?

Although the process by which this anthology was created remains something of a mystery, having been assembled in stages over a long period of time, it is widely recognized as producing a very significant meta-story. Although its diversity of authorship and genre give ammunition to those who wish to dismantle the story into contradictory parts, there is more here to unite than divide. The anthology itself, which abounds in intertextual references, provides most of the literary context within which its contents may be understood. There is not a book within the whole collection that can be interpreted satisfactorily in isolation from the rest. Each book contributes something special to the meta-story and, in turn, the meta-story offers a framework within which each book may be best interpreted. In this regard, the long-standing principle of interpreting Scripture by Scripture makes considerable practical sense.

Given the complexity of the Bible as a literary anthology, outlining its meta-story is not easy. The approach adopted here is to begin at the end. As is often the case, a story's conclusion provides a good guide to the themes and ideas dominant throughout. By resolving an intricate plot that runs throughout a story, a good denouement sheds light on the entire story. While recognizing that there are limitations to this approach, it is nevertheless one way of attempting to determine the main elements of the meta-story.

The final chapters of Revelation, which form the starting point for our study, contain visions that look to the future and anticipate the creation of a new earth and a new heaven. As we shall see, this brings to fulfilment a process that started with the creation of the present earth, as described in the opening chapters of Genesis. The very strong links between Genesis 1 – 3 and Revelation 20 – 22 suggest that these passages frame the entire biblical meta-story.

Detailed evidence for this will be provided in the chapters that follow. To base this study on the visions of Revelation 20 – 22 may seem to some to invite major problems at the outset. The apocalyptic nature of these visions requires that caution must be exercised in reading them. Not everything can be taken literally. Jesus Christ is unlikely to resemble an actual lamb and the New Jerusalem may not be a gigantic cube in shape. Due allowance must be given for the symbolic nature of elements within John's visions. This does not mean, however, that everything in the visions must be viewed as merely symbolic. As I shall argue, the new earth and the new heavens are very likely to have much in common with the present cosmos.

This brief study does not attempt to be exhaustive, but rather indicative, outlining some of the central themes that run throughout the Bible. Overall, the material is presented using broad brush strokes designed to show the general shape of the meta-story. Where others, to the author's knowledge, have provided a more detailed discussion, reference is made in footnotes. In places it has become evident that further research still needs to be undertaken to produce a more refined understanding. In attempting to delineate the major themes of the biblical meta-story, I am conscious that aspects of what follows may need to be emended in the light of constructive criticism and/or further evidence.

There is something of value in seeing the big picture, for it frequently enables us to appreciate the details more clearly. The scholarly tendency to 'atomize' biblical texts is often detrimental to understanding them. By stripping passages out of their literary contexts meanings are imposed upon them that were never intended by their authors. I hope this study goes a little way to redressing this imbalance, for biblical scholarship as a whole has not articulated clearly the major themes that run throughout Scripture. Since these themes were an integral part of the thought world of the biblical authors, an appreciation of them may significantly alter our reading of individual books.

Good theology always has pastoral implications. Doctrine and praxis ought to be closely related. For this reason, our study of the main themes of the biblical meta-story occasionally moves into

the area of application. The truths revealed are extremely important for shaping the lifestyle choices we make. However, because
the application of scriptural truth often needs to take into account
cultural diversity, the observations made here are suggestive rather
than comprehensive.

2. FROM SACRED GARDEN TO HOLY CITY: EXPERIENCING THE PRESENCE OF GOD

As the book of Revelation moves towards a conclusion, the apostle John recounts one final, fascinating vision to add to those he has already witnessed. He introduces it with these words:

> Then I saw a new heaven and a new earth, for the first heaven and the first earth had passed away, and the sea was no more. And I saw the holy city, new Jerusalem, coming down out of heaven from God, prepared as a bride adorned for her husband. And I heard a loud voice from the throne saying, 'Behold, the dwelling place of God is with man. He will dwell with them, and they will be his people, and God himself will be with them as their God.' (Rev. 21:1–3)

John's attention is drawn to a holy city that possibly fills the new earth.[1] As the voice from the throne announces, here God will live

---

1. G. K. Beale, *The Temple and the Church's Mission: A Biblical Theology of the Dwelling Place of God*, New Studies in Biblical Theology 17 (Leicester: Apollos, 2004), pp. 23–25, supports this position. J. D. Levenson, *Creation*

alongside human beings.[2] With this remarkable vision of God coming to dwell with humanity on a new earth the biblical meta-story comes to an end.

Yet, the Bible begins with a similar picture. Genesis opens by recounting how God creates an earth, into which he places a human couple, Adam and Eve. This first earth, as I shall argue later, is designed to be a divine residence, for here God intends to coexist with people. However, the divine plan for this first earth is soon disrupted when the human couple, due to their disobedience, are driven from God's presence. The complex story that follows centres on how the earth can once more become a dwelling place shared by God and humanity.

By providing a closely matched beginning and end, the opening chapters of Genesis and the final chapters of Revelation undoubtedly frame the biblical meta-story. To quote Jon Levenson, 'Eschatology is like protology.'[3] Yet, while *Endzeit* resembles *Urzeit*, there is progression. Whereas Genesis presents the earth as a potential building site, Revelation describes a finished city. Underlying the construction of this city is the expectation that God will reside within it, sharing its facilities with people from every nation.

Although it may not be immediately apparent, the theme of

Footnote 1 (*continued*)

    and the Persistence of Evil: The Jewish Drama of Divine Omnipotence (San Francisco: Harper & Row, 1988), pp. 89–90, observes that in Isa. 65:17–18 the name Jerusalem appears to be used as a metonym for 'heaven and earth'.

2. This point is picked up later in Rev. 22:3–4: 'No longer will there be anything accursed, but the throne of God and of the Lamb will be in it, and his servants will worship him. They will see his face, and his name will be on their foreheads.'

3. J. D. Levenson, 'The Temple and the World', *Journal of Religion* 64 (1984), p. 298. In a similar vein, M. Barker, *The Gate of Heaven: The History and Symbolism of the Temple in Jerusalem* (London: SPCK, 1991), p. 68, writes, 'The prophets looked forward to a time when the End would be like the Beginning, and everything would be restored to its original state.'

God's presence on the earth is especially significant for understanding the biblical meta-story. Before focusing on the details, a brief overview may helpfully establish its importance. This will sketch out in general terms the overall pattern that runs from Genesis to Revelation.

Overview

The opening chapters of Genesis assume that the earth will be God's dwelling place.[4] This expectation, however, is swiftly shattered when Adam and Eve disobey God and are expelled from his presence. While people continue to live on the earth, God's presence is associated with heaven.[5] From there he occasionally descends to meet with selected individuals, although these encounters are always relatively brief and sometimes unexpected. When God reveals himself, it is always for a particular purpose. This pattern is found throughout almost all of Genesis and the first half of Exodus.

In the second half of Exodus a major new development occurs, linked to the divine rescue of the enslaved Israelites from Egypt. At Mount Sinai God enters into a special, covenant relationship with the people. This results in the construction of a lavishly decorated tent that becomes God's dwelling place in the midst of the Israelite camp. This event represents a major advance forward in the biblical meta-story, for God now resides permanently with one nation.

---

4. Evidence for this comes in the next section.

5. We see this reflected in Jacob's dream of a ladder ascending to heaven (Gen. 28:12–17). While the title 'God of heaven' is rarely used in the Pentateuch, coming only in Gen. 24:3, 7, it is commonly found in the books of Ezra, Nehemiah and Daniel (Ezra 1:2; 5:11–12; 6:9–10; 7:12, 21, 23; Neh. 1:4–5; 2:4, 20; Dan. 2:18–19, 37, 44). Various psalms speak of God looking down from heaven (Pss 2:4; 11:4; 14:2; 33:13; 53:2). D. E. Gowan, *Eschatology in the Old Testament* (Philadelphia: Fortress, 1986), p. 113, states, 'Heaven thus plays a minor role in OT eschatology compared to its prominence later on.'

Soon after the Israelites' initial settlement in the land of Canaan the tabernacle is set up at Shiloh in the tribal region of Ephraim and appears to have remained there for many years (Josh. 18:1; 1 Sam. 1:3).[6] In due course, according to the books of Samuel, the Shiloh sanctuary is replaced by a new temple constructed in Jerusalem during the reign of Solomon. Dedicated by Solomon in his eleventh year as king (c. 959 BC), this ornately decorated structure becomes God's permanent residence. Due to the temple, the entire walled city of Jerusalem is also perceived as being God's dwelling place. Consequently, for almost 400 years God coexists in a unique way with the citizens of Jerusalem.

A major reversal of this occurs when in 586 BC the Babylonians raze the temple and destroy the walls of Jerusalem. This temporary state of affairs is eventually overturned when the Persian king Cyrus gives permission in 538 BC for exiled Jews to return to Judah and rebuild the temple. While the process is slow, the completed temple is dedicated in 516 BC, but not before the prophets Haggai and Zechariah have had to intervene in order to encourage the people of Judah to complete the reconstruction. As the books of Haggai and Zechariah highlight, the restoration of the temple was divinely sanctioned, underlining God's ongoing commitment to Jerusalem and its population. The walls of the city, however, remain largely in ruins, a situation later remedied when the Persian king Artaxexes I appoints Nehemiah as Governor of Judea in 444 BC. In spite of opposition, Nehemiah oversees the renovation of the city walls. While the evidence is ambiguous,

---

6. While the evidence is limited, several factors suggest that the tabernacle became a permanent fixture at Shiloh. Judg. 18:31 implies that the 'house of God', *bêt-hā'ĕlōhîm*, was located at Shiloh for some time, and 1 Sam. 1:9 refers to Eli sitting at the gate of the 'temple of the LORD', *hêkal yhwh*, in Shiloh. 1 Sam. 1:24 recounts how Samuel was brought to the 'house of the LORD', *bêt-yhwh*, at Shiloh, where he obviously lived for some years. Judg. 21:19 and 1 Sam. 1:3 both suggest that Shiloh was the location to which Israelites travelled annually to celebrate a feast before the Lord. Cf. M. Haran, *Temples and Temple-Service in Ancient Israel* (Oxford: Clarendon, 1978), pp. 198–202.

God was probably perceived as once more dwelling within the city of Jerusalem.[7] The next significant development in the biblical meta-story is the coming of Jesus. As the opening chapter of John's Gospel affirms, Jesus, as God, tabernacles among human beings (John 1:14).[8] The incarnation is a further development of the concept of God living on the earth. For this reason Jesus can speak of his

---

7. Although there are clear statements about God's glory filling the tabernacle (Exod. 40:34–35) and the Solomonic temple (1 Kgs 8:10–11; cf. 2 Chr. 7:1–2), no similar event is described in the biblical literature concerning the temple built after the exile. R. T. Beckwith, 'The Temple Restored', in T. D. Alexander and S. Gathercole (eds.), *Heaven on Earth: The Temple in Biblical Theology* (Carlisle: Paternoster, 2004), p. 72, observes that the 'Second Temple lacked five things which the First Temple possessed, namely, the fire, the ark, the Urim and Thummim, the oil of anointing and the Holy Spirit [of prophecy]'. These items are listed in the Jerusalem Talmud (*Ta'anit* 2.1; *Makkot* 2.4–8) and the Babylonian Talmud (*Yoma* 21b). The absence of these 'visible tokens' of God's presence indicates that the Holy of Holies was empty. M. Barker, *The Great High Priest: The Temple Roots of Christian Liturgy* (London: T. & T. Clark, 2003), p. 147, observes that, according to Josephus, the Holy of Holies was empty when the Roman general Pompey entered it in 63 BC. Barker, *Gate of Heaven*, p. 141, notes that according to *Numbers Rabbah* 15.10, five things would be restored to the temple in the age of the Messiah: the fire, the ark, the menorah, the Spirit and the cherubim. However, according to G. I. Davies, 'The Presence of God in the Second Temple and Rabbinic Doctrine', in W. Horbury (ed.), *Templum Amicitiae*, Journal for the Study of the New Testament, Supplement Series 48 (Sheffield: JSOT Press, 1991), pp. 32–36, there is evidence from the Second Temple period that some Jews considered God to be dwelling in the temple. For example, Matt. 23:21 records Jesus as saying, 'And whoever swears by the temple swears by it and by him who dwells in it.'

8. All of John 1:14, 'And the Word became flesh and dwelt among us, and we have seen his glory, glory as of the only Son from the Father, full of grace and truth,' resonates with vocabulary reminiscent of the tabernacle being filled with the glory of God (see Exod. 40:34–35).

own body as a temple, as in his comment 'Destroy this temple, and in three days I will raise it up' (John 2:19).[9]

The death, resurrection and ascension of Jesus paves the way for another significant step in the process by which God comes to inhabit the earth alongside human beings. Jesus hints at this in his conversation with the woman at the well in Samaria when their discussion focuses on the place where God is to be worshipped.

> The woman said to him, 'Sir, I perceive that you are a prophet. Our fathers worshipped on this mountain, but you say that in Jerusalem is the place where people ought to worship.' Jesus said to her, 'Woman, believe me, the hour is coming when neither on this mountain nor in Jerusalem will you worship the Father.' (John 4:19–21)

With the coming of the Holy Spirit on the day of Pentecost God's presence, previously associated with the Jerusalem temple, is now linked to the newly created church. The church, which quickly comes to include Jews, Samaritans and Gentiles, becomes the new temple of God. Wherever the followers of Jesus meet, God is present with them by his Spirit. Consequently, as the church expands throughout the earth, God's dwelling place is also extended. Coinciding with this new development, as Jesus predicted, the Jerusalem temple is destroyed by the Romans in AD 70.

While the ever-expanding church replaces the Jerusalem temple as God's residence on earth, the biblical meta-story records one further development before the process of God inhabiting the whole earth reaches completion. As the book of Revelation reveals, there is yet to come a time when all that is evil will finally be removed from the present earth. At that stage, when God makes all

---

9. At the trial of Jesus, the witnesses reinterpret what Jesus said. According to Matt. 26:61, 'This man said, "I am able to destroy the temple of God, and to rebuild it in three days."' Mark 14:58 states, 'We heard him say, "I will destroy this temple that is made with hands, and in three days I will build another, not made with hands."' In both of these passages, as in John 2:19, the Greek term for temple is *naos*, which probably refers to the 'inner sanctuary' rather than the whole temple complex.

things new, his presence and glory will fill a rejuvenated earth. This is what John sees in his vision recorded in Revelation 21 – 22.

This brief overview provides a basic framework for understanding how the motif of divine presence on the earth is an important part of the biblical meta-story. I shall now add flesh to these bones by exploring how the associated concept of 'temple' enables us to follow the flow of the biblical story from the sacred Garden of Eden in Genesis to the New Jerusalem of Revelation.

The motif of temple

The description of the New Jerusalem in Revelation 21 – 22 contains features that have strong associations with the temple Solomon constructed. The dimensions of the city and the materials composing it are somewhat peculiar. Revelation 21:15–17 describes them as follows:

> And the one who spoke with me had a measuring rod of gold to measure the city and its gates and walls. The city lies foursquare; its length the same as its width. And he measured the city with his rod, 12,000 stadia. Its length and width and height are equal. He also measured its wall, 144 cubits by human measurement, which is also an angel's measurement. The wall was built of jasper, while the city was pure gold, clear as glass. (Rev. 21:15–18)

As befits the apocalyptic nature of Revelation, the portrayal of the city is far from ordinary. Although the numbers may be symbolic, as is often the case in this type of literature, they nevertheless convey something of the immensity of the city. Its dimensions run to some 1,380 miles (2,220 kilometres) for each side in terms of length, breadth and height.[10] While the very size of the city is

---

10. John records that the distance for each side is '12,000 stadia'. The Greek term *stadios*, from which we derive the English word 'stadium', denotes the track used by athletes in ancient Greece. These tracks, which varied somewhat in length, were on average about 185 metres in length.

striking, even by modern standards,[11] its shape is even more unusual: it is a perfect cube.

The symmetrical dimensions of the New Jerusalem are most unusual for a city. It is as high as it is long or wide. Interestingly, however, the proportions of the city match those of the Holy of Holies, the inner sanctuary of the temple, the only other cube specifically mentioned in the Bible. As 1 Kings 6:20 states, 'The inner sanctuary was twenty cubits long, twenty cubits wide, and twenty cubits high.' The New Jerusalem also resembles the Holy of Holies in that both are made of gold. While, according to 1 Kings 6:20, the inner sanctuary was overlaid with gold, Revelation 21:18 records that 'the city was pure gold'.[12]

As golden cubes, the Holy of Holies and New Jerusalem are clearly connected. Since God dwells inside both of these structures, we may reasonably conclude that the entire New Jerusalem is an expanded Holy of Holies.[13] This idea is reflected in Revelation 21:22: 'And I saw no temple in the city, for its temple is the Lord God the Almighty and the Lamb.' By associating the temple with God, John appears to imply that the whole city is a sanctuary.[14] Undoubtedly, in John's vision the New Jerusalem is portrayed as a temple-city. This end-time picture takes on special significance when we consider what the whole biblical meta-story says about the earth as God's dwelling place.

The temple-garden of Eden

Having observed that the New Jerusalem is a gigantic temple-city in which God lives, it is noteworthy that the Garden of Eden is

---

11. The base of the New Jerusalem is half the size of the continent of Europe.

12. The main furnishings of the tabernacle were also gold-plated. In the Bible, gold is often associated with the divine presence.

13. We shall see later that the Holy of Holies was perceived as a mini-cosmos and as such modelled God's design for the real cosmos.

14. The Greek term *naos*, here translated 'temple', refers to the sanctuary.

portrayed in the opening chapters of Genesis as a divine sanctuary. As Gordon Wenham observes:

> The garden of Eden is not viewed by the author of Genesis simply as a piece of Mesopotamian farmland, but as an archetypal sanctuary, that is a place where God dwells and where man should worship him. Many of the features of the garden may also be found in later sanctuaries, particularly the tabernacle or Jerusalem temple. These parallels suggest that the garden itself is understood as a sort of sanctuary.[15]

While Wenham views the garden as a 'sort of sanctuary', it may be more accurate to designate it a temple-garden, adopting John Walton's suggestion that the garden is attached to Eden, with Eden itself being the temple.[16]

The case for Eden being a divine residence rests largely on the striking parallels that exist between the garden and later Israelite sanctuaries. Wenham helpfully lists the main similarities between the Garden of Eden and the tabernacle and/or Jerusalem temple:[17]

- Eden and the later sanctuaries were entered from the east and

---

15. G. J. Wenham, 'Sanctuary Symbolism in the Garden of Eden Story', *Proceedings of the World Congress of Jewish Studies* 9 (1986), p. 19.

16. J. H. Walton, 'Eden, Garden of', in T. D. Alexander and D. W. Baker (eds.), *Dictionary of the Old Testament: Pentateuch* (Downers Grove: IVP; Leicester: IVP, 2003), p. 202, observes that in Gen. 2:10 'the water flows *from* Eden and waters the garden'.

17. Wenham, 'Sanctuary Symbolism', pp. 19–25. A largely overlapping list is provided by G. K. Beale, 'The Final Vision of the Apocalypse and its Implications for a Biblical Theology of the Temple', in T. D. Alexander and S. Gathercole (eds.), *Heaven on Earth: The Temple in Biblical Theology* (Carlisle: Paternoster, 2004), pp. 197–199; cf. Beale, *Temple and the Church's Mission*, pp. 66–80; 'Eden, the Temple, and the Church's Mission in the New Creation', *Journal of the Evangelical Theological Society* 48 (2005), pp. 7–10.

guarded by cherubim (Gen. 3:24; Exod. 25:18–22; 26:31; 36:35; 1 Kgs 6:23–29; 2 Chr. 3:14).[18]

- The tabernacle menorah (or lampstand) possibly symbolizes the tree of life (Gen. 2:9; 3:22; cf. Exod. 25:31–35).[19] Arboreal decorations adorned the temple.[20]
- The Hebrew verbs *'ābad*, 'to serve, till', and *šāmar*, 'to keep, observe, guard', used in God's command to the man 'to work it (the garden) and take care of it' (Gen. 2:15), are found in combination elsewhere in the Pentateuch only in passages that

18. Barker, *Gate of Heaven*, p. 57, writes, 'Solomon built the temple as a garden sanctuary; the walls of the *hekal* were decorated with golden palm trees and flowers, set with precious stones; the bronze pillars were decorated with pomegranate patterns and the great lamp was a stylized almond tree.'

19. C. L. Meyers, *The Tabernacle Menorah: A Synthetic Study of a Symbol from the Biblical Cult*, American Schools of Oriental Research Dissertation Series 2 (Missoula: Scholars Press, 1976), pp. 169–172.

20. V. Hurowitz, 'YHWH's Exalted House: Aspects of the Design and Symbolism of Solomon's Temple', in J. Day (ed.), *Temple and Worship in Biblical Israel*, Library of Hebrew Bible / Old Testament Studies 422 (London: T. & T. Clark, 2005), p. 84, draws attention to the treelike decorations on the two pillars that stood by the entrance to the sanctuary. He writes, 'Finally, we must bear in mind that the columns were topped with capitals bearing floral and arboreal elements (*šûšan*, "lily"; *rimmōnîm*, "pomegranates"; *śĕbākîm*, "tangled branches"). They are, in fact, stylized trees. To be sure, columns at the entrances of temples are referred to in ancient Near Eastern literature and depicted on numerous terra cotta temple models found in the land of Israel. I would like to conjecture, however, that in the context of a Temple reflecting a divine garden, these two treelike columns, standing at the entrance to the Temple in the middle of the court, may have represented the two trees which, according to the tradition reflected in J, were at the middle of the Garden of Eden (Gen. 2.9b, translating according to the Masoretic accentuation and Onqelos): "And the Tree of Life was in the middle of the garden, as was the Tree of Knowledge of Good and Evil."'

While Hurowitz's proposal is interesting, it is unnecessary to establish a link between the temple and Eden. Even if this specific suggestion is rejected, there are still sufficient points of contact to connect the two.

describe the duties of the Levities in the sanctuary (cf. Num. 3:7–8; 8:26; 18:5–6).[21]

• Gold and onyx, mentioned in Genesis 2:11–12, are used extensively to decorate the later sanctuaries and priestly garments (e.g. Exod. 25:7, 11, 17, 31).[22] Gold, in particular, is one of the main materials used in the construction of the tabernacle and the temple.

Two further features add weight to these observations, although by themselves they are inconclusive:

• The Lord God walks in Eden as he later does in the tabernacle (Gen. 3:8; cf. Lev. 26:12; Deut. 23:15; 2 Sam. 7:6–7).
• The river flowing from Eden (Gen. 2:10) is reminiscent of Ezekiel 47:1–12, which envisages a river flowing from a future Jerusalem temple and bringing life to the Dead Sea. The fact that Eden must be an elevated location, possibly a mountain, also supports the idea that it is a sanctuary, for God's presence is frequently associated with mountains.[23]

---

21. U. Cassuto, *Commentary on Genesis*, vol. 1 (Jerusalem: Magnes, 1964), pp. 122–123.
22. There are about one hundred references to gold and seven to onyx in the Exodus account of the building of the tabernacle. Various precious stones are also associated with Eden in Ezek. 28:13.
23. Ezek. 28:13–16 refers to 'Eden, the garden of God' as 'the holy mountain of God'. For a fuller discussion of the links between sanctuary and mountain, see J. M. Lundquist, 'The Common Temple Ideology of the Ancient Near East', in T. G. Madsen (ed.), *Temple in Antiquity: Ancient Records and Modern Perspectives*, The Religious Studies Monograph Series 9 (Provo, Utah: Religious Studies Center, Brigham Young University, 1984), pp. 59–60; R. J. Clifford, 'The Temple and the Holy Mountain', in T. G. Madsen (ed.), *Temple in Antiquity: Ancient Records and Modern Perspectives*, The Religious Studies Monograph Series 9 (Provo, Utah: Religious Studies Center, Brigham Young University, 1984), pp. 107–124; Beale, *Temple and the Church's Mission*, pp. 145–148.

While all of the evidence cited so far derives from Genesis 2:4 –
3:24, Genesis 1:1 – 2:3 also hints at the possibility that the earth
will be God's temple. As John Walton observes:

> On the seventh day we finally discover that God has been working to
> achieve a rest. This seventh day is not a theological appendix to the
> creation account, just to bring closure now that the main event of creating
> people has been reported. Rather, it intimates the purpose of creation and
> of the cosmos. God does not set up the cosmos so that only people will
> have a place. He also sets up the cosmos to serve as his temple in which
> he will find rest in the order and equilibrium that he has established.[24]

Further evidence that the contents of Genesis 1:1 – 2:3 have
been influenced by priestly or temple concerns has been observed
by Peter Kearney, Moshe Weinfeld and Joseph Blenkinsopp.
Kearney notes a correspondence between the divine instructions
for building the tabernacle and the six days of creation.[25] Weinfeld
suggests that the special interest shown in Genesis 1:14 for feast
days, weeks and years, and in Genesis 2:1–3 for the Sabbath,
reflects matters of priestly interest.[26] Blenkinsopp, picking up on
the anthropological studies of Mary Douglas, sees a connection
between the division of the cosmos into sky, earth and seas in
Genesis 1 and the categorization of animals, birds and fish as clean
or unclean in the 'priestly' dietary regulations of Leviticus 11:1–47
and Deuteronomy 14:3–21.[27] On the basis of these observations,

---

24. J. H. Walton, 'Creation', in T. D. Alexander and D. W. Baker (eds.),
    Dictionary of the Old Testament: Pentateuch (Downers Grove: IVP; Leicester:
    IVP, 2003), p. 161.
25. P. J. Kearney, 'Creation and Liturgy: The P Redaction of Ex 25–40',
    Zeitschrift für die alttestamentliche Wissenschaft 89 (1977), pp. 375–387.
26. M. Weinfeld, 'Sabbath, Temple, and the Enthronement of the Lord – the
    Problem of the "Sitz im Leben" of Genesis 1:1–2:3', in A. Caquot and M.
    Delcor (eds.), *Mélanges Bibliques et Orientaux en L'honneur de M. Henri
    Cazelles*, Alter Orient und Altes Testament 212 (Kevelaer: Butzon &
    Bercker, 1981), pp. 501–512.
27. J. Blenkinsopp, *Sage, Priest, Prophet: Religious and Intellectual Leadership in*

Genesis 1 – 3 provides a strong basis for believing that the Garden of Eden was envisaged as part of a divine sanctuary. The absence of references to sacrifices and altars should not detract from seeing temple imagery in the opening chapters of Genesis. Since no one had yet sinned, there was no need for atonement sacrifices.

If Genesis portrays the Garden of Eden as a sanctuary or temple-garden, a number of things follow: (1) Since the garden is a place where divinity and humanity enjoy each other's presence, it is appropriate that it should be a prototype for later Israelite sanctuaries. This explains why many of the decorative features of the tabernacle and temple are arboreal in nature.[28] (2) Because they met God face to face in a holy place, we may assume that Adam and Eve had a holy or priestly status. Only priests were permitted to serve within a sanctuary or temple. (3) Although it is not stated, the opening chapters of Genesis imply that the boundaries of the garden will be extended to fill the whole earth as human beings are fruitful and increase in number. Greg Beale observes:

> As Adam and Eve were to begin to rule over and subdue the earth, it is plausible to suggest that they were to extend the geographical boundaries of the Garden until Eden extended throughout and covered the whole earth.[29]

Understood in the light of ancient Near Eastern practices, an increasing population would create a city around the temple. Through time, the whole earth would become a holy garden-city. While Genesis 2 merely introduces the start of this process, the

---

Ancient Israel, Library of Ancient Israel (Louisville: Westminster John Knox, 1995), pp. 101–104.

28. For detailed descriptions of the features of the tabernacle and Solomonic temple, see respectively, R. E. Averbeck, 'Tabernacle', in T. D. Alexander and D. W. Baker (eds.), *Dictionary of the Old Testament: Pentateuch* (Downers Grove: IVP; Leicester: IVP, 2003), pp. 807–827; Hurowitz, 'YHWH's Exalted House', pp. 63–110.

29. Beale, 'Final Vision of the Apocalypse', p. 201. See also Beale, 'Eden, the Temple', pp. 10–11.

long-term outcome is the establishment of an arboreal temple-city where God and humanity coexist in perfect harmony. Interpreted along these lines, the opening chapters of Genesis enable us to reconstruct God's blueprint for the earth. God intends that the world should become his dwelling place. Remarkably, this blueprint is eventually brought to completion through the New Jerusalem envisaged in Revelation 21 – 22.

However, the biblical meta-story reveals that the process from blueprint to final reality is suddenly interrupted with tragic consequences for the whole of creation. To comprehend this we must focus carefully on the events recorded in Genesis 3. While Genesis 2 draws attention to the privileged, holy status of Adam and Eve, Genesis 3 reveals how, when tested by the serpent, they fail to fulfil one of the main priestly responsibilities placed upon them.

In Genesis 2:15 the man is divinely commissioned to 'work and keep' the garden. Interestingly, the verb 'keep', in Hebrew, šāmar, may also be translated 'guard, protect'. In Deuteronomy 5:12 the same verb is used to instruct the Israelites to keep or guard the sanctity of the Sabbath. In all likelihood, Adam was commissioned to keep or guard the garden so that it would remain holy. This was a normal task associated with any sanctuary. However, by siding with the serpent the human couple fail in their priestly duty. Beale puts it like this:

> When Adam failed to guard the temple by sinning and letting in a foul serpent to defile the sanctuary, he lost his priestly role, and the cherubim took over the responsibility of 'guarding' the Garden temple: God 'stationed the cherubim . . . *to guard* the way to the tree of life' (so Gen. 3:24; see also Ezek. 28:14, 16).[30]

The same idea is picked up by Richard Middleton:

> While *'ādām* is placed in the garden to till/work and 'keep' (*šāmar*) it (2:15), the cherubim are placed at the east of the garden to 'guard' (*šāmar*) the way to the tree of life (3:24). . . . when *'ādām* is expelled from

---

30. Beale, *Temple and the Church's Mission*, p. 70.

the garden, all that is left to do is to 'till' or 'work' the ground (3:23). The task of keeping or guarding the garden has been passed on to others.[31]

By obeying the serpent, rather than God, Adam and Eve fail to maintain the sanctity of the temple-garden. Consequently, they are deprived of their priestly status and expelled from the sanctuary complex. No longer do they have immediate access to God; no longer do they live within the temple-garden. All importantly, their actions jeopardize the fulfilment of God's blueprint that the whole earth should become a holy garden-city. The very ones meant to extend God's dwelling place throughout the earth are excluded from his presence.

One of the immediate consequences of Adam and Eve's rebellion against God is the disruption of the harmonious relationship that exists between the man and the ground. Genesis 2 underlines the importance of this relationship by describing how the man is formed from the ground; the wordplay on the names *'ādām*, 'man/Adam', and *'ādāmâ*, 'ground', reinforces this link. The man's punishment in Genesis 3:17–19 involves an ongoing struggle that will require him to toil arduously in order to provide food. Although it is not developed in detail, the subsequent chapters of Genesis indicate that continued human wrongdoing exacerbates this problem. This ongoing tension is reflected in the naming of Noah (Gen. 5:29), for the hope is held out that he will in some way alleviate the pain of toiling the ground.

Eventually, the increasing violence of humanity causes God to destroy the majority of human beings through a flood. Close verbal links with Genesis 1 indicate that the flood narrative is deliberately structured in order to convey the idea that this is an act of recreation.[32] As Tikva Frymer-Kensky observes, the flood

---

31. J. R. Middleton, *The Liberating Image: The Imago Dei in Genesis 1* (Grand Rapids: Brazos, 2005), p. 59.

32. G. V. Smith, 'Structure and Purpose in Genesis 1–11', *Journal of the Evangelical Theological Society* 20 (1977), pp. 310–311, writes, 'When Gen. 1 and 2 are compared with 8 and 9, one begins to perceive the extent to which the author uses repeated phrases and ideas to build the structural

cleanses the earth from the defilement caused by human wrong-doing:

> It is the filling of the earth with *ḥāmas* [violence] and its resultant pollution that prompts God to bring a flood to physically erase everything from the earth and start anew. The flood is not primarily

---

Footnote 32 (*continued*)

relationships within the units. The following relationships are found: (a) Since man could not live on the earth when it was covered with water in chaps. 1 and 8, a subsiding of the water and separation of the land from the water took place, allowing the dry land to appear (1:9–10; 8:1–13); (b) "birds and animals and every creeping thing that creeps on the earth" are brought forth to "swarm upon the earth" in 1:20–21, 24–25 and 8:17–19; (c) God establishes the days and seasons in 1:14–18 and 8:22; (d) God's blessing rests upon the animals as he commands them to "be fruitful and multiply on the earth" in both 1:22 and 8:17; (e) man is brought forth and he receives the blessing of God: "Be fruitful and multiply and fill the earth" in 1:28 and 9:1,7; (f) Man is given dominion over the animal kingdom in 1:28 and 9:2; (g) God provides food for man in 1:29–30 and 9:3 (this latter regulation makes a direct reference back to the previous passage when it includes the statement, "As I have given the green plant"); and (h) in 9:6 the writer quotes from 1:26–27 concerning the image of God in man. The author repeatedly emphasizes the fact that the world is beginning again with a fresh start. But Noah does not return to the par-adise of Adam, for the significant difference is that "the intent of man's heart is evil" (Gen 8:21).'

G. J. Wenham, 'Flood', in W. A. VanGemeren (ed.), *New International Dictionary of Old Testament Theology and Exegesis*, vol. 4 (Carlisle: Paternoster; Grand Rapids: Zondervan, 1996), p. 642, observes that the 'parallels between the first creation and the re-creation after the Flood suggest that Noah should be seen as a second Adam'. Thus both are commanded to 'be fruitful and increase in number' (Gen. 1:28; 9:1, 7). However, Wenham suggests that Noah is distinguished from Adam in that he is portrayed as being 'righteous' and 'blameless' (Gen. 6:9). He comments, 'Repeatedly the narrative insists, "Noah did everything just as God commanded him." He apparently kept the Sabbath (8:10, 12), distinguished between clean

an agent of punishment . . . but a means of getting rid of a thoroughly polluted world and starting again with a clean, well-washed one.[33]

While the receding of the flood waters marks a new beginning, human nature has not changed. People still have the propensity to sin and defile the earth. For this reason, God places obligations upon Noah and his family after the flood that are specifically designed to minimize the future defilement of the ground by people (Gen. 9:1–7).

In the light of God's blueprint for the earth, the early chapters of Genesis conclude with a highly ironic account (Gen. 11:1–9). Human beings set about building a city with a tower that will reach up to the heavens in order that humankind will not be dispersed throughout the earth. This reverses the divine plan, for God is interested in making the whole earth his residence by filling it with holy people. In marked contrast, the people of Babel[34] attempt to access heaven and avoid filling the earth.[35] Babel represents the antithesis of what God intends.

When we grasp the true intention of the human city-builders,

---

and unclean animals, and was in a covenant relationship with God (6:18). In all these ways he acts like a model Israelite. Finally, on emerging from the ark Noah offered a sacrifice whose pleasing aroma prompted the Lord to declare that he would never destroy the world again in a flood. Here Noah is portrayed as exercising a priestly ministry on behalf of the rest of humankind, just as Israel would later be called to act as a kingdom of priests on behalf of all the nations in the world (cf Exod 19:6).'

33. T. Frymer-Kensky, 'The Atrahasis Epic and Its Significance for Our Understanding of Genesis 1–9', *Biblical Archaeologist* 40 (1977), p. 153.

34. In Hebrew the term *bābel* is also the name for Babylon. I shall say more about Babylon in chapter 7, for it appears throughout the biblical meta-story.

35. Although God has given us human beings the capacity to build cities, we do not have the ability to ensure they will provide an environment harmonious, congenial and pleasant for every citizen. What modern city does not have slums, traffic pollution and red-light districts?

it is clear that their project is not as innocent as it may at first seem.[36] On the contrary, what we have here is an account in which all the God-given abilities of human beings are deliberately focused on creating a society where God is redundant. Confident in their own capacity to meet every challenge, the inhabitants of this human city view the Creator as irrelevant.

At this point, we need to pause and ponder. Is there not a sense in which modern Western culture images Babel? Do not the aspirations of these ancient city-builders reflect those of contemporary society? As one writer has put it:

> What a wealth of human meanings converge in the single image of Babel! It is an ambivalent image, evoking powerful feelings of a wide range. On one side we can see the human longings for community, achievement, civilization, culture, technology, safety, security, permanence and fame. But countering these aspirations we sense the moral judgment against idolatry, pride, self-reliance, the urge of material power and the human illusion of infinite achievement. It is a picture of misguided human aspirations ending in confusion – in literary terms an episode of epic proportions that follows the downward arc of tragedy.[37]

In the light of God's initial creation project, the account of Babel is a stark reminder of how perverted human nature has become.

God's original blueprint is for the whole earth to become a temple-city filled with people who have a holy or priestly status. Tragically, the actions of Adam and Eve endanger the fulfilment of this project. In spite of this, God graciously and mercifully

---

36. The recent attempt of T. Hiebert, 'The Tower of Babel and the Origin of the World's Cultures', *Journal of Biblical Literature* 126 (2007), pp. 29–58, to reinterpret the Babel story in a positive way fails to give sufficient attention to the overall context in which the story comes. If there is a positive aspect to the outcome to the story, this is due to divine intervention and the overturning of the aspirations of the builders.

37. Anonymous, 'Babel, Tower of', in L. Ryken, J. C. Wilhoit and T. Longman III (eds.), *Dictionary of Biblical Imagery* (Downers Grove: IVP; Leicester: IVP, 1998), p. 67.

embarks on a lengthy process designed to reverse this setback and bring to completion his creation scheme. In the chapters that follow we shall observe different aspects of God's redemptive activity. For the present, however, we shall focus on those measures that involve the re-establishment of his presence upon the earth.

The tabernacle

Important links exist between the Garden of Eden and the tabernacle. As we shall shortly observe, the construction of the latter is a significant step towards the fulfilment of God's initial plan that the earth should become his dwelling place. However, prior to the setting up of the tabernacle as God's portable residence, various sacrificial sites existed that, according to Beale, were 'impermanent, miniature forms of sanctuaries'.[38] These sacred sites, mentioned mainly in conjunction with the patriarchs of Genesis 12 – 50, have a number of elements in common. First, they are normally associated with theophanies that involve God restating the commission in Genesis 1:28 that human beings are to be fruitful, fill the earth and rule over it (see Gen. 9:1, 7; 12:2–3; 17:2, 6, 8, 20; 22:17–18; 26:3–4, 24; 28:3–4; 35:11–12; cf. 41:52; 47:27; 48:4; 49:22). Secondly, linked to the theophany is the construction of an altar, sometimes on a mountain (see Gen. 8:20; 12:7–8; 13:4, 18; 22:9; 26:25; 33:20; 35:1, 3, 7).

Two examples of these temporary sanctuaries are particularly noteworthy. The first comes in Genesis 22 when Abraham constructs an altar on Mount Moriah. According to 2 Chronicles 3:1, Moriah is the location where Solomon later builds the house of the Lord in Jerusalem. As a result of Abraham's willingness to offer Isaac as a sacrifice, the conditional promises of Genesis 12:1–3 are guaranteed by a divine oath.[39] The second example

---

38. Beale, 'Eden, the Temple', p. 14.

39. See T. D. Alexander, *From Paradise to the Promised Land: An Introduction to the Pentateuch*, 2nd ed. (Carlisle: Paternoster; Grand Rapids: Baker, 2002),

concerns Jacob's night vision of God when fleeing from Isaac (Gen. 28:12–17). In response to the divine promises that echo those previously given to Abraham and Isaac, Jacob constructs an altar.[40] To underline the significance of both the occasion and the promises, Jacob designates the location Bethel 'House of God' (Gen. 28:19). When Jacob returns to Canaan after his lengthy sojourn in Paddan-aram, the Lord appears to him again and encourages him to dwell at Bethel (Gen. 35:1–15). After Jacob builds an altar to the Lord there, God speaks to him once more, reaffirming the promises made previously (Gen. 35:11–12).

While the various sacrificial sites mentioned in Genesis 12 – 50 are not viewed as permanent sanctuaries, they clearly foreshadow the tabernacle and temple. Moreover, the promises given to the patriarchs build on God's creation blueprint that the whole earth shall become his dwelling place as holy people populate it. While Genesis anticipates this development, the book of Exodus advances the meta-story by introducing the tabernacle.

As part of his restoration process, God commissions the construction of a special tent, the manufacture of which is described in considerable detail in the second half of Exodus. Somewhat later, features of the tabernacle are replicated in the temple. Without going into the details of the tabernacle and its furnishing,[41] it consisted of three distinctive areas. A curtained barrier formed an enclosed rectangular courtyard, with an entrance on the east side. Inside this courtyard stood the tabernacle, a large tent divided into two sections. Entered from the east, the first room of the tent was the Holy Place. In this part stood the menorah, table of the showbread and incense altar. A pair of curtains, embroi-

---

Footnote 39 (continued)

pp. 145–153; cf. P. R. Williamson, *Sealed with an Oath: Covenant in God's Unfolding Purpose*, New Studies in Biblical Theology 23 (Downers Grove: IVP; Leicester: Apollos, 2007), pp. 77–93.

40. The divine promises of Gen. 28:13–15 echo those in 12:1–3; 22:16–18; 26:3–5.

41. For a general discussion of the tabernacle and its furnishings, see Alexander, *From Paradise*, pp. 192–203.

dered with cherubim separated the Holy Place from the Holy of Holies. This latter room was the inner sanctum wherein was placed the ark of the covenant. This rectangular box served a double function, being both the footstool of a throne and a chest.[42] Understood as a footstool, the ark of the covenant extends the heavenly throne to the earth; this is where the divine king's feet touch the earth.[43] Consequently, the tabernacle links heaven and earth.[44] As a chest, the ark of the covenant stores

---

42. It is sometimes claimed that the ark itself was the throne of God. R. E. Clements, *God and Temple* (Oxford: Basil Blackwell, 1965), pp. 28–35, traces the origin of this idea to a study by W. Reichel, *Über vorhellenischen Götterculte* (Vienna: Hölder 1897). While some evidence points in this direction, the case is far from convincing, as Clements clearly demonstrates.

43. 2 Chr. 9:18 briefly describes a human throne and footstool: 'The throne had six steps and a footstool of gold, which were attached to the throne.' C. L. Seow, 'Ark of the Covenant', in D. N. Freedman (ed.), *Anchor Bible Dictionary*, vol. 1 (New York: Doubleday, 1992), p. 389, notes that 'footstools regularly came with the throne in the ANE'. And 'The cherubim thrones of the sarcophagus of Ahiram and the ivory plaque of Megiddo both show boxlike footstools at the base of the throne. The god El, the enthroned deity par excellence among West Semitic deities, also has a stool (*hdm*, as in Hebrew) on which he places his feet (*CTA* 4.4.29–30; *ANET*; 133).' The ark is clearly designated a footstool in 1 Chr. 28:2. Pss 99:5 and 132:7 offer an invitation to worship at God's footstool. Further support for the ark being God's footstool comes from Isa. 60:13: 'The glory of Lebanon shall come to you, / the cypress, the plane, and the pine, / to beautify the place of my sanctuary, / and I will make the place of my feet glorious.' Isa. 66:1 (cf. Acts. 7:49) also draws a distinction between the throne of God and the footstool: 'Heaven is my throne, / and the earth is my footstool.' Ps. 11:4 may well be alluding to the same point when it states, 'The LORD is in his holy temple; / the LORD's throne is in heaven.' Seow rejects the idea that the ark itself was the throne. In passing, it is also worth noting that Lam. 2:1 associates Jerusalem with the footstool of God.

44. Solomon's prayer at the dedication of the temple draws attention to a special link between heaven and earth (1 Kgs 8:30–51; 2 Chr. 6:22–39). While Solomon requests that God should listen or hear from heaven his

various items. The most important of these are the treaty or covenant documents that set out the obligations placed upon the Israelites by God.[45]

The importance of the tabernacle is reflected in the number of chapters devoted in Exodus to describing its construction (Exod. 25 – 31, 35 – 40). Three aspects of this special tent link it to God's plans for the earth.

First, as already noted, the tabernacle has features that associate it closely with the Garden of Eden. As divine sanctuaries, both are entered from the east and cherubim guard their entrances. The golden menorah that stood in the Holy Place may have been designed specifically to resemble the tree of life. Like Adam, the Levites are instructed to 'serve (or minister) and guard' the sanctuary (Num. 3:7–8; 8:26; 18:5–6). These parallels suggest that the construction of the tabernacle marks the continuation of God's plans for the Garden of Eden. Further evidence in support of this will be given below.

Secondly, the tabernacle becomes the dwelling place of God on earth. Various features support the idea that God lived within the tent. The term used most frequently to denote the tabernacle is *miškān*, 'dwelling' (e.g. Exod. 25:9; 26:1; 27:9, 38:21; 40:9; Lev. 8:10;

Footnote 44 (*continued*)

dwelling place (1 Kgs 8:30, 39, 43, 49; 2 Chr. 6:21, 23, 30, 33, 39), the locations from which supplicants may pray vary from within the temple (1 Kgs 8:31, 33; 2 Chr. 6:22, 24) to outside the land (1 Kgs 8:38; 2 Chr. 6:38). Yet even those outside the land are still expected to pray towards the temple (1 Kgs 8:38; 2 Chr. 6:38). Clements, *God and Temple*, p. 68, observes that quite frequently in the Psalms 'we discover that Yahweh's dwelling in heaven, and his presence on Mount Zion are mentioned in the same psalm, without any consciousness of contradiction between the two' (e.g. Pss 11:4; 14:2, 7; 20:2, 6; 76:2, 8; 80:1, 14).

45. Seow, 'Ark of the Covenant', vol. 1, p. 389, notes that footstools associated with ancient Near Eastern deities were often boxlike containers into which treaty documents were placed. The ark of the covenant, also known as the 'ark of the testimony' (e.g. Exod. 25:22; 30:6; 39:35; Num. 4:5; 7:89), served a similar function (Exod. 40:20; Deut. 10:5; 1 Kgs 8:9).

Num. 1:50–51; 3:7–8; 4:16; 5:17; 7:1; 9:15), and the furniture within it consisted of a chest, a table for food and a lampstand, items that point to its use as a home. The extensive use of gold in the manufacture of these objects reflects the importance of the one for whom they were fashioned.

When the tent was finally erected, Exodus 40:34–35 records that God's glory filled the tent and remained within it. As a result, Moses was unable to enter it due to the divine presence. Later, when God guided the people on their journey through the wilderness to Canaan, the divine presence, which appeared as a cloud by day and fire by night, was intimately associated with the tabernacle. If the people were to move camp, the cloud departed from the tabernacle and went in front of them. Presumably, when this happened the tent was dismantled. Later, when the journey was completed and the tabernacle reassembled, the cloud returned to it. The brief description of this in Numbers 9:15–22 clearly underscores that the tabernacle was perceived as God's abode:

> On the day that the tabernacle was set up, the cloud covered the tabernacle, the tent of the testimony. And at evening it was over the tabernacle like the appearance of fire until morning. So it was always: the cloud covered it by day and the appearance of fire by night. And whenever the cloud lifted from over the tent, after that the people of Israel set out, and in the place where the cloud settled down, there the people of Israel camped. . . . Whether it was two days, or a month, or a longer time, that the cloud continued over the tabernacle, abiding there, the people of Israel remained in camp and did not set out, but when it lifted they set out. (Num. 9:15–17, 22)

Another pointer to the tabernacle being a divine residence is the fact that Moses met regularly with God at the tent. This function is underlined by another of the titles given to the tabernacle; it is frequently designated the 'tent of meeting', *'ōhel mô'ēd* (e.g. Exod. 27:21; 28:43; 29:4; 40:2; Lev. 1:1; 3:2; Num. 1:1; 2:2). We may helpfully compare the arrangement for this Tent of Meeting with an earlier, temporary one set up outside the Israelite camp (Exod. 33:7). With this first tent, when Moses went inside, God's glory surrounded it, with the tent curtains a barrier. In the case of the tabernacle, erected at the centre of the camp, Moses remained outside while God was within, the tent curtains once more separating them. God's presence inside the tabernacle indicated it was his dwelling place.

Finally, God's presence inside the tabernacle was reflected in the exceptionally holy status attributed to the Holy of Holies. Within the tabernacle, the inner sanctum was the holiest location. The further one moved away from the Holy of Holies, the less holy places became.[46] These differing levels of holiness are reflected in the objects, people, dress and accessibility associated with each part of the sanctuary. While other parts of the tabernacle were viewed as holy, they were so to lesser degrees, depending on their distance from the Holy of Holies.[47] The intensity of holiness associated with the inner sanctum reinforces the idea that the Holy One of Israel was present there. In support of this, Haran observes that the ritual acts within the tabernacle reflected the presence of the divine king by catering to the various senses (e.g. smell, taste, touch, sight):

> Taken together, the six regular rites performed inside the tabernacle . . .
> are at once seen to embrace almost all the human senses, and to cater, as
> it were, for almost all man's possible needs. The incense provides for the
> sense of smell, the lamps for the sense of sight, while the loaves of
> bread are a symbol of the need for food. The bells attract the sense of
> hearing, the stones on the ephod and the breastpiece awaken the 'sense'
> of memory, and the diadem on the high priest's forehead evokes the
> 'sense' of grace (for even these last two qualities could be conceived,
> by the ancients, as manifestations of spiritual or 'sensorial' activity).[48]

---

46. The use of the term *miqdāš* for the sanctuary points to its holy nature.
47. A more detailed discussion of this is found in Haran, *Temples and Temple-Service*, pp. 158–188, 205–229; Alexander, *From Paradise*, pp. 206–215. See also P. P. Jenson, *Graded Holiness: A Key to the Priestly Conception of the World*, Journal for the Study of the Old Testament, Supplement Series 106 (Sheffield: JSOT Press, 1992).
48. Haran, *Temples and Temple-Service*, p. 216.

Naturally, the idea of God dwelling inside a tent needs to be handled carefully. It does not necessarily mean that his presence was restricted to this location. As already noted, the identification of the ark of the covenant as a footstool points to a heavenly throne, indicating that God's being was not contained within the tabernacle alone. However, Nahum Sarna is mistaken when he writes:

> the sanctuary is not meant to be understood literally as God's abode, as are other such institutions in the pagan world. Rather, it functions to make perceptible and tangible the conception of God's immanence, that is, the indwelling of the Divine Presence in the camp of Israel, to which the people may orient their hearts and minds.[49]

The tabernacle was much more than a symbol of God's immanence. The various features noted above point to it being his dwelling place on the earth. Here his presence was experienced in a unique way.

Thirdly, the tabernacle was probably also viewed as a model of the cosmos.[50] The case for this is not beyond dispute, for much of

---

49. N. M. Sarna, *Exodus*, Jewish Publication Society Torah Commentary (Philadelphia: Jewish Publication Society, 1991), p. 158. Sarna comes to this conclusion largely on the basis that when God remarks in Exod. 25:8 and 29:45 about living among the Israelites, he makes no reference to the tabernacle.

50. See Levenson, 'Temple and the World', pp. 283–298; Barker, *Gate of Heaven*, pp. 104–132; C. R. Koester, *The Dwelling of God: The Tabernacle in the Old Testament, Intertestamental Jewish Literature, and the New Testament*, Catholic Biblical Quarterly Monograph Series 22 (Washington: Catholic Biblical Association of America, 1989), pp. 59–63. For a discussion of how the tabernacle was linked to creation in later Jewish literature, for example Josephus and Philo, see C. T. R. Hayward, *The Jewish Temple: A Non-Biblical Sourcebook* (London: Routledge, 1996). In suggesting that the tabernacle was a microcosm, I am inclined to view the Holy of Holies as representing the earth. In doing so, I part company with those who see the Holy of Holies as signifying heaven. M. Barker, *On Earth as It Is in*

the evidence is circumstantial. It is noted, for example, that temples in the ancient Near East were often viewed as microcosms, models of the cosmos.[51] As regards the tabernacle, this is

Footnote 50 (*continued*)

> *Heaven: Temple Symbolism in the New Testament* (Edinburgh: T. & T. Clark, 1995), p. 8, favours a two-part representation: 'The temple buildings were a representation of the universe. They were the centre of the ordered creation, the source of its life and stability. The *hekal* [Holy Place] represented the Garden of Eden, the created world, and the holy of holies was heaven, the place of the presence of God.' Elsewhere, Barker, *Gate of Heaven*, p. 105, writes, 'The *hekal* represented the earth and the *debir* [Holy of Holies] the heavens; between them was the veil which separated the holy place from the most holy (Exod. 26.33). The veil represented the boundary between the visible world and the invisible, between time and eternity.'
>
> Adopting a slightly different approach, Beale, *Temple and the Church's Mission*, p. 48, writes, 'the three parts of Israel's temple represented the three parts of the cosmos: the outer court symbolized the visible earth (both land and sea, the place where humans lived); the holy place primarily represented the visible heavens (though there was also garden symbolism); the holy of holies stood for the invisible heavenly dimension of the cosmos where God dwelt (apparently not even the high priest who entered there once a year could see because of the cloud from the incense which he was to put on the fire; cf. Lev. 16:32)'. See also Beale, 'Eden, the Temple', pp. 16–18. For an outright rejection of the idea that the temple represented the cosmos, see R. de Vaux, *Ancient Israel: Its Life and Institutions*, 2nd ed. (London: Darton, Longman & Todd, 1965), pp. 328–329.

51. H. H. Nelson, 'The Significance of the Temple in the Ancient Near East: Part I. The Egyptian Temple', *Biblical Archaeologist* 7 (1944), pp. 47–48, notes that in Egypt the temple was 'pictured as a microcosm of the world . . . Its ceiling is painted blue for the sky and is studded with a multitude of golden stars. . . . The floor of the temple is similarly conceived of as the earth out of which plants grow.' Cf. G. E. Wright, 'The Significance of the Temple in the Ancient Near East: Part III. The Temple in Palestine-Syria', *Biblical Archaeologist* 7 (1944), pp. 66–67, 74–75; H. W. Turner, *From Temple*

conveyed through the use of fabrics that are blue, purple and scarlet in colour, representing the 'variegated colors of the sky'.[52] In line with this the lights of the tabernacle are designated by the Hebrew term *mā'ôr*, which is also used to denote the sun, moon and stars in Genesis 1:14–16.[53]

Subtle links have also been observed between the account of the building of the tabernacle and the creation of the earth. To those already noted on page 24, we may add the following. Middleton draws attention to how Bezalel, who oversees the construction of the tabernacle, is portrayed using terminology associated with the creation of the earth. He writes:

> As overseer of tabernacle construction, Bezalel is filled (Exodus 31:3) with 'wisdom' *(ḥokmâ)*, 'understanding' *(tĕbûnâ)*, and 'knowledge' *(da'at)*, precisely the same triad by which God is said to have created the world in Proverbs 3:19–20. To this is added that Bezalel is filled with 'all crafts'

---

to Meeting House: The Phenomenology and Theology of Places of Worship (The Hague: Mouton, 1979), pp. 26–31, 35–37, 57–60. H. W. Nibley, 'What Is a Temple?', in T. G. Madsen (ed.), *Temple in Antiquity: Ancient Records and Modern Perspectives*, The Religious Studies Monograph Series 9 (Provo, Utah: Religious Studies Center, Brigham Young University, 1984), p. 22, writes, 'We can summarize a hundred studies of recent date in the formula: a temple, good or bad, is a scale-model of the universe.' W. J. Dumbrell, 'Genesis 2:1–17: A Foreshadowing of the New Creation', in S. J. Hafemann (ed.), *Biblical Theology: Retrospect and Prospect* (Downers Grove: IVP; Leicester: Apollos, 2002), p. 58, n. 14, comments, 'The tabernacle or temple stands as a representation of the cosmos, with God's plan eventually being that all of creation becomes precisely this.'

52. Beale, 'Eden, the Temple', p. 16.

53. Ibid., p. 17, n. 26, writes, 'Josephus, *J. W.* 5.210–14, says that the "tapestry" hanging over the outer entrance into the temple "typified the universe" and on it "was portrayed a panorama of the heavens." The same may have well been the case with the outer part of the curtain separating the Holy of Holies from the Holy Place, since also according to Josephus, all of the curtains in the temple contained "colours seeming so exactly to resemble those that meet the eye in the heavens" (Josephus, *Ant.* 3.132).'

or 'all works' *(kol-mĕlā'kâ)*, the very phrase used in Genesis 2:2–3 for 'all the works' that God completed in creation. Therefore, not only does the tabernacle replicate in microcosm the macrocosmic sanctuary of the entire created order, but these verbal resonances suggest that Bezalel's discerning artistry in tabernacle-building images God's own construction of the cosmos.[54]

Picking up on another parallel between the tabernacle and Genesis 1, Mark Smith writes:

Commentators beginning with Martin Buber and Franz Rosenzweig have observed that Exodus 39–40 consciously echoes the end of the priestly creation account (Exod. 39.43a//Gen. 1.31a; Exod. 39.32a//Gen. 2.1; Exod. 40.33b//Gen. 2.2a; and Exod. 39.43b//Gen. 2.3a). Exodus 39–40 is thereby connected to the creation story of Genesis: while the account of Genesis marks the creation of the world, the creation language of Exodus 39–40 heralds the new creation of Israel's cultic life with its deity.[55]

Later, the concept of the tabernacle as a microcosm was transferred to the temple.[56] As models of the ideal cosmos, the

---

54. Middleton, *Liberating Image*, p. 87.

55. M. S. Smith, *The Pilgrimage Pattern in Exodus*, Journal for the Study of the Old Testament, Supplement Series 239 (Sheffield: Sheffield Academic Press, 1997), pp. 116–117. See U. Cassuto, *Commentary on Exodus* (Jerusalem: Magnes, 1967), pp. 476–477, 483; R. P. Gordon, 'The Week That Made the World: Reflections on the First Pages of the Bible', in J. G. McConville and K. Möller (eds.), *Reading the Law: Studies in Honour of Gordon J. Wenham*, Library of Hebrew Bible / Old Testament Studies 461 (Edinburgh: T. & T. Clark, 2007), pp. 234–235.

56. It is sometimes suggested that the author's comment in Ps. 78:69 that God 'built his sanctuary like the high heavens, / like the earth, which he has founded for ever' points to the temple being a microcosm. However, as de Vaux, *Ancient Israel*, p. 328, rightly observes, 'all this verse means is that God's choice of Sion as his dwelling-place . . . is definitive, and as enduring as the heavens and the earth'.

tabernacle and the temple are designed to remind people of God's original purpose for the world.

Since the tabernacle and temple were both perceived as being models of the earth, it is unsurprising that tent and building metaphors are used in the Old Testament to describe the created world.[57] The author of Psalm 104:2 states, 'He stretches out the heavens like a tent.'[58] In a similar vein, Job 38:4–7 pictures the cosmos being constructed like a building:

> Where were you when I laid the foundation of the earth?
> Tell me, if you have understanding.
> Who determined its measurements – surely you know!
> Or who stretched the line upon it?
> On what were its bases sunk,
>   or who laid its cornerstone, when the morning stars sang together
>   and all the sons of God shouted for joy?

Other passages see the earth as a building with foundations and pillars (Prov. 3:19; 8:27; Pss 33:7; 75:3; 104:5; 119:90; Job 28:26; Isa. 48:13; 51:13,16; Zech. 12:1; Amos 9:6). These descriptions of the earth may have been influenced by the Israelites' perception of the tabernacle and temple as cosmic models. We should, therefore, be cautious in comparing and contrasting Israelite cosmology with modern understandings of the universe's structure. From the limited evidence available to us it is difficult to judge whether the Israelites viewed the tent and building descriptions of the earth as metaphorical or real.

Linked to both Eden and the cosmos, the tabernacle, as a

---

57. Levenson, *Creation*, pp. 78–87.

58. Ps. 19:4–5 says, 'Their measuring line goes out through all the earth, / and their words to the end of the world. / In them he has set a tent for the sun, / which comes out like a bridegroom leaving his chamber, / and, like a strong man, runs its course with joy.' Compare also Isa. 40:22, 'It is he who sits above the circle of the earth, / and its inhabitants are like grasshoppers; / who stretches out the heavens like a curtain, / and spreads them like a tent to dwell in.'

model, conveys the idea that the whole earth is to become God's dwelling place. 'The temple was a small-scale model and symbolic reminder to Israel that God's glorious presence would eventually fill the whole cosmos.'[59] Furthermore, in reality it represented an important step towards the fulfilment of this project, for with its construction God took up residence on the earth. With good reason Smith comments that 'with the book of Exodus Israel enters into the cosmic plan which Yahweh laid out at the beginning of the world'.[60] Yet, while the building of the tabernacle is a positive step towards the fulfilment of God's creation blueprint, his actual abode is restricted to a relatively small area. Moreover, although the land of Canaan offers the possibility of a return to Edenic fruitfulness (cf. Gen. 13:10), it continues as an imperfect environment. At best it is a foretaste of something better still to come.[61]

The Jerusalem temple

Soon after the Israelites enter the land of Canaan, the tabernacle is set up at Shiloh in the tribal district of Ephraim. The choice of Shiloh as the central location for the Lord's sanctuary is in keeping with the expectation that the first monarchy of Israel would come from the tribe of Ephraim.[62] However, due to the increasing waywardness of the Ephraimites, as reflected especially in the book of Judges and the early part of Samuel, God abandons the sanctuary at Shiloh. As 1 Samuel 2:12–17 reveals, God's departure is prompted by the corrupt behaviour of the Shiloh priests. The

---

59. Beale, 'Eden, the Temple', p. 18.
60. M. S. Smith, *Pilgrimage Pattern in Exodus*, p. 117.
61. We see this developed in Isa. 51:3; Ezek. 36:35; Joel 2:3.
62. See T. D. Alexander, 'The Regal Dimension of the *tolĕdôt ya'ăqob*:
    Recovering the Literary Context of Genesis 37–50', in J. G. McConville
    and K. Möller (eds.), *Reading the Law: Studies in Honour of Gordon J. Wenham*,
    Library of Hebrew Bible / Old Testament Studies 461 (Edinburgh: T. &
    T. Clark, 2007).

tragic significance of this event is conveyed by the wife of Phinehas when she names her soon-to-be-orphaned son 'Ichabod, saying, "The glory has departed from Israel!'" (1 Sam. 4:21). Although it appears that the Philistines have captured the Lord and overpowered him, the events of 1 Samuel 4:19–22 demonstrate that God has *allowed* himself to be taken captive. The toppling of Dagon's statue and the plagues that come upon the Philistines are powerful indicators that the Lord is in control (1 Sam. 5:1–12).

Eventually, with David's public appointment as king of Israel and the capture of Jerusalem, the ark of the covenant is brought to the city. The significance of these events is underlined in the final part of Psalm 78. The divine rejection of Ephraim and Shiloh is matched by the selection of David and Jerusalem (Zion). God's choice of David as king is confirmed by his choice of dwelling place; the thrones of the Israelite king and the divine king are now located side by side in the same city. This convergence represents an important development in the biblical meta-story, especially when the building of a temple on Mount Zion follows it.

David's desire to construct a temple for the Lord in Jerusalem is prompted by the incongruity he observes between his own palace and the tabernacle (2 Sam. 7:2). From David's perspective it is inappropriate that his own royal residence should be grander than God's abode. While David is motivated by a concern for God's honour, the Lord intervenes and prohibits him from constructing a temple. Through a wordplay on the term 'house' (*bayit*), God promises that he will build a house for David (i.e. a dynasty) and that David's son will build a house for God (i.e. a temple). This divine commitment is called a 'covenant' in Psalm 89:3, although this term is not used in 2 Samuel 7, where these events are narrated.

In due course David's son Solomon succeeds to the throne and builds a magnificent temple in Jerusalem. Following his dedication prayer, the glory of the Lord fills the new sanctuary. The account of this in 1 Kings 8:10–11 (cf. 2 Chr. 7:1–2) strongly echoes the description of God's glory filling the tabernacle in Exodus 40:34–35, indicating that the Jerusalem temple has now superseded the tabernacle.

Undoubtedly, the temple is viewed as the Lord's dwelling place on earth. As Carol Meyers observes:

The very terminology used for the building ('house,' 'palace') and the emphasis on the extraordinary nature of its design and fabrication together provide symbolic statements that God is in residence on Zion. The furnishings meet the 'needs' of the building's occupant, with the glory of those furnishings signifying the Glory within.[63]

Like the tabernacle, the temple complex also exhibits varying degrees of holiness:

Every category of structure, furniture, ritual, and human attendants is arrayed in a continuum, from the profane territory outside the sacred precinct, to the somewhat holy and pure character of the courtyard area with its bronze implements and its access to the public, to the holier and hence more pure and precious gold-adorned *hêkāl*, to which only certain priests had access, and finally to the inner sanctum, the place where God's glory rests. The innermost room was the essence of holiness and thus off-limits to all but the chief priest, only once a year and only after he attained an exceptional state of purity (at least in Second Temple times).[64]

As with the tabernacle, the exceptionally holy nature of the temple's inner sanctum indicates that it is God's residence. With good reason Meyers concludes that 'the existence of the concentric circles, as it were, of increasing holiness signified that the Holiest One of all could be found at the sacred center'.[65]

When the Jerusalem temple replaces the tabernacle as God's earthly abode, the Edenic and cosmic features associated with the tent transfer to the permanent building.[66] In line with this, the

---

63. C. L. Meyers, 'Temple, Jerusalem', in D. N. Freedman (ed.), *Anchor Bible Dictionary*, vol. 6 (New York: Doubleday, 1992), p. 360.

64. Ibid.

65. Ibid. The same point is made by Haran, *Temples and Temple-Service*, pp. 205–229, concerning the tabernacle.

66. For a fuller discussion, see P. Pitkänen, 'From Tent of Meeting to Temple: Presence, Rejection and Renewal of Divine Favour', in T. D. Alexander and S. Gathercole (eds.), *Heaven on Earth: The Temple in Biblical Theology* (Carlisle: Paternoster, 2004), pp. 23–34.

decor of the temple includes arboreal imagery, with, for example, carvings of lilies and pomegranates decorating the tops of the pillars.[67] The construction of the temple by Solomon transforms the status of Jerusalem as a city. It now becomes in a unique way the city of God. According to Psalms 78:68 and 132:13, the Lord chooses Jerusalem to be his dwelling place. Since God's creation project is to create a temple-city that will fill the whole earth, it is easy to see how Jerusalem is viewed as partially fulfilling God's plan. Consequently, Jerusalem/Zion becomes a model of God's creation blueprint and reflects in microcosm what God intends for the whole earth. However, it is not the final product.

As the dwelling place of God on earth, the temple-city of Jerusalem is in miniature what God intends for the whole world.[68] This explains why certain psalms praise the Lord by extolling the virtues of Jerusalem as the city of God. We see this, for example, in Psalm 48:

> Great is the LORD and greatly to be praised
> in the city of our God!

---

67. M. S. Smith, *Pilgrimage Pattern in Exodus*, p. 100, highlights this link between the temple and Eden. He writes, 'Solomon's choice of palmette and cherub motif to adorn the walls and doors conveys to Temple visitors that the Temple proper recreated the Garden of Eden, Yahweh's terrestrial residence.' See also Barker, *Gate of Heaven*, pp. 68–103; L. E. Stager, 'Jerusalem as Eden', *Biblical Archaeology Review* 26 (2000), pp. 38–47, 66.

68. Beale, 'Eden, the Temple', p. 19, comments, 'the land of promise, the land of Israel, was repeatedly called the "Garden of Eden" (cf. Gen 13:10; Isa 51:3; Joel 2:3; Ezek 36:35) partly perhaps because Israel was to expand the limits of the temple and of their own land to the ends of the earth in the same manner as should have Adam. That this was Israel's ultimate task is apparent from a number of Old Testament passages prophesying that God will finally cause the sacred precinct of Israel's temple to expand and first encompass Jerusalem (see Isa 4:4–6; 54:2–3, 11–12; Jer 3:16–17; Zech 1:16–2:11), then the entire land of Israel (Ezek 37:25–28), and then the whole earth (Dan 2:34–35, 44–45; cf. also Isa 54:2–3).'

His holy mountain, beautiful in elevation,
  is the joy of all the earth,
Mount Zion, in the far north,
  the city of the great King.
Within her citadels God
  has made himself known as a fortress. . . .

Walk about Zion, go around her,
  number her towers,
consider well her ramparts,
  go through her citadels,
that you may tell the next generation
  that this is God,
our God for ever and ever.
  He will guide us for ever.
  (Ps. 48:1–3, 12–14)

As the final verses of this psalm indicate, those who dwell in Zion are blessed because of the Lord's presence. This theme is echoed in Psalms 132:13–18, 133:1–3 and 147:12–14.

The extension of God's residence to include the whole city of Jerusalem possibly accounts for the attention given to the large quantities of gold that flowed into the city in the time of Solomon. As the author of Chronicles records, 'And the king made silver and gold as common in Jerusalem as stone' (2 Chr. 1:15). If gold, as used in the tabernacle and the temple, is associated with God's presence, then the presence of gold throughout Jerusalem signifies that the whole city has become his dwelling place.[69]

The exceptional nature of Jerusalem as the city of God is affirmed in Psalm 87, although here the emphasis is upon those privileged to enjoy citizenship:

On the holy mount stands the city he founded;
  the LORD loves the gates of Zion

---

69. This feature anticipates the New Jerusalem, which is made of gold (Rev. 21:18).

more than all the dwelling places of Jacob.
Glorious things of you are spoken,
   O city of God. *Selah*

Among those who know me I mention Rahab and Babylon;
   behold, Philistia and Tyre, with Cush –
   'This one was born there,' they say.
And of Zion it shall be said,
   'This one and that one were born in her';
   for the Most High himself will establish her.
The LORD records as he registers the peoples,
   'This one was born there.' *Selah*

Singers and dancers alike say,
   'All my springs are in you.'
(Ps. 87:1–7)

In keeping with these positive portrayals of Zion as the city of God, pilgrimages to Jerusalem were significant events because they provided an opportunity to come close to the Lord. The author of Psalm 84 conveys well the sense of joy and longing that permeated the whole experience of travelling to Jerusalem in order to be within the temple courts:

How lovely is your dwelling place,
   O LORD of hosts!
My soul longs, yes, faints
   for the courts of the LORD;
my heart and flesh sing for joy
   to the living God.

Even the sparrow finds a home,
   and the swallow a nest for herself,
   where she may lay her young,
at your altars, O LORD of hosts,
   my King and my God.
Blessed are those who dwell in your house,
   ever singing your praise! *Selah*

> Blessed are those whose strength is in you,
>   in whose heart are the highways to Zion.
> (Ps. 84:1–5)

The experience of travelling to Jerusalem in order to worship the Lord transformed the pilgrimage into a special occasion. Smith captures well the significance of such times for the true worshipper:

> In sum, the pilgrimage was like visiting paradise and temporarily recapturing the primordial peaceful and abundant relationship with God. It involved both holiness and pleasure, sacred and aesthetic space. It was an experience imbued with holiness, the beauty of the divine dwelling, and the very presence of God. The pilgrims' experience in the Temple was global in its effects. It saturated the psalmists' senses with all kinds of wonders: abundant food and incense, music and singing, gold and silver, palm trees, water and cherubs. This joyful experience led further to an experience of awe and holiness in the presence of God.[70]

Quite naturally this positive portrayal of the pilgrim's experience draws heavily upon Psalms 120 – 134, a section of the Psalter devoted to songs used by those who ascended to the temple.

While the Old Testament biblical meta-story moves to something of a peak with the construction of the Jerusalem temple during the reign of Solomon, thereafter comes a period of sustained decline, halted occasionally only by the reigns of a few righteous Davidic kings. Eventually, the accumulated failure of the kings and citizens of Jerusalem leads to the destruction of the temple and the overthrow of the city. That this should be undertaken by the Babylonians is highly ironic in the light of how Genesis 11 portrays Babel as being the antithesis of God's creation blueprint.[71]

Throughout the period of the Davidic dynasty Jerusalem and the temple are both theologically significant. Undoubtedly, this

---

70. M. S. Smith, *Pilgrimage Pattern in Exodus*, p. 109.
71. In Hebrew the names 'Babel' and 'Babylon' are identical.

was fostered by the expectation that God would establish on the earth a temple-city. However, if Jerusalem was to reflect God's creation blueprint, then its citizens needed to be exceptionally holy. Yet, as the biblical meta-story reveals, the inhabitants of Jerusalem proved to be no more righteous than those of other cities. They repeatedly fell below the standards of holiness necessary to live in the presence of God.

The book of Isaiah illustrates well the contrast between what God expects of the Jerusalemites and what they do. The opening chapter contains a damning indictment of the city's leadership, comparing them to the citizens of Sodom and Gomorrah. Even the sacrifices meant to atone for human sin are abhorrent to God:

> Ah, sinful nation,
>> a people laden with iniquity,
> offspring of evildoers,
>> children who deal corruptly!
> They have forsaken the LORD,
>> they have despised the Holy One of Israel,
>> they are utterly estranged. . . .

> Hear the word of the LORD,
>> you rulers of Sodom!
> Give ear to the teaching of our God,
>> you people of Gomorrah!
> 'What to me is the multitude of your sacrifices?
>> says the LORD;
> I have had enough of burnt offerings of rams
>> and the fat of well-fed beasts;
> I do not delight in the blood of bulls,
>> or of lambs, or of goats.

> 'When you come to appear before me,
>> who has required of you
>> this trampling of my courts?
> Bring no more vain offerings;
>> incense is an abomination to me.
> New moon and Sabbath and the calling of convocations –

I cannot endure iniquity and solemn assembly.
Your new moons and your appointed feasts
   my soul hates;
they have become a burden to me;
   I am weary of bearing them.
When you spread out your hands,
   I will hide my eyes from you;
even though you make many prayers,
   I will not listen;
   your hands are full of blood.'
(Isa. 1:4, 10–15)

This vivid picture of eighth-century Jerusalem highlights a major discrepancy between what the city should be as the temple-city of God and what it is in reality. From this starting point, the book of Isaiah moves in an interesting direction. Without attempting to discuss every facet of this important Old Testament text, one of its striking features is the way in which it envisages the future transformation of Jerusalem. Barry Webb rightly observes:

> The vision of the book moves, in fact, from the historical Jerusalem of the eighth century (under judgment) to the new Jerusalem of the eschaton, which is the centre of the new cosmos and symbol of the new age. To this new Jerusalem the nations come (66.18–21; cf. 60.1–22) so that ultimately the nations find their salvation in Zion . . .[72]

---

72. B. G. Webb, 'Zion in Transformation: A Literary Approach to Isaiah', in D. J. A. Clines, S. E. Fowl and S. E. Porter (eds.), *The Bible in Three Dimensions*, Journal for the Study of the Old Testament, Supplement Series 87 (Sheffield: JSOT Press, 1990), p. 71. W. J. Dumbrell, *The End of the Beginning: Revelation 21–22 and the Old Testament* (Grand Rapids: Baker, 1985), p. 5, writes, 'Isaiah is dominated by Jerusalem imagery. The book's structure is, as we will demonstrate, informed by Jerusalem orientated theology. Commencing (Isa 1) with a depiction of absolute corruption seizing the city (c740–690 BC), the prophecy concludes (66:20–24) with the emergence of a New Jerusalem as God's holy mountain. Further, it is to this mountain the world will go in a pilgrim

Something of this future transformation is anticipated in Isaiah 2:2–5, which speaks about what 'shall come to pass in the latter days':

It shall come to pass in the latter days
   that the mountain of the house of the LORD
shall be established as the highest of the mountains,
   and shall be lifted up above the hills;
and all the nations shall flow to it,
   and many peoples shall come, and say:
'Come, let us go up to the mountain of the LORD,
   to the house of the God of Jacob,
that he may teach us his ways
   and that we may walk in his paths.'
For out of Zion shall go the law,
   and the word of the LORD from Jerusalem.
He shall judge between the nations,
   and shall decide disputes for many peoples;
and they shall beat their swords into plowshares,
   and their spears into pruning hooks;

---

age of worship. It is clear from the final chapters of this great prophecy that the New Jerusalem and the New Creation are intimately linked. This link is sharpened in 65:17–18, where the New Jerusalem entails a New Creation. The New Jerusalem is thus a symbol of the New Creation and is finally presented as an obvious juxtaposition with the city initially described. There is thus good reason to see this book as a "tale of two cities" (a motif on which the book of Revelation is largely based).'

R. E. Clements, 'The Davidic Covenant in the Isaiah Tradition', in A. D. H. Mayes and R. B. Salters (eds.), *Covenant as Context: Essays in Honour of E. W. Nicholson* (New York: Oxford University Press, 2003), p. 65, observes that two themes form the backbone of the entire Isaiah book: 'God's chosen dynasty of kings and the glory of the holy city from which it ruled.' The relationship between the Davidic dynasty and Jerusalem (the city of David) is an important element within the biblical meta-story and extends throughout both Testaments.

nation shall not lift up sword against nation,
　　neither shall they learn war any more.
O house of Jacob,
　　come, let us walk
　　in the light of the LORD.

When Isaiah comments here about the mountain of the house of the Lord being established as the highest of the mountains, he is not speaking simply about the altitude of Mount Zion. As Donald Gowan observes:

> This is a theological, not a topographical, statement. In the mythology of the ancient Near East, the World Mountain was an important theme, and its meaning in myth reveals to us what the OT intended to say by speaking of the height of Zion. The World Mountain was the highest point on earth, located at the center of the earth, the point from which creation began, and thus the point par excellence where God could be encountered.[73]

Isaiah's use of mountain imagery underlines that God himself will be exalted in majesty as he exercises supreme authority over the whole earth. This expectation brings to fulfilment God's creation blueprint, for it anticipates the Lord dwelling in a temple-city that will fill the whole earth. While a variety of passages in Isaiah contribute to this future hope, Isaiah 65:17–25 is perhaps one of the most significant:[74]

'For behold, I create new heavens
　　and a new earth,
and the former things shall not be remembered
　　or come into mind.
But be glad and rejoice for ever
　　in that which I create;

---

73. Gowan, *Eschatology in the Old Testament*, pp. 11–12.
74. There are a number of significant similarities between Isa. 65:17–25 and John's vision of the New Jerusalem in Rev. 21 – 22.

for behold, I create Jerusalem to be a joy,
and her people to be a gladness.
I will rejoice in Jerusalem
and be glad in my people;
no more shall be heard in it the sound of weeping
and the cry of distress.
No more shall there be in it
an infant who lives but a few days,
or an old man who does not fill out his days,
for the young man shall die a hundred years old,
and the sinner a hundred years old shall be accursed.
They shall build houses and inhabit them;
they shall plant vineyards and eat their fruit.
They shall not build and another inhabit;
they shall not plant and another eat;
for like the days of a tree shall the days of my people be,
and my chosen shall long enjoy the work of their hands.
They shall not labour in vain
or bear children for calamity,
for they shall be the offspring of the blessed of the LORD,
and their descendants with them.
Before they call I will answer;
while they are yet speaking I will hear.
The wolf and the lamb shall graze together;
the lion shall eat straw like the ox,
and dust shall be the serpent's food.
They shall not hurt or destroy
in all my holy mountain,' says the LORD.

This passage undeniably envisages a radically different future world. The description of human longevity and harmonious coexistence involving predatory animals indicates that this new earth has none of the deficiencies of the present one. Significantly, in verses 17–18 the creation of the 'new heavens and a new earth' parallels the creation of Jerusalem (cf. Isa. 24:23).[75] The repeated

---

75. As noted earlier, Rev. 21:1–3 does the same.

use of the Hebrew verb *bārā'*, 'to create', suggests that Jerusalem is deliberately equated here with the new heavens and the new earth.[76] They are one and the same.

The description of a divinely created Jerusalem in Isaiah 65 is part of a sequence of passages that portray the future in terms of a transformed city. Isaiah 60 anticipates a time when the light and glory of the Lord will fill a totally renewed Jerusalem, dispelling the present darkness that covers the earth (Isa. 60:2):

> Whereas you have been forsaken and hated,
>   with no one passing through,
> I will make you majestic for ever,
>   a joy from age to age.
> You shall suck the milk of nations;
>   you shall nurse at the breast of kings;
> and you shall know that I, the LORD, am your Saviour
>   and your Redeemer, the Mighty One of Jacob.
>
> Instead of bronze I will bring gold,
>   and instead of iron I will bring silver;
> instead of wood, bronze,
>   instead of stones, iron.
> I will make your overseers peace
>   and your taskmasters righteousness.
> Violence shall no more be heard in your land,
>   devastation or destruction within your borders;
> you shall call your walls Salvation,
>   and your gates Praise.
>
> The sun shall be no more
>   your light by day,
> nor for brightness shall the moon
>   give you light;
> but the LORD will be your everlasting light,
>   and your God will be your glory.

---

76. Levenson argues this in more detail, *Creation*, pp. 89–90.

Your sun shall no more go down,
    nor your moon withdraw itself;
for the LORD will be your everlasting light,
    and your days of mourning shall be ended.
(Isa. 60:15–20)

As the final verses of this passage reveal, the presence of God within this future city will bring so much light that sun and moon will be redundant.[77] This exceptionally positive description of life within a future, renewed Jerusalem bears little resemblance to the historical city of the eighth to sixth centuries BC. Ironically, while the book of Isaiah looks forward to the presence of God filling a new Jerusalem, the sixth century BC witnesses the reverse. The destruction of the temple by the Babylonians in 586 BC brings to an end, at least temporarily, God's coexistence with the population of Jerusalem. While the reality of this experience is the opposite of the expectations contained in the book of Isaiah, the hope lived on that God would yet fulfil his creation blueprint through a transformed Jerusalem.

Although the razing of the Jerusalem temple in 586 BC seems a major reversal of God's purposes for the people of both the southern kingdom, Judah,[78] and Ephraim, the northern kingdom, the contemporary prophet Ezekiel brings to the Jewish exiles in Babylon a remarkable message of hope regarding the future. In spite of focusing on God's devastating judgment upon the population of Jerusalem, the book of Ezekiel, like Isaiah, contributes much to the theme of God's presence on the earth.

Ezekiel comes from a priestly family and is thus expected to serve in the temple, but is deported to Babylon in 597 BC at the age of twenty-five.[79] Five years later he has the first of a series of

---

77. The same theme is found in Rev. 21:11, 23 and 22:5.

78. The impact of this catastrophe upon the people of Judah is captured well in the book of Lamentations.

79. According to K. A. Kitchen, *On the Reliability of the Old Testament* (Grand Rapids: Eerdmans, 2003), p. 44, the Babylonian Chronicle dates the capture of Jerusalem by Nebuchadrezzar II to 2 Adar (15/16 March 597). See 2 Kgs 24:10–11.

visions through which God speaks to him over the next twenty years. To his utter amazement Ezekiel witnesses the almost indescribable chariot-throne of God coming towards him in Babylonia, with God in all his glory seated upon it. While Ezekiel might possibly have hoped to see the glory of God within the Jerusalem temple, as Isaiah had done (Isa. 6:1–5), nothing could have prepared him for this extraordinary event. To the exiled priest, this vision was a powerful reminder that the sovereign Lord had not abandoned his people.

God's initial messages to Ezekiel, however, chillingly predict that Jerusalem and its temple will soon be destroyed. In a vision that transports Ezekiel to the temple itself, he witnesses the 'image of jealousy' alongside the altar, seventy elders of Israel offering incense to 'every form of creeping things and loathsome beasts, and all the idols of the house of Israel', women mourning for Tammuz and twenty-five men bowing down to the sun (Ezek. 8:3–16). In the light of these idolatrous activities, God says to Ezekiel, 'Son of man, do you see what they are doing, the great abominations that the house of Israel are committing here, to drive me far from my sanctuary' (Ezek. 8:6)? In the chapters that follow, Ezekiel witnesses the departure of 'the glory of the God of Israel' from the temple as judgment is executed upon the inhabitants of Jerusalem who have not sighed and groaned over all the abominations done in the city (cf. Ezek. 9:4).[80] The idolatry, bloodshed and injustice of the people has forced God to leave the temple and the city.

Several factors, however, indicate that God takes no delight in abandoning the temple and Jerusalem. As John Taylor observes, in Ezekiel 10 'it was only a partial departure: from inner sanctum to threshold, as if the Lord is reluctant to leave and is almost pressurized into moving further away from the idolatrous epicentre that

---

80. There is irony in the fact that the people's sin is compounded by their belief that God has abandoned the land. As God says to Ezekiel, 'The guilt of the house of Israel and Judah is exceedingly great. The land is full of blood, and the city full of injustice. For they say, "The Lord has forsaken the land, and the Lord does not see"' (Ezek. 9:9).

was once his dwelling place'.[81] God's reluctance to leave the city is further reflected in Ezekiel 11:23, which portrays God as moving 'from the midst of the city' to a 'mountain that is on the east side of the city'. The Lord looks upon the city with a sense of regret, longing to return there.

While the opening chapters of Ezekiel centre on the departure of the divine presence from Jerusalem,[82] chapters 40–48 record another vision that focuses on God's return to a restored land and a new temple. At the time of this vision the Jerusalem temple has already been reduced to ruins by the Babylonians. Coming in 572 BC, twenty years after his first vision, Ezekiel's final vision is a long and detailed portrayal of an idealized replacement temple, set within a renewed city.[83] There is an artificiality to the lengthy vision that suggests its contents are to be taken as symbolic. For example, the river that flows from the centre of the temple keeps on growing, despite the lack of tributaries adding to it (Ezek. 47:1–6) and its waters desalinate the Dead Sea (Ezek. 47:8–10). In marked contrast to Ezekiel's earlier visions of judgment, the emphasis here is upon the return of God's presence. Significantly, the vision concludes with *yerušalayim*, 'Jerusalem', being renamed *yhwh-šammâ*, 'the LORD is there' (Ezek. 48:35).

81. J. B. Taylor, 'The Temple in Ezekiel', in T. D. Alexander and S. Gathercole (eds.), *Heaven on Earth: The Temple in Biblical Theology* (Carlisle: Paternoster, 2004), p. 67.

82. For a fuller treatment of this, see J. F. Kutsko, *Between Heaven and Earth: Divine Presence and Absence in the Book of Ezekiel*, Biblical and Judaic Studies from the University of California, San Diego, 7 (Winona Lake: Eisenbrauns, 2000).

83. Taylor, 'Temple in Ezekiel', pp. 67–69, sets out briefly the case for seeing chapters 40–48 as 'idealized and essentially symbolic in character and intention'. He suggests that the following factors favour this approach: (1) There is no divine command authorizing the reconstruction of this temple; it will be built by God himself. (2) The details provided are insufficient to enable the vision to be made a reality: only a ground plan is given; there is no partition wall around the inner court; no furniture is mentioned.

Although Ezekiel's vision in chapters 40–48 is a highly idealized picture of the future, it communicates powerfully, like the concluding chapters of Isaiah, that God is still committed to making the whole earth his dwelling place, establishing in the process a temple-city.

The same theme is echoed in the post-exilic prophetic book of Zechariah. In particular, Zechariah 8 looks forward to a transformed city in which God will dwell:

> Thus says the LORD: I have returned to Zion and will dwell in the midst of Jerusalem, and Jerusalem shall be called the faithful city, and the mountain of the LORD of hosts, the holy mountain. . . . Thus says the LORD of hosts: behold, I will save my people from the east country and from the west country, and I will bring them to dwell in the midst of Jerusalem. And they shall be my people, and I will be their God, in faithfulness and in righteousness. (Zech. 8:3, 7–8)

Commenting on the expectations outlined in Zechariah 8, Gowan writes:

> The good life that Zechariah projects for the inhabitants of Jerusalem is a mixture of the material and the spiritual. Peace, prosperity, and security are dominant themes, but his is no secular city. What makes it all possible is God, who carries out his purpose (8:2, 6, 11, 13b–15), and the source of the good life in Zion is the presence of Yahweh in its midst. Zechariah 8 begins, 'I will return to Zion and will dwell in the midst of Jerusalem,' and it ends, 'we have heard that God is with you.'[84]

These future expectations were clearly intended to encourage Zechariah's contemporaries in the late sixth century BC to finish rebuilding the temple. While the completed structure was unable to match the splendour of the temple constructed by Solomon, its erection was a powerful signal that God was still concerned to fulfil his creation blueprint. The subsequent rebuilding of the walls of Jerusalem, in the face of stern opposition, further confirmed

---

84. Gowan, *Eschatology in the Old Testament*, p. 6.

that the departure of God from Jerusalem at the start of the Babylonian exile was merely temporary. In spite of the setbacks of the sixth century, Jerusalem and its temple still feature in the plan by which God will establish his presence throughout the world.[85] With good reason, Gowan argues that Zion is central to Old Testament eschatology. This is demonstrated by the number of passages in the prophetic books that anticipate a future transformed Jerusalem. In all, Gowan identifies forty-three references in Isaiah, thirteen in Jeremiah, ten in Ezekiel and eight in Zechariah.[86] The large number of passages that focus on a future Jerusalem is certainly sufficient to justify Gowan's claim. However, as we have noted, the expectations associated with Jerusalem envisage a greatly transformed city and go far beyond a mere restoration of the city to its pre-exilic glory. Taking into account the rich variety of images used to describe the future Jerusalem, it seems likely that they all derive from the concept of the whole earth becoming God's temple-city.

---

85. Ibid., p. 9: 'Despite the embarrassment of the fall of Jerusalem and with it the end of all that Judeans trusted in; despite their eventual acceptance of the tragedy as fully merited judgement for their own sins, they could not, it seems, abandon that symbol of the city of God built on his holy mountain in favour of something better.' While Gowan is correct in highlighting the stigma attached to the fall of Jerusalem for the Judeans, it is God, not the people, who refuses to abandon the city.

86. Gowan (ibid.) lists the following passages: Isa. 1:24–26; 2:2–4; 4:2–6; 11:6–9; 18:7; 24:21–23; 25:6–8; 26:1; 27:13; 28:16; 29:8; 30:19–26; 30:29; 31:4–5; 32:14–20; 33:5–6; 33:17–24; 34:8; 35:10; 37:30–32; 40:2, 9; 41:27; 44:24–28; 45:13; 46:13; 48:2; 49:14–26; 51:1–3, 9–11, 12–16; 52:1–10; 54:1–17; 56:3–8; 57:11–13; 59:20; 60:10–14; 61:1–11; 62:1–12; 65:17–25; 66:1, 6, 10–14, 18–21; Jer. 3:14–18; 27:22; 29:10–14; 30:18–22; 31:6, 10–14, 23, 38–40; 32:36–41, 44; 33:4–16; 50:4–5; Ezek. 16:59–63; 17:22–24; 20:40–44; 34:20–30; 37:24–28; 40:2; 43:12; 45:6–8; 47:1–12; 48:35; Zech. 1:14–17; 2:1–12; 3:2; 8:1–23; 9:9–10; 12:1–9; 13:1; 14:1–21. In addition, Gowan notes that 'Jerusalem as the ideal city' is mentioned in Dan. 9:2, 24–26; Joel 3:17–21; Obad. 15–21; Hag. 2:9; Mal. 3:4; Mic. 4:1–13; Zeph. 3:14–20. See also Dumbrell, *End of the Beginning*, pp. 5–27.

Thus far, our survey of the biblical meta-story in the Old Testament has centred largely on the movement from Eden to tabernacle to Jerusalem temple. Although the construction of the tabernacle and later the Jerusalem temple are positive developments, overturning some of the barriers to the fulfilment of God's initial plans for the earth, the subsequent destruction of the temple by the Babylonians in 586 BC is a telling reminder that major obstacles still remain before God's blueprint will be fully realized. While the post-exilic reconstruction of the temple and the rebuilding of the city walls are evidence that God is still determined to complete his creation project, further measures are necessary in order for this to be achieved. As the preceding centuries have revealed, the sinfulness of the Jerusalemites prevents God's presence from expanding outward from the city. Since its population continues to be wayward, Jerusalem cannot easily evolve into the final reality.[87] In the light of this, the next stage in the biblical meta-story introduces an important transformation that involves the replacement of the Jerusalem temple by a new and very different edifice.

The church as temple

In moving from the Old Testament to the New Testament, we discover that the Jerusalem temple is replaced by the church and, with its outward expansion from Jerusalem to the ends of the earth, God's dwelling place also spreads outward. As we shall see below, this transition is bound to the incarnation of Jesus Christ, in whom the concepts of temple and body are united. This association provides an important theological basis for understanding how the church, as the body of Christ, is also the temple of God.

Although the church plays an important role in both modelling

---

87. The book of Malachi reveals that even in the post-exilic period the temple was defiled by those who served and worshipped there. Christ's remarks about Jerusalem in Matt. 23:37 and Luke 13:34 convey something of God's frustration at the city's response to its privileged status.

and partially realizing God's creation blueprint for the earth, it too, like the Jerusalem temple, has limitations. For the ultimate realization of God's purposes for the world we must look to the New Jerusalem of Revelation 21 – 22.

Without exhausting all of the evidence that points to the church superseding the Jerusalem temple, the following observations demonstrate this transition.

The concept of the church as God's dwelling place plays a significant role within the apostle Paul's letter to the Ephesians. Addressing a largely Gentile audience he comments:

> So then you are no longer strangers and aliens, but you are fellow citizens with the saints and members of the household of God, built on the foundation of the apostles and prophets, Christ Jesus himself being the cornerstone, in whom the whole structure, being joined together, grows into a holy temple in the Lord. In him you also are being built together into a dwelling place for God by the Spirit. (Eph. 2:19–22)

Undoubtedly, Paul views the church corporately as being God's temple. 'Paul pictured each local church as providing God with a spiritual habitation in that locality (Eph 2:22) and as growing together with all the other churches into one holy, universal sanctuary for the Lord's indwelling.'[88] Using building imagery, he sees

---

88. P. W. Comfort, 'Temple', in G. F. Hawthorne, R. P. Martin and D. G. Reid (eds.), *Dictionary of Paul and his Letters* (Leicester: IVP; Downers Grove: IVP, 1993), p. 925. On the basis of Eph. 2:6, D. Peterson, 'The New Temple: Christology and Ecclesiology in Ephesians and 1 Peter', in T. D. Alexander and S. Gathercole (eds.), *Heaven on Earth: The Temple in Biblical Theology* (Carlisle: Paternoster, 2004), p. 168, argues that the temple here is 'a heavenly, rather than a local, assembly'. A similar position is adopted by P. T. O'Brien, 'The Church as a Heavenly and Eschatological Entity', in D. A. Carson (ed.), *Church in the Bible and the World* (Exeter: Paternoster, 1987), pp. 101–103. He writes, 'Here at Eph. 2 the temple is God's heavenly abode, the place of his dwelling. Yet that temple is his people in whom he lives by his Spirit. Believers on earth, recipients of this circular letter, are linked with the heavenly realm in and through the Spirit of the risen

the apostles and prophets as the foundation, with Jesus Christ being the cornerstone (*akrogōniaiou*) around which the whole structure is created.[89] Although Paul envisages God as already residing in this biological temple, he also sees it as still growing.[90] Paul is not contemplating here the personal growth of individual believers, but rather the corporate growth of the church. This is clearly reflected in the use of 'being joined together' (*synarmologoumenē*) and 'being built together' (*synoikodomeisthe*).[91]

Footnote 88 (*continued*)

Lord.' However, the weight of evidence favours seeing Eph. 2:19–22 as referring to the local church. It is possible to take 2:6 and 2:19–22 as referring to heavenly and earthly temples respectively, for in the Old Testament both temples are linked.

89. M. Turner, 'Ephesians', in D. A. Carson, R. T. France, J. A. Motyer and G. J. Wenham (eds.), *New Bible Commentary (21st Century Edition)* (Leicester: IVP, 1994), p. 1233, underlines the importance of Christ for the whole structure: 'all is built on Christ, supported by Christ, and the lie or shape of the continuing building is determined by Christ, the cornerstone'. According to Peterson, 'New Temple', p. 165, the cornerstone is 'the primary stone of the foundation'.

90. R. J. McKelvey, *The New Temple: The Church in the New Testament*, Oxford Theological Monographs (London: Oxford University Press, 1969), p. 117, comments, 'Viewed as the building the church is still under construction; viewed as the temple, however, it is an inhabited dwelling.' T. G. Gombis, 'Being the Fullness of God in Christ by the Spirit: Ephesians 5:18 in its Epistolary Setting', *Tyndale Bulletin* 53 (2002), p. 261, observes, 'Verse 21 states that though the building has been built (*epoikodomēthentes*), it is "being joined together" (*synarmologoumenē*) and is "growing (*auxei*) into a holy temple in the Lord". In verse 22, they are "being built up (*synoiko-domeisthe*) into a dwelling of God by the Spirit". So, while the church as the dwelling place of God by the Spirit is an accomplished reality, it is also a process which stands in need of being increasingly actualised.'

91. The Greek terms Paul employs here are constructed using the prefix *syn-*, 'together with, in company with'. In passing, it is worth noting that L. J. Kreitzer, 'The Messianic Man of Peace as Temple Builder: Solomonic Imagery in Ephesians 2:13–22', in J. Day (ed.), *Temple and Worship in Biblical*

Apart for the presence of building terminology in Ephesians 2:21–22, the concept of the church as God's dwelling place is also reflected in Paul's use of terms associated with the concept of 'filling'. Paul's prayer for the Ephesians is that they 'may be filled with all the fullness of God' (Eph. 3:19). Paul alludes here to the image of the tabernacle and temple being filled with God's glory. This train of thought also underlies his instruction that the believers in Ephesus are to 'be filled by the Spirit' (Eph. 5:18). Paul commands them as a group to be the dwelling place of God by his Spirit. They will achieve this by

> addressing one another in psalms and hymns and spiritual songs, singing and making melody to the Lord with all your heart, giving thanks always and for everything to God the Father in the name of our Lord Jesus Christ, submitting to one another out of reverence for Christ. (Eph. 5:19–21)[92]

Although Paul stresses in Ephesians the importance of the church being filled with the presence of God through the Holy Spirit, he says relatively little about the process of temple-building. This is reversed in 1 Corinthians, where Paul also writes about the church being the temple of God.

In the Corinthian correspondence Paul refers on several occasions to the church as God's temple. He does so first in 1 Corinthians 3:16–17: 'Do you[93] not know that you are God's temple and that God's Spirit dwells in you? If anyone destroys

---

Israel, Library of Hebrew Bible / Old Testament Studies 422 (London: T. & T. Clark, 2005), pp. 484–512, finds allusions in Eph. 2 to Solomon and the construction of the Jerusalem temple.

92. Commenting on this passage, Gombis, 'Being the Fullness', p. 271, writes, 'The church is to be the temple of God, the fullness of Christ by the Spirit *by* being the community that speaks God's word to one another, sings praises to the Lord, renders thanksgiving to God for all things in the name of the Lord Jesus Christ, and lives in relationship characterised by mutual submission.'

93. The Greek for 'you' is plural in vv. 16 and 17.

God's temple, God will destroy him. For God's temple is holy, and you are that temple.'

Later, in 1 Corinthians 6:19, he comments, 'Or do you[94] not know that your body is a temple of the Holy Spirit within you, whom you have from God?'[95] In 2 Corinthians 6:16 Paul writes, 'What agreement has the temple of God with idols? For we are the temple of the living God; as God said, "I will make my dwelling among them and walk among them, and I will be their God, and they shall be my people."' By way of explanation, McKelvey writes:

> the apostle evidently understands God's presence in the church as much more than a type of the divine indwelling in the old sanctuary or the fulfilment of the prophecy that God would again dwell with his people after the exile, for he supplements the LXX verb 'walk among' with the much stronger verb 'live in'. In other words, God no longer dwells *with* his people in a sanctuary which they make for him; he dwells *in* them, and *they* are his temple.[96]

Paul's argument in this passage draws strongly upon Old

---

94. Again, 'you' and 'your' are plural in this verse. Paul is not speaking here of the bodies of *individual* believers, but the *corporate* body of the church.

95. Many scholars interpret Paul's comment 'your body is a temple of the Holy Spirit' as implying that each individual believer is a temple of God. So, for example, Comfort, 'Temple', p. 924, writes, 'Each person who has been spiritually united to the Lord is his holy dwelling place; his or her body belongs to the Lord and must not be given to or joined with a prostitute.' However, Paul's use of the singular forms 'body' and 'temple' in conjunction with the plural pronoun 'you' would seem more naturally to fit with the view that the local church is the temple of God. If Paul had intended otherwise, he would surely have said, 'do you not know that your *bodies* are the temples of the Holy Spirit' (my italics). Further reasons in favour of 'body' denoting the whole church in Corinth are offered by T. Holland, *Contours of Pauline Theology: A Radical New Survey of the Influences on Paul's Biblical Writings* (Fearn: Mentor, 2004), p. 127.

96. McKelvey, *New Temple*, p. 95.

Testament practices. If idols were excluded from the tabernacle and temple, they can have no place within the new temple of the church.

Although the term 'temple' is not used in 1 Corinthians 14:25, when he remarks that an unbeliever 'will worship God and declare that God is really among you', Paul obviously assumes that the assembled church forms a divine dwelling place. It is also highly likely, as Brian Rosner has argued, that 'the expulsion of the sinner in 1 Corinthians 5 is in order to restore the holiness of God's temple, the church'.[97] Beale also finds evidence of temple imagery in 2 Corinthians 4:16 – 5:5.[98]

According to David Peterson, the expression 'temple of God' in 1 Corinthians 3:16 'marks out the Corinthian church as the divine sanctuary where God's Spirit dwells'.[99] This comes at the end of a passage in which Paul focuses on the theme of building. He begins in 3:10 by observing that he has been gifted by God to be 'a skilled master builder' or 'director of works' (*architektōn*).[100] While Paul describes his own role in terms of overseeing and directing the construction work, he observes that others are

97. B. S. Rosner, 'Temple and Holiness in 1 Corinthians 5', *Tyndale Bulletin* 42 (1991), p. 137.

98. Beale, *Temple and the Church's Mission*, pp. 256–259. E. E. Ellis, '2 Corinthians 5:1–10 in Pauline Eschatology', *New Testament Studies* 6 (1960), pp. 211–224, suggests that in 2 Cor. 5 Paul's reference to a 'house not made with hands, eternal in the heavens' refers to the corporate body of Christ conceived as a new temple.

99. Peterson, 'New Temple', p. 162. O'Brien, 'Church', p. 100, writes, 'the congregation at Corinth is itself the dwelling-place of God. His tabernacling on earth is not apart from his people; rather, it is an indwelling within them (note v. 16, "the Spirit of God dwells *in you*["]; v. 17, "the temple of God ... you are").'

100. Here Paul alludes to the way in which God gifted Bezalel for the task of constructing the tabernacle (see Exod. 31:2–5). In Ephesians Paul draws attention to apostles, prophets, evangelists, pastors/teachers as 'craftsmen' whose task is to equip others 'for the work of ministry, for building up the body of Christ'.

involved in this building process. In Paul's thinking, every Christian is gifted by God to contribute to the process of constructing the church as God's temple. Both here and in Ephesians 4:7 Paul indicates that those who build are equipped to do their various tasks by God's grace through the Holy Spirit.[101]

Paul cautions those who build. He stresses the importance of building upon the right foundation, Jesus Christ. He also exhorts them to work earnestly and competently. The quality of how someone builds is illustrated using different kinds of materials. The first four of these (gold, silver, precious stones, wood) were used in the construction of the Jerusalem temple. To these Paul adds 'hay' and 'straw' as types of material that will not survive if burned with fire. Pointing to a future divine assessment of how each person has contributed to the building process, Paul urges the Corinthian believers to co-operate in creating a 'a sacred community of people indwelt by the Spirit of God'.[102]

The image of the church as a temple is probably also found in 1 Peter 2:4–6, part of a longer passage that abounds in Old Testament allusions:

> As you come to him, a living stone rejected by men but in the sight of God chosen and precious, you yourselves like living stones are being built up as a spiritual house, to be a holy priesthood, to offer spiritual sacrifices acceptable to God through Jesus Christ. For it stands in Scripture: 'Behold, I am laying in Zion a stone, a cornerstone chosen and precious, and whoever believes in him will not be put to shame.'

While the image of living stones being built into a spiritual house resonates with what Paul says in Ephesians 2:19–22, the lack of any specific reference to a temple has caused some scholars to

---

101. W. Hildebrand, *An Old Testament Theology of the Spirit of God* (Peabody: Hendrickson, 1995), pp. 194–195, observes that in the Old Testament those responsible for the construction of the tabernacle and the Jerusalem temple are specially equipped to do so by the Spirit of God (Exod. 31:2–5; 1 Chr. 28:11–19).

102. Peterson, 'New Temple', p. 162.

suggest that temple imagery is not present in this passage.[103] However, Beale links 1 Peter 2:4–6 with Revelation 11 and proposes that we have here 'the conception of God's saints being the true temple of God's presence . . . and extending that presence throughout the earth by means of their witness'.[104]

The idea of the church being the new temple of God, replacing the Jerusalem temple, is also reflected in the Gospel of Luke and its sequel, the book of Acts.[105] A distinctive feature of Luke's Gospel is the special attention it gives to the temple. From the outset Luke draws attention to the temple in his selection of infancy stories. Only in Luke do we read of Zechariah's encounter with the angel at the altar of incense in the sanctuary (1:8–23) and the bringing of Jesus to the temple as a baby (2:22–38). This latter passage introduces Simeon and Anna, who both affirm at the temple the significance of the newborn child. Only Luke records Jesus' visit at the age of twelve to the temple (2:41–51).[106] Later, the temple courts are the location where Jesus teaches after coming to Jerusalem (19:47; 20:1; 21:37–38; 22:53). Finally, Luke concludes his Gospel by observing that the disciples 'were continually in the temple blessing God' (24:53). Although Luke's portrayal of the temple is the most

103. O'Brien, 'Church', p. 104.

104. Beale, *Temple and the Church's Mission*, p. 332.

105. A more detailed treatment of the temple in Luke's Gospel is provided by P. M. Head, 'The Temple in Luke's Gospel', in T. D. Alexander and S. Gathercole (eds.), *Heaven on Earth: The Temple in Biblical Theology* (Carlisle: Paternoster, 2004), pp. 102–119. For a discussion of the temple in Acts, see Beale, *Temple and the Church's Mission*, pp. 201–244; 'The Descent of the Eschatological Temple in the Form of the Spirit at Pentecost: Part 1: The Clearest Evidence', *Tyndale Bulletin* 56.1 (2005), pp. 73–102; 'The Descent of the Eschatological Temple in the Form of the Spirit at Pentecost: Part 2: Corroborating Evidence', *Tyndale Bulletin* 56.2 (2005), pp. 63–90.

106. Head, 'Temple in Luke's Gospel', p. 111, notes that the text of Luke 2:49 refers ambiguously to the temple. Following D. D. Sylva, 'The Cryptic Clause *en tois tou patros mou dei einai me* in Lk 2:49b', *Zeitschrift für die neutestamentliche Wissenschaft und die Kunde der älteren Kirche* 78 (1987), pp. 132–140, he translates *en tois tou patros mou* as 'among the things of my father'.

extensive and positive of all the Gospels, he too records Jesus' comment regarding its destruction (21:5–6) and mentions the rending of the temple curtain (23:45; cf. Matt. 27:51; Mark 15:38).[107] With a number of references to the disciples worshipping there, the Jerusalem temple continues to be prominent in the opening chapters of Acts (2:46; 3:1–3; 5:20–21, 42). However, as Luke's account of the early church progresses, the Jerusalem temple becomes less and less significant. At one level, the diminution of the temple may be viewed simply as reflecting the manner in which the book of Acts follows the expansion of the church from Jerusalem to Samaria and on to Rome. As the focus of attention moves away from Jerusalem, it is only natural that the temple diminishes in importance.

However, another factor may better account for this shift in emphasis. According to Beale, the coming of the Spirit at Pentecost in Acts 2 is best understood as paralleling those occasions in the Old Testament when God came to fill with his presence the tabernacle (Exod. 40:34–35) and temple (1 Kgs 8:10–11; 2 Chr. 7:1–2).[108] This temple imagery is confirmed by Peter's use of Joel 2:28–32 to explain the significance of this extraordinary event. As Peterson observes:

> Prophecies about the restoration of Israel after the Babylonian exile included the promise of the gift of God's Spirit, as the means by which he would dwell in or among his people and bless them in a new way (e.g. Joel 2:28–32; Isa. 44:3–5; Ezek. 36:27–28; 37:14).[109]

---

107. The temple also features in Luke's account of the temptation of Jesus (Luke 4:9–11). T. Longman III and D. G. Reid, *God Is a Warrior*, Studies in Old Testament Biblical Theology (Grand Rapids: Zondervan, 1995), p. 96, observe, 'Luke's placement of the temptation at the Jerusalem temple as the last of the three probably reflects his own desire to foreshadow Jerusalem as the final place of triumph, as well as his noticeable emphasis on Jerusalem as the geographical center of redemptive history (cf. Lk 9:31, 51, 53; 19:28).'

108. Beale, *Temple and the Church's Mission*, pp. 201–216; Beale, 'Spirit at Pentecost: Part 2', pp. 64–66.

109. Peterson, 'New Temple', pp. 162–163.

In Acts the process of believers being incorporated into the new, organic temple of God occurs in stages. The Jerusalem Pentecost is followed by two similar occurrences: the first involves the coming of the Spirit upon Samaritans (8:14–17); the next centres on the Gentiles in Cornelius' house, who receive the Spirit (10:44–47). These closely related events are highly significant for our understanding of how the new temple of God incorporates people from all nations. Steve Walton comments:

> The stories in Acts represent, as it were, the cusp of the change from a localized view of God dwelling in the Temple to what we might call a universalized view, in which God is available, and reveals himself, anywhere and everywhere. Luke says implicitly what Paul or Hebrews or 1 Peter or John or Revelation say explicitly, but does not express their view outright because he is concerned to describe faithfully the historical process of development.[110]

The creation of the church as the dwelling place of God involves a subtle but significant shift in emphasis. Whereas in the Old Testament God was perceived as dwelling *among* his people, in the New Testament he is viewed as dwelling *within* his people. As R. E. Clements notes:

> The ancient promises that God would dwell with his people were eagerly taken up by Christians and applied to the Church, the Body of Christ, in which God dwelt by the Holy Spirit. The major difference between the new fulfilment and the old promise is that whereas the Old Testament had spoken of a dwelling of God among men, the New Testament speaks of a dwelling of God within men by the Holy Spirit.[111]

---

110. S. Walton, 'A Tale of Two Perspectives? The Place of the Temple in Acts', in T. D. Alexander and S. Gathercole (eds.), *Heaven on Earth: The Temple in Biblical Theology* (Carlisle: Paternoster, 2004), p. 149.

111. Clements, *God and Temple*, p. 139; cf. A. J. Köstenberger, *John*, Baker Exegetical Commentary on the New Testament (Grand Rapids: Baker, 2004), p. 141.

The fact that God, through the Holy Spirit, did not indwell believers in the Old Testament period does not exclude them from being regenerate, as J. M. Hamilton demonstrates in his book *God's Indwelling Presence*. In both testaments regeneration is not dependent upon the indwelling of the Holy Spirit within an individual. Rather indwelling is tied to the concept of temple:

> Indwelling does exist in the old covenant, but it is not each individual that is indwelt. In the old covenant God indwelt the temple. In the new covenant the people of God *are* the temple, and God dwells *in* them.[112]

As an organic, growing building the church, as the new temple of God, takes its shape from Jesus Christ, the cornerstone (Eph. 2:20), a concept that has its origins in Jesus' own teaching (see Matt. 21:42; Mark 12:10; Luke 20:17; cf. Acts 4:11). John's Gospel also witnesses to this link between Jesus and the temple. In addition to John 1:14, which speaks of Jesus 'tabernacling' in the world, John 2:19–21 reports that Jesus said:

> 'Destroy this temple, and in three days I will raise it up.' The Jews then said, 'It has taken forty-six years to build this temple, and will you raise it up in three days?' But he was speaking about the temple of his body.

In the light of Jesus' claim to be the temple of God, it is noteworthy that Mark's Gospel highlights the part played by the temple establishment in opposing Jesus. Kent Brower, who helpfully outlines the development of the conflict between Jesus and the temple authorities in Mark, writes:

> This conflict brought God's judgment on the very heart of the temple system through the death of the messiah, the Son of God. But this judgment also carried with it the conviction that God's purposes for

---

112. J. M. Hamilton, *God's Indwelling Presence: The Holy Spirit in the Old and New Testaments*, New American Commentary Studies in Bible and Theology (Nashville: B. & H., 2006), p. 160 (italics in original).

the temple would be realized through Jesus and His new covenant community.[113]

As Mark's Gospel highlights, the failure of the temple establishment to recognize Jesus as the divinely appointed heir to the Davidic throne is a significant factor in the transition from the Jerusalem temple to the church as God's dwelling place. The Gospel passages that present Christ's own body as a temple also help us understand how the church can be a temple constructed of people. Since Christ's body is the temple of God and since, as Paul repeatedly emphasizes, Christians are those who are 'in Christ', it naturally follows that the church, as the body of Christ, is also the temple of God. On the basis of this, Edmund Clowney observes:

> The church's existence as the body-temple depends totally on the resurrection body of Christ in which the church is raised up, and on the Spirit of Christ by which the church lives. Paul's appeals for the unity of the church are drawn from the unity of the body of Christ as the true and final temple. For Paul the body and the temple go together: the breaking down of the middle wall of the temple creates one body; the New Temple grows as a body (Eph. 2:21); the body is built as a temple (Eph. 4:12, 16). Christ is the cornerstone of the structure, the Lord in whom the New Temple exists.[114]

---

113. K. E. Brower, ' "Let the Reader Understand": Temple and Eschatology in Mark', in K. E. Brower and M. W. Elliott (eds.), *The Reader Must Understand': Eschatology in Bible and Theology* (Leicester: Apollos, 1997), p. 143.

114. E. P. Clowney, 'The Final Temple', *Westminster Theological Journal* 35 (1973), pp. 184–185. While Clowney helpfully draws attention to the significance of the relationship between Christ's body as the temple of God and the church as the temple of God, he mistakenly views individual Christians as temples. For example, he writes, 'Just as the church is one with Christ in his body and as his body-temple, so the individual believer is a temple of the Lord' (p. 185). However, a careful analysis suggests that Paul frequently adopts a corporate understanding of the term 'body' (cf. Holland, *Contours of Pauline Theology*, pp. 85–110).

This connection between the body and temple is highly significant and clearly influences how the New Testament writers understand the church.

While the New Testament gives particular attention to the church as the temple of God, the concept of 'city' retreats somewhat into the background. Given the dispersed nature of the church, this is hardly surprising. Nevertheless, citizenship within a divine city remains part of the Christian hope. In Galatians 4:21–31 the apostle Paul contrasts the 'present Jerusalem', which he associates with slavery to the law, with the 'Jerusalem above', which brings freedom. And in Philippians 3:20 he writes, 'Our citizenship is in heaven, and from it we await a Saviour, the Lord Jesus Christ.' The author of Hebrews also develops the idea of a divine city in the final sections of his letter. In Hebrews 11:8–10, with reference to Abraham, we read:

> By faith Abraham obeyed when he was called to go out to a place that he was to receive as an inheritance. And he went out, not knowing where he was going. By faith he went to live in the land of promise, as in a foreign land, living in tents with Isaac and Jacob, heirs with him of the same promise. For he was looking forward to the city that has foundations, whose designer and builder is God.

The writer obviously believes that God had promised Abraham that one day the patriarch would dwell in a divinely constructed city. This is no ordinary city, for God is both the architect and builder. Several verses later, after commenting on Sarah's faith, the subject of the promised city is reintroduced:

> These all died in faith, not having received the things promised, but having seen them and greeted them from afar, and having acknowledged that they were strangers and exiles on the earth. For people who speak thus make it clear that they are seeking a homeland. If they had been thinking of that land from which they had gone out, they would have had opportunity to return. But as it is, they desire a better country, that is, a heavenly one. Therefore God is not ashamed to be called their God, for he has prepared for them a city. (Heb. 11:13–16)

These additional remarks reveal that Abraham, Sarah, Isaac and Jacob did not receive this city, designed and built by God, before they died. Rather, they inherit it after death.

Towards the end of his exhortatory letter, the author of Hebrews urges his readers to set their hope on a heavenly city. Like the patriarchs and Sarah who lived some 2,000 years earlier, they too will, by faith, inherit a city. However, the city is not to be found here and now. As the author remarks, 'For here we have no lasting city, but we seek the city that is to come' (Heb. 13:14).

We began this chapter by noting that Revelation 21 – 22 antici-pates a new earth dominated by a golden city of immense proportions in which God resides. Observing that the origins of this temple-city may be traced back to the opening chapters of Genesis, our survey of the theme of divine presence reveals a fas-cinating and coherent progression from Eden to tabernacle to Jerusalem temple to church to New Jerusalem. This distinctive framework is not only important for understanding the biblical meta-story, but it enables us, as we shall see in our remaining chap-ters, to understand better complementary themes that run in parallel from the initial chapters of Genesis to the final chapters of Revelation.

3. THROWN FROM THE THRONE: RE-ESTABLISHING THE SOVEREIGNTY OF GOD

In the preceding chapter we proposed that the New Jerusalem of Revelation 21 – 22 represents the fulfilment of God's original blueprint for the earth. From the outset of creation, God intended that the earth would become a holy garden-city in which he would dwell alongside human beings. However, the disobedience of Adam and Eve jeopardized this divine project. Expelled from God's presence, the first human couple were stripped of their priestly status. In addition, through their unholy behaviour they and subsequent generations defiled the earth. Those who were meant to facilitate God's creation plan now prevented it from being fulfilled.

In the process of recovering the earth as his dwelling place, God progressively established the tabernacle, the Jerusalem temple and the church. In differing ways each of these functioned as a model resembling God's ultimate ambition for the world. Additionally, all three herald new stages in the process by which God himself gradually begins to inhabit the earth. Ultimately, God's presence will fill the New Jerusalem, bringing to completion his creation project.

The throne of God

Building on the theme of God's presence, we shall now consider another of the important images found in John's final vision. Revelation 22:1–3 draws attention to the divine throne:

> Then the angel showed me the river of the water of life, bright as crystal, flowing from the throne of God and of the Lamb through the middle of the street of the city . . . No longer will there be anything accursed, but the throne of God and of the Lamb will be in it, and his servants will worship him.

The divine throne reappears in a number of visions in the book of Revelation. Perhaps the most detailed comes in 4:1–4:

> After this I looked, and behold, a door standing open in heaven! And the first voice, which I had heard speaking to me like a trumpet, said, 'Come up here, and I will show you what must take place after this.' At once I was in the Spirit, and behold, a throne stood in heaven, with one seated on the throne. And he who sat there had the appearance of jasper and carnelian, and around the throne was a rainbow that had the appearance of an emerald. Around the throne were twenty-four thrones, and seated on the thrones were twenty-four elders, clothed in white garments, with golden crowns on their heads.

References to the throne of God draw attention to his kingship, one of the major themes in Revelation. By highlighting the divine throne, John's final vision reveals that the creation of the New Jerusalem consolidates God's absolute authority over everything that exists upon the earth.

At first sight this claim may not seem especially noteworthy. Is God not already sovereign over everything? Surely, by his very nature God is King of kings and Lord of lords. However, the biblical meta-story indicates that God's sovereignty does not extend unchallenged over the present earth. To appreciate why this is so, we need to return to the opening chapters of Genesis.

Adam and Eve as God's viceroys

In Genesis 1 – 2 Adam and Eve are endowed with a holy or priestly status that enables them to serve in the temple-garden and have direct access to God. In addition, the human couple are appointed as God's viceroys to govern the earth on his behalf. Genesis 1 underlines this in two distinctive ways. First, they are directly instructed by God to exercise dominion over all of the other creatures made by him:

> Then God said, 'Let us make man in our image, after our likeness. And let them have dominion over the fish of the sea and over the birds of the heavens and over the livestock and over all the earth and over every creeping thing that creeps on the earth.' So God created man in his own image, in the image of God he created him; male and female he created them. And God blessed them. And God said to them, 'Be fruitful and multiply and fill the earth and subdue it and have dominion over the fish of the sea and over the birds of the heavens and over every living thing that moves on the earth.' (Gen. 1:26–28)

Through commissioning human beings to govern all land animals, birds and fish, God sets them apart from all other creatures and gives them a royal status. By repeating this point twice within three verses, the author of Genesis 1 underscores the divine delegation of authority to humankind to rule over the earth.

The second reason for believing that Adam and Eve were commissioned to be God's viceroys is less obvious to modern readers. The concept of royalty underlies the expression 'image of God'. In the ancient Near East, in both Egypt and Mesopotamia, the phrase 'image of God' was commonly linked to kings. The king was the living 'image of a god'. Here is how Ramses II (1290–1224 BC) describes his divine-image status:

> Utterance of the divine king, Lord of the Two Lands, lord of the form of Khepri, in whose limbs is Re, who came forth from Re, whom Ptah-Tatenen begat, King Ramses II, given life; to his father, from whom he came forth, Tatenen, father of the gods: 'I am thy son whom thou hast placed upon thy throne. Thou hast assigned to me thy kingdom, thou

hast fashioned me in thy likeness and thy form, which thou hast assigned to me and hast created.'[1]

As this quotation reveals, kingship and divine image go hand in hand. With good reason, Richard Middleton writes:

the writer of Genesis 1 portrays God as king presiding over 'heaven and earth,' an ordered and harmonious realm in which each creature manifests the will of the creator and is thus declared 'good.' Humanity is created *like* this God, with the special role of representing or imaging God's rule in the world.[2]

To be made in the 'image of God' is to be given regal status.[3]

As well as ruling over other creatures, the first human couple, as God's representatives, are instructed to be fruitful and fill the earth. Implicit in this instruction is the idea that God's authority will be extended throughout the earth as people increase in

---

1. J. H. Breasted, *Ancient Records of Egypt*. Vol. 3: *The Nineteeth Dynasty* (Chicago: University of Chicago Press, 1906), p. 181.

2. J. R. Middleton, *The Liberating Image: The Imago Dei in Genesis 1* (Grand Rapids: Brazos, 2005), p. 26.

3. Ibid., pp. 52–53: 'Many scholars identify the *imago Dei* with rule without further ado. Thus Robert Davidson, noting that "context is the safest guide to meaning," asserts that "image and likeness are defined by what *follows*, to rule." Likewise H. D. Preuss concludes that the meaning of the likeness to God in 1:26 "emerges only from the broader context (v. 28) and is explained as a cooperative sharing in dominion." Many interpreters who deny that the image is simply equivalent to rule nevertheless take this verse to mean that rule is an important subsidiary component of the image, typically related to the image as its result or consequence. But this is not exactly a justified reading of the syntax of 1:26, since a Hebrew jussive with unconverted *wāw* (*wĕyirdû*, and let them rule) that follows a cohortative (*na'ăśeh*, let us make) always expresses the intention or aim of the first-person perspective (singular or plural) represented by the cohortative. The syntax, in other words, points to "rule" as the *purpose*, not simply the consequence or result, of the *imago Dei.*'

number and spread outwards. Again, knowledge of the ancient Near Eastern background sheds further valuable light on this instruction to fill the earth. In the ancient Near East a ruler's image was set up in distant parts of his kingdom in order to indicate that his authority reached there.[4] As images of God, human beings are to perform a similar function. Taken in conjunction with their holy status, Adam and Eve are to be fruitful so that their descendants may, as priest-kings, extend God's temple and kingdom throughout the earth.[5] This was God's blueprint for the created world.

Against this background, the familiar account in Genesis 3 of how the serpent deceives the woman and the man into disobeying God is highly significant. In the light of their royal status and their divine commission to rule over the animals, it is especially noteworthy that Adam and Eve obey the serpent's instructions rather than those of God. By submitting to the serpent, Adam and Eve fail to exercise their God-given dominion over this crafty animal.

Adam and Eve's disobedience to God is an act of the utmost treachery. On the one hand, they knowingly betray the Creator who has entrusted them with his authority to govern the earth. On the other hand, they give their allegiance to a cunning creature who challenges God's authority with the deliberate intention of overturning his careful ordering of creation.

By betraying God and obeying the serpent, the royal couple dethrone God. Adam and Eve, commissioned by God to play a central role in the building of his holy garden-city, not only forfeit

---

4. G. von Rad, *Old Testament Theology*, vol. 1 (Edinburgh: Oliver & Boyd, 1962), pp. 146–147.

5. In Hebrew the term for 'temple', *hêkāl*, may also be translated as 'palace'. In the ancient Near East a temple was perceived as a divine palace. Consequently, temple and kingdom are intimately connected concepts. Dumbrell, 'Genesis 2:1–17', pp. 53–65, develops the idea that Adam is a king-priest with the role of expanding Eden into a worldwide sanctuary. The role of ancient Near Eastern kings as temple-builders is noted by A. S. Kapelrud, 'Temple Building, a Task for Gods and Kings', *Orientalia* 32 (1963), pp. 56–62.

their priestly status but also betray the trust placed in them to govern the earth. The ones through whom God's sovereignty was to be extended throughout the earth side with his enemy. By heeding the serpent they not only give it control over the earth, but they themselves become its subjects.[6]

Although Adam and Eve are expelled from God's presence, human beings retain the capacity to exercise dominion. However, due to their rebellious behaviour, God's authority structures are overturned. The divine ordering of creation is rejected by the human couple, with disastrous consequences for all involved. Harmony gives way to chaos. As the early chapters of Genesis go on to reveal, people exercise dominion in the cruellest of ways. Violence towards other creatures, both human and animal, is the hallmark of fallen humanity. Not only do we witness Cain killing his brother, Abel (Gen. 4:8), but in Genesis 6:13 God tells Noah that he is going 'to make an end of all flesh, for the earth is filled with violence through them'.

Against this background, the rest of the biblical story is especially interested in describing how the sovereignty of God will be restored and extended over the whole earth. How will God's kingdom be established throughout the world? How will his throne be set up in the holy garden-city that is to fill the earth? How will human beings be rescued from the control of the enemy and be enabled to fulfil the purpose for which God created them? These are the important questions raised by Adam and Eve's rebellion against God.

To see how the restoration of God's sovereignty over the earth is described in the rest of the Bible, we shall focus briefly on Israel as a theocracy and the church as the kingdom of God.

---

6. D. G. McCartney, 'Ecce Homo: The Coming of the Kingdom as the Restoration of Human Vicegerency', Westminster Theological Journal 56 (1994), p. 15, comments, 'By dethroning man on earth, Satan thought to dethrone God's reign on earth.' We shall consider the nature and identity of the serpent in more detail in chapter 4.

The theocracy of Israel

As the biblical meta-story moves from creation blueprint to final reality, the establishment of Israel as a nation ruled over by the Lord God is an exceptionally important development. This unique theocracy is initiated when God brings the descendants of Abraham, Isaac and Jacob to Mount Sinai and enters into a covenant relationship with them. The covenant at Sinai, as we shall see shortly, bestows on the Israelites a royal and priestly status. This is significant, for the opening chapters of Genesis reveal that the fulfilment of God's creation project requires the existence of priest-kings who will extend God's temple-city throughout the earth. Although Adam and Eve were given this special status when created, they subsequently forfeited it by rebelling against God. Against this background, the designation of the Israelites as priest-kings indicates that the creation of Israel as a theocracy will contribute to the completion of God's creation project.

While the making of the Sinai covenant is an important new development in the biblical meta-story, its origins may be traced back to the patriarch Abraham and his special relationship with God. Indeed, the whole exodus event is anticipated in Genesis 15:13–16, where God reveals to Abraham through a distinctive covenant ceremony that his descendants will be enslaved in a foreign land before returning to settle in the land of Canaan. This divine promise comes in the context of Abraham having just encountered the priest-king Melchizedek, an event that has an important bearing on understanding the development of God's special relationship with Abraham and his descendants.

Genesis 14 recounts Abraham's dramatic rescue of his nephew Lot, abducted by four kings: Chedorlaomer, king of Elam; Tidal, king of Goiim; Amraphel, king of Shinar; and Arioch, king of Ellasar. These kings have already defeated five kings, 'the king of Sodom, the king of Gomorrah, the king of Admah, the king of Zeboiim, and the king of Bela (that is, Zoar)' (v. 8). With help from several allies, Abraham successfully defeats the four eastern kings and rescues Lot. When he returns victorious, two kings come to greet him. Their rendezvous is described as follows:

After his return from the defeat of Chedorlaomer and the kings who were with him, the king of Sodom went out to meet him at the Valley of Shaveh (that is, the King's Valley). And Melchizedek king of Salem brought out bread and wine. (He was priest of God Most High.) And he blessed him and said,

'Blessed be Abram by God Most High,
  Possessor of heaven and earth;
and blessed be God Most High,
  who has delivered your enemies into your hand!'

And Abram gave him a tenth of everything. And the king of Sodom said to Abram, 'Give me the persons, but take the goods for yourself.' But Abram said to the king of Sodom, 'I have lifted my hand to the LORD, God Most High, Possessor of heaven and earth, that I would not take a thread or a sandal strap or anything that is yours, lest you should say, "I have made Abram rich." I will take nothing but what the young men have eaten, and the share of the men who went with me. Let Aner, Eshcol, and Mamre take their share.' (Gen. 14:17–24)

The actions of the two kings who meet Abraham provide a fascinating contrast.[7] Melchizedek is both king of Salem and priest of God Most High. As a priest-king, probably linked to Jerusalem,[8] his name means 'My king is righteous'. Melchizedek blesses Abraham by acknowledging that God Most High is both the 'possessor/getter of heaven and earth' and the one who has delivered Abraham's enemies into his hand. By way of contrast to Melchizedek, the unnamed king of Sodom makes no reference to God but offers Abraham all the goods taken in plunder.

Two distinctive forms of kingship are represented by the kings of Salem and Sodom. Melchizedek displays the kind of kingship

---

7. The discussion that follows is indebted to J. G. McConville, 'Abraham and Melchizedek: Horizons in Genesis 14', in R. S. Hess, P. E. Satterthwaite and G. J. Wenham (eds.), *He Swore an Oath: Biblical Themes from Genesis 20–50*, 2nd ed. (Grand Rapids: Baker; Carlisle: Paternoster, 1994), pp. 93–118.

8. Poetic parallelism in Ps. 76:2 equates Salem with Zion.

acceptable to God. As a priest-king he acknowledges God's right to exercise sovereignty over the earth.[9] The king of Sodom, in marked contrast, typifies earthly or godless kingship that places sovereignty in the power of the individual. Such kingship extols the virtue of becoming wealthy by grasping all one can, regardless of the consequences for others.

By affirming the truthfulness of what Melchizedek has to say and rejecting the offer of the king of Sodom, Abraham indicates his own commitment to be a righteous priest-king. Abraham will not inherit the earth through the use of aggressive military power, although clearly his defeat of the eastern kings indicates he has the capacity to do so. Rather, he looks to God to provide for his future well-being.

As this story reveals, corrupted human kingship is about taking possession of the earth and using power to control others. Divinely instituted kingship is quite different. It seeks to re-establish God's sovereignty on the earth in line with the divine mandate given to human beings when first created. Because these two forms of kingship are mutually incompatible, they naturally come into conflict.

While Melchizedek is clearly presented as the priest-king of Salem, we should also observe that Abraham himself displays both royal and priestly characteristics. The events of Genesis 14 indicate that Abraham is no ordinary semi-nomadic pastoralist. His military exploits very definitely place him on a par with kings. Years later, Abimelech, the king of Gerar, establishes a friendship treaty with Abraham (Gen. 21:22–34), the ratification of which suggests that the local king views Abraham as his equal. Abraham's 'royal' status is also indicated when the inhabitants of Hebron designate him a 'prince of God' (Gen. 23:6). While Abraham is never called a king, these observations suggest he is

---

9. On the basis of Ps. 110 the author of Hebrews argues that Jesus' priesthood resembles that of Melchizedek (Heb. 5:4–10; 6:19 – 7:17). Although very little is known about this king of Salem, the author of Hebrews argues that his royal priesthood is superior to the Levitical priesthood divinely instituted on Mount Sinai to serve within the tabernacle.

one in all but name. Moreover, the Lord covenants with Abraham that kings will be among his descendants (Gen. 17:6; cf. 17:16).

Alongside these features, indicative of royal standing, Abraham undertakes activities that suggest he has a priestly status. We see this especially in the building of altars and the offering of sacrifices (Gen. 12:7–8; 13:4, 18; 22:1–13; cf. 15:9–10). In addition, Abraham encounters God on various occasions and receives divine communications (Gen. 12:1–3; 13:14–17; 15:1, 4–5, 7, 9, 13–16, 18–21; 17:1–22; 18:1–33; 21:12–13; 22:1, 12, 15–18). His special relationship with God suggests he enjoys a status equivalent to that of a priest, although he is never designated as one.[10]

The royal and priestly characteristics displayed by Abraham parallel to a certain extent features associated with Noah, Abraham's ancestor. Like Abraham, Noah constructs an altar and offers sacrifices. While there is no record of Noah engaging with kings, he exercises dominion over birds, animals and creeping things by preserving them from the flood. In line with this, Noah is blessed by the Lord in terms that closely echo Genesis 1:28. He and his descendants are to multiply and fill the earth (Gen. 9:1, 7). Encouraged by God, they are to fulfil the creation mandate previously given to Adam and Eve. However, the accompanying remarks and instructions in Genesis 9:2–6 suggest that Noah and his descendants will struggle to exercise dominion over the earth as God originally intended.

In the light of God's repeated mandate to fill the earth, the call of Abraham takes on special significance. Promised both land and descendants, Abraham is summoned by God to form a new nation that will subsequently play an important role in establishing Jerusalem as a unique temple-city. While this outcome is not stated, the repeated promise that Abraham's descendants will be fruitful and multiply alludes back to God's creation blueprint (e.g. Gen. 17:6, 20; 26:22; 28:3; 35:11; 41:52; 47:27; 48:4; cf. 15:5; 22:17; 26:4; 32:12).[11]

---

10. Abraham is, however, called a 'prophet' by God in Gen. 20:7.

11. This connection is noted by N. T. Wright, *The New Testament and the People of God*, Christian Origins and the Question of God 1 (London: SPCK,

In the light of God's creation mandate, the book of Exodus begins with the interesting observation 'But the people of Israel were fruitful and increased greatly; they multiplied and grew exceedingly strong, so that the land was filled with them' (Exod. 1:7). While at one level, the numerical growth of the Israelites prompts Pharaoh to oppress them, within the literary context of the Pentateuch as a whole, this extraordinary expansion prepares for the creation of Israel as God's special, holy nation. Although Exodus begins with the enslavement of the Israelites to Pharaoh, it concludes with their becoming the priest-kings of the Lord.

Immediately following the arrival of the Israelites at Mount Sinai, God speaks privately to Moses:

> Thus you shall say to the house of Jacob, and tell the people of Israel: You yourselves have seen what I did to the Egyptians, and how I bore you on eagles' wings and brought you to myself. Now therefore, if you will indeed obey my voice and keep my covenant, you shall be my treasured possession among all peoples, for all the earth is mine; and you shall be to me a kingdom of priests and a holy nation. These are the words that you shall speak to the people of Israel. (Exod. 19:3–6)

The phrase especially significant for our purposes is 'a kingdom of priests'. The Hebrew original probably denotes 'a body of priests ruling as kings', 'a royal priesthood'.[12] At the heart of God's plans for the people of Israel is the idea that they will become priest-kings. They are to fulfil the role that God had originally allocated through Adam and Eve to all human beings. Not surprisingly, in the light of Adam and Eve's disobedience, this passage emphasizes the necessity of obeying God. To reject the Lord's commands is to deny this kingship. The Israelites cannot be genuine priest-kings and simultaneously disregard God's instructions.

Footnote 11 (continued)

1993), pp. 262–263, although he does not associate it with the earth being established as the dwelling place of God.

12. The earliest Greek translation of this passage is *basileion hierateuma*, 'royal priesthood'.

God's speech in Exodus 19:3–6 refers back to the rescue of the people from slavery in Egypt. Since the sweep of biblical history is about how divine kingship will be established on the earth, the book of Exodus presents us with an interesting example of how this will be achieved. In the opening chapter the author of Exodus states that the fruitfulness of the Israelites is perceived as a threat by the king of Egypt:

> But the people of Israel were fruitful and increased greatly; they multiplied and grew exceedingly strong, so that the land was filled with them. Now there arose a new king over Egypt, who did not know Joseph. And he said to his people, 'Behold, the people of Israel are too many and too mighty for us. Come, let us deal shrewdly with them, lest they multiply, and, if war breaks out, they join our enemies and fight against us and escape from the land.' Therefore they set taskmasters over them to afflict them with heavy burdens. They built for Pharaoh store cities, Pithom and Raamses. (Exod. 1:7–11)

The remarkable increase of the Israelites loudly echoes the divine command of Genesis 1 to be fruitful and fill the earth. Implicit in this is the possibility that they will establish God's temple-city on the earth. However, the new king of Egypt feels threatened by them and sets them to work building cities for his own benefit. In this scenario we see a conflict between God's blueprint for the earth and how those who have dethroned God have corrupted it. The account of the divine deliverance of the Israelites from oppression in Egypt is deeply significant. In essence it describes how God rescues people from the consequences of human sin with the intention of establishing both his sovereignty and dwelling place on the earth. Interestingly, both of these themes are picked up in the victory song of the Israelites in Exodus 15:

> Who is like you, O LORD, among the gods?
>> Who is like you, majestic in holiness,
>> awesome in glorious deeds, doing wonders?
> You stretched out your right hand;
>> the earth swallowed them.

> You have led in your steadfast love the people whom you have
>   redeemed;
>   you have guided them by your strength to your holy abode. . . .
> You will bring them in and plant them on your own mountain,
>   the place, O Lord, which you have made for your abode,
>   the sanctuary, O Lord, which your hands have established.
> The Lord will reign for ever and ever.
> (Exod. 15:11–13, 17–18)

The story of the exodus is about moving from one kingdom to another; it is about escaping corrupt human kingship and experiencing loving, divine kingship; it is about becoming priest-kings and entering into God's sanctuary where he reigns for ever.[13]

Unsurprisingly, the exodus from Egypt was viewed by the ancient Israelites as the greatest redemptive event of their entire history. Through the annual festivals held to commemorate God's deliverance of the people from slavery, each new generation became aware of its significance. Moreover, as Ninow highlights, the exodus was presented to later generations in a way that made them participants in the original event.[14] The exodus was not merely a past event but an ongoing activity. Even those who had never been in Egypt were meant to see themselves as having been liberated from there.[15]

---

13. Quite deliberately this paradigm of divine salvation is later applied to a new exodus brought about by Jesus Christ. I shall say more about this in chapter 5.

14. F. Ninow, *Indicators of Typology within the Old Testament: The Exodus Motif*, Friedensauer Schriftenreihe A4 (Frankfurt am Main: Lang, 2001), pp. 115–120. For example, Deut. 5:2–4 states, 'The Lord our God made a covenant with us in Horeb. Not with our fathers did the Lord make this covenant, but with us, who are all of us here alive today. The Lord spoke with you face to face at the mountain, out of the midst of the fire' (cf. Deut. 6:20–25; cf. Josh. 24:6–7).

15. Given the centrality of the exodus in Israel's cultic life, it is no surprise that it became the great paradigm for God's redemptive activity. For example, it features prominently in the book of Isaiah, which looks

By accepting God as their divine king and giving their total allegiance to him, the Israelites enjoyed the special privilege of being priest-kings. This set them apart from every other nation. As a consequence of this, God came to live among them in the specially constructed tabernacle (Exod. 25 – 31, 35 – 40).

With the tabernacle at its heart, the layout of the Israelite camp resembled those of ancient Near Eastern kings when they embarked on military campaigns.[16] The divine king's tent was located in the centre with his army spread around him.[17] Given its location and lavish furnishings the Israelites would undoubtedly have perceived the tabernacle as a royal tent, its occupant being the king. In line with this, the gold-plated ark of the covenant adorned with cherubim was viewed as the footstool of his throne.[18]

With the establishment of Israel as a theocracy and the construction of the tabernacle, the throne of God was set up on the earth. However, although the Israelites acclaimed God as the Lord of all the earth, in reality citizens of other nations recognized his sovereignty only rarely. The Old Testament describes an ongoing tension regarding the reign of God over both Abraham's descendants and those of other nations. While Psalms 93 – 99 invite worshippers to acknowledge wholeheartedly that the Lord reigns, this does not reflect the normative experience of all Israelites. For example, during the period of the divided monarchy, Elijah's encounter with the prophets of Baal on Mount Carmel reveals

---

forward, especially in chs. 40–48, to a future exodus for those Israelites who have been dispersed among the nations. The centrality of the exodus in Paul's writings has recently been highlighted by T. Holland, *Contours of Pauline Theology: A Radical New Survey of the Influences on Paul's Biblical Writings* (Fearn: Mentor, 2004).

16. See K. A. Kitchen, 'The Tabernacle – a Bronze Age Artefact', *Eretz Israel* 24 (1993), pp. 119–129, esp. 123; 'The Desert Tabernacle: Pure Fiction or Plausible Account?', *Biblical Research* 16 (2000), pp. 14–21; *On the Reliability*, pp. 275–283.

17. The military nature of the Israelite camp was underlined by the taking of a census of those able to go to war (see Num. 1:2–3, 45).

18. See chapter 2, n. 43 above (p. 33).

that the sole kingship of the Lord was seriously threatened: many Israelites were apparently content to worship Baal as their divine king.

One of the most vivid descriptions of divine kingship comes in Isaiah 6. In the eighth century BC, when the reality of God's sovereignty over the nation of Judah was largely dismissed as irrelevant by the leading citizens of Jerusalem, God revealed himself in all his majestic splendour to the prophet Isaiah. The vision is highly significant, for, given his calling to rebuke the royal house of David, Isaiah needs to be thoroughly convinced of God's supreme power. Isaiah's vision is a stark reminder that the leading citizens of Jerusalem rejected God's sovereignty; their worship was only nominal and consequently highly offensive to the Lord. In addition, given Isaiah's acknowledgment of his own uncleanness and of having seen 'the king, the LORD of hosts', the vision transforms his perception of the Judean monarchy. As Dumbrell observes:

> The temple on which the Jerusalem cult was centred was also the divine 'palace' and as such was the seat of Israel's final political authority. Israel's worship was intended to be a recognition of this fact. Perhaps Isaiah is acknowledging in chapter 6 that he also had uncritically accepted the prosperity of the age of Uzziah as a mark of divine favour. The disorders which had effected the central core of Israel's responses to Yahweh (cf. 1:10–20) represent ultimate rejection of Yahweh's rule, and thus an abrogation of the covenant.[19]

The whole history of Israel as a theocracy witnesses to the fact that the Israelites continually challenged and undermined God's sovereignty. The recurring theme of the prophets is Israel's faithlessness to its sovereign God. While the establishment of Israel as a theocracy advanced God's creation blueprint, this development was constantly marred by the failure of all the people to acknowledge God's kingship unreservedly. As an expression of divine rule on earth, the Israelite theocracy had major limitations.

---

19. W. J. Dumbrell, *The End of the Beginning: Revelation 21–22 and the Old Testament* (Grand Rapids: Baker, 1985), p. 9.

Nevertheless, the hope existed that God's kingship would eventually be universally acknowledged. Consequently, the book of Daniel anticipates a time when earthly kingdoms will be replaced by a divine kingdom (Dan. 2:1–49; 7:1–28), and the post-exilic book of Zechariah looks forward to a day when 'the LORD will be king over all the earth' (14:9).[20]

The church and the kingdom of God

When we move to the New Testament, the theocracy of Israel is replaced by the kingdom of God, which is inaugurated through the coming of Jesus. The establishment of this kingdom, one of the central ideas of the Gospels, is intimately associated with who Jesus is and what he does. Kingdom ideology underlies Matthew's portrayal of Jesus as the Son of David who fulfils Old Testament expectations. From beginning to end the Gospel of Matthew is permeated with ideas and themes associated with royalty. In keeping with this, Matthew summarizes the teaching of both John the Baptist and Jesus in the sentence 'Repent, for the kingdom of heaven is at hand' (Matt. 3:2 for John; Matt. 4:17 for Jesus).[21]

To comprehend the importance of the New Testament emphasis upon the coming of the kingdom of God, we need to appreciate that this involves the re-establishment of human beings as God's viceroys. As Dan McCartney has perceptively observed, 'The arrival of the reign of God is the *reinstatement of the originally intended divine order for earth, with man properly situated as God's vicegerent.*'[22] By way of expounding this, McCartney argues that the

---

20. Compare also Obad. 21, 'Saviours shall go up to Mount Zion / to rule Mount Esau, / and the kingdom shall be the LORD's.'

21. Matthew prefers to use the expression 'kingdom of heaven' rather than 'kingdom of God'. However, the two expressions denote the same entity. For a fuller discussion, see G. R. Beasley-Murray, *Jesus and the Kingdom of God* (Grand Rapids: Eerdmans; Exeter: Paternoster, 1986).

22. McCartney, '*Ecce Homo*', p. 2.

reinstatement of human vicegerency centres on Jesus Christ, for as a *human* he receives the kingdom:

> Before his incarnation, the eternal Son was not a man, and thus did not
> rule as a man. Philippians 2, for example, speaks of the preincarnate
> Christ as equal with God. However, Christ received the 'name above
> every name' and the homage of every knee and tongue only after, and as
> reward for, his incarnation, suffering, and death. Similarly, Col 1:15–20
> speaks of Christ as the firstborn of all *creation* because all things were
> created in him, etc., but he is the head of the *church* because he is the
> 'firstborn from the dead . . . having reconciled to himself all things,
> whether on earth or in heaven, making peace by the blood of his cross.'
> Heb 2:9 states that Jesus was 'made for a little while lower than the
> angels' *so that* everything might be subject to him, he being crowned with
> glory and honor because of the suffering of death. And Rom 1:3–4
> speaks of Jesus being appointed Son of God in power, which, as J.
> Murray pointed out, is not a declaration of his eternal sonship but his
> instatement *as man* to the position of sovereignty.[23]

This emphasis upon the *human* aspect of Jesus' kingship is important, for it distinguishes his reign as king from that of God the Father.[24] In line with this the apostle Paul observes in 1 Corinthians 15:24–28 that ultimately, when all things are subject to him, Jesus will deliver the kingdom over to the Father:

> Then comes the end, when he delivers the kingdom to God the Father
> after destroying every rule and every authority and power. For he must
> reign until he has put all his enemies under his feet. The last enemy to

---

23. Ibid. The reference in the final sentence is to J. Murray, *The Epistle to the Romans* (Grand Rapids: Eerdmans, 1968), p. 10.
24. This is not to claim that the kingdom of God and the kingdom of Christ are two separate entities. As McCartney, '*Ecce Homo*', p. 16, correctly observes, 'The kingdom of God and the kingdom of Christ are the same entity (Eph 5:5, 21), not only because Christ is God, for as God Christ has always reigned with the Father. It is because Christ is now a man, and as man rules as human vicegerent.'

be destroyed is death. For 'God has put all things in subjection under his feet.' But when it says, 'all things are put in subjection,' it is plain that he is excepted who put all things in subjection under him. When all things are subjected to him, then the Son himself will also be subjected to him who put all things in subjection under him, that God may be all in all.

Paul's argument here rests on the premise that God has delegated authority to another, in support of which he quotes Psalm 8:6.[25] When the one to whom authority has been delegated (in this instance Jesus Christ) has subdued all his enemies, he himself will still remain subject to God the Father.

Although Paul anticipates that Christ will deliver the kingdom to the Father when 'the end' comes, for the present Jesus Christ has been exalted to the right hand of the Father from where he reigns. As Jesus himself reveals to his disciples after his resurrection, 'All authority in heaven and on earth has been given to me' (Matt. 28:18). Making the same point, the author of Hebrews speaks of seeing Jesus 'crowned with glory and honour because of the suffering of death' (Heb. 2:9).[26]

Without repeating every detail of McCartney's helpful discussion of Jesus as vicegerent, he argues that the New Testament presents Jesus as fulfilling 'OT expectations of the restoration of human vicegerency'.[27] To support this claim, he provides a short summary of the Old Testament evidence for human vicegerency. In doing so, he highlights the following points: (1) The concept of human vicegerency finds its origins in Genesis.[28] (2) The restoration of human vicegerency is linked to the divine promises to the

---

25. Ps. 8 refers to humanity in general. Ps. 8:6 is used in a similar way in Heb. 2; see pp. 93–94.

26. The theme of Jesus reigning at God's right hand dominates the opening chapter of Hebrews.

27. McCartney, 'Ecce Homo', p. 8.

28. Ibid., p. 3: 'God's rule of earth was, in the original order of creation, accomplished through the agency of man's vicegerency. When man fell, he spoiled his vicegerency; man was cast out of the garden, and the earth was no longer compliant in its subjection to him.'

patriarchs. (3) 'In the Davidic theocracy, a typological and imperfect human vicegerency was reinstated as partial fulfilment of the promise to Abraham.'[29] (4) The concept of human vicegerency is reflected in various psalms (e.g. Pss 2; 8; 45) and the writings of the prophets (e.g. Isa. 9:6–7). (5) The restoration of human vicegerency is 'effected by the anointing by the Spirit'.[30] (6) 'The restoration of God's kingdom is the restoration of his vicegerent's kingdom, just as the absence of the anointed king meant the absence of God's kingdom (cf. Jer 8:19f.: "Is YHWH not in Zion? Is her King no longer there?").'[31]

Evidence for the fulfilment of these expectations in Jesus is easy to find. As heir to the Davidic throne, Jesus is anointed by the Holy Spirit at his baptism, while, with words reminiscent of Psalm 2:7, God the Father acknowledges Jesus as his royal 'Son' or vicegerent. Then, as I shall discuss more fully in the next chapter, Jesus confirms his status as vicegerent by overcoming Satan, a foretaste of which is provided in the temptation account that immediately follows Jesus' baptism (see Matt. 3:13 – 4:11; cf. Mark 1:9–13; Luke 3:21–22; 4:1–13).[32]

---

29. Ibid. McCartney notes that in the Old Testament there is a looking forward to a time 'when David's greater Son will rule a perfect kingdom as God's vicegerent (Ps 80:17: "But let thy hand be upon the *man* of thy right hand, the *son of man* whom thou hast made strong for thyself!" Cf. 2 Sam 7:14).'

30. McCartney, '*Ecce Homo*', p. 4. He writes, 'The empowerment by the Spirit is why God's vicegerent is "the anointed one," the Christ. God is not himself the anointed king; he is the one who anoints. Anointing is appointment and empowerment to act in God's place. J. Gray observes: "Anointing was known in Egypt as a rite by which the authority of the Pharaoh was delegated to officials and to vassal kings in Syria in the 15th century, and it has been argued that it symbolized the strengthening of a person so anointed with special ability."' The quotation in the passage is from J. Gray, *The Biblical Doctrine of the Reign of God* (Edinburgh: T. & T. Clark, 1979), p. 274, n. 1.

31. McCartney, '*Ecce Homo*', p. 6.

32. Whereas Matthew and Mark immediately follow the baptism of Jesus with the account of his temptation, Luke introduces his genealogy, which

While the New Testament clearly affirms the importance of Jesus' role as a human vicegerent, it also anticipates the extension of vicegerency to other human beings. According to McCartney:

> This was already hinted at in the OT. Psalm 8, for example, speaks of humanity in general as the recipient of dominion (v. 6). In Daniel 7, after the vision of the representative 'one like a son of man' receiving dominion, the 'saints of the Most High' also obtain this everlasting dominion (vv. 18, 27).[33]

The extension of Christ's vicegerency to others is clearly stated by the author of Hebrews. In chapter 2, he affirms that human vicegerency will be established over the 'world to come', because this is God's intention for humanity. Contrasting the role of human beings with that of angels and quoting part of Psalm 8, the author of Hebrews writes:

> Now it was not to angels that God subjected the world to come, of which we are speaking. It has been testified somewhere,
>
> > 'What is man, that you are mindful of him,
> >   or the son of man, that you care for him?
> > You made him for a little while lower than the angels;
> >   you have crowned him with glory and honour,
> >   putting everything in subjection under his feet.'
>
> Now in putting everything in subjection to him, he left nothing outside his control. At present, we do not yet see everything in subjection to him. (Heb. 2:5–8)

Throughout these verses, the author of Hebrews is speaking of humanity ('man') in general. He anticipates a time when their status as God's viceroys will be re-established and everything will

---

deliberately associates Jesus with Adam, both being called God's son. By doing so, Luke underlines the idea of Jesus being a vicegerent like Adam.

33. McCartney, '*Ecce Homo*', p. 17 (italics original).

be subject to them. Having affirmed this, the author of Hebrews then proceeds to focus on Jesus Christ, who having 'for a little while' been 'made lower that the angels' is now 'crowned with glory and honour because of the suffering of death, so that by the grace of God he might taste death for everyone' (Heb. 2:9). In highlighting this, the author of Hebrews proceeds to underline the importance of Jesus becoming a human being:

> For he [Jesus Christ] who sanctifies and those who are sanctified all have one origin. That is why he is not ashamed to call them brothers, saying,
>
> > 'I will tell of your name to my brothers;
> > in the midst of the congregation I will sing your praise.'
> > (Heb. 2:11–12)

By becoming a perfect human vicegerent in the present, Jesus Christ is able to re-establish the vicegerent status of other human beings in the future. In doing so, Christ may be considered a 'second Adam'. To quote McCartney:

> According to Paul, mankind lost his vicegerency in Adam, but gains it again in Christ. In Rom 5:17, Adam's sin resulted in the 'reign' of death displacing man, but through the one man Jesus Christ, those who have received the abounding of grace will reign in life. Similarly in 1 Cor 15:45: 'The first man Adam became a living being, but the last Adam became a life-giving spirit.' Paul goes on to say in v. 48 that 'just as we have borne the image of the man of dust, we shall also bear the image of the man of heaven.'[34]

The establishment of Christ's vicegerency is undoubtedly one of the central ideas associated with the kingdom of God in the New Testament. Christ's human reign is intimately tied to God's creation blueprint. By reigning as a man, Christ will enable the earth to be filled with those who are priest-kings. However, the completion of this is located in the future. As McCartney observes:

---

34. Ibid., p. 19.

For us the restoration to vicegerency is not yet fully here (cf. Hebrews 2). But it is our hope. 'If we suffer we shall also reign with him' (1 Tim 2:12). Note Rom 8:15–23: 'You did not receive a spirit that makes you a slave again to fear, but you received the Spirit of sonship [i.e., kingship, because] . . . if we are children then we are heirs, heirs of God and co-heirs with Christ.' As heirs of God and fellow heirs with Christ, we expect a time when the inheritance will be fully ours. This is why Paul regards 'the sufferings of this present time' as 'not worth comparing with the glory that is to be revealed to [or "in"] us.'[35]

In line with this, the Beatitudes in Matthew 5:2–10 contain an interesting contrast between present and future rewards. Whereas the rewards of verses 2 and 10, which frame the Beatitudes, are in the present ('for theirs is the kingdom of heaven'), all of the other rewards are future orientated: they shall be comforted; they shall inherit the earth; they shall be satisfied; they shall receive mercy; they shall see God; they shall be called sons of God. This distinction is significant, for it underscores that although the kingdom of God (the reign of Christ) is a present reality, the consummated kingdom awaits his return in glory. Only then will the vicegerency of all believers be fully and perfectly established.

Although Jesus' ministry, death, resurrection and ascension initiate the kingdom of God, the parables of Matthew 13 indicate that for the subsequent phase of human history the citizens of God's kingdom will coexist on the earth with the wicked. The kingdom associated with Jesus Christ's first coming does not bring to an end all evil on earth. The parables of the wheat and weeds, and the fishing net, both anticipate a future separation of the good and the bad at the end of this age. While the divine kingdom is growing, evil powers constantly oppose it. Only at Christ's second coming in royal splendour will the world be purged of everything opposed to God's presence and sovereignty. Only at that stage will redeemed humanity experience the full reality of being God's viceroys.

In awaiting Christ's return, his followers are called to obey him

---

35. Ibid., p. 20.

without hypocrisy. Acknowledging Jesus as king must go beyond
mere words. As Jesus put it:

> Not everyone who says to me, 'Lord, Lord,' will enter the kingdom of
> heaven, but the one who does the will of my Father who is in heaven.
> On that day many will say to me, 'Lord, Lord, did we not prophesy in
> your name, and cast out demons in your name, and do many mighty
> works in your name?' And then will I declare to them, 'I never knew
> you; depart from me, you workers of lawlessness.' (Matt. 7:21–23)

By living in obedience to Christ, his disciples participate in the
establishment of God's kingdom on the earth. This kingdom is not
restricted by national boundaries, but is gradually expanding to fill
the whole earth. Yet, although this divine kingdom continues to
grow, with more and more people acknowledging the supreme sovereignty of God, many of the earth's inhabitants defiantly refuse to
enthrone God as their Lord. As we shall see in chapter 4, the battle
for control of the earth continues to rage. Ultimately, however,
God will be victorious and his throne will be exalted in the golden
garden-city that will one day fill a transformed earth.

In the light of these observations, it is unsurprising that the
motif of priest-kings should be applied to those who acknowledge
the reign of Christ. With good reason 1 Peter 2:9 describes the
church as a royal priesthood, closely echoing Exodus 19: 'But you
are a chosen race, a royal priesthood, a holy nation, a people for his
own possession, that you may proclaim the excellencies of him
who called you out of darkness into his marvellous light.' This
passage presents the followers of Jesus Christ as having a royal and
priestly status. As such they are heirs to the creation mandate that
centred on the extension of God's temple-city throughout the
whole world. The same idea is reflected in Revelation 5:10: 'and you
have made them a kingdom and priests to our God, and they shall
reign on the earth'.[36] G. B. Caird notes the significance of this:

---

36. A similar affirmation is made in Rev. 1:5b–6: 'To him who loves us and has
    freed us from our sins by his blood and made us a kingdom, priests to his
    God and Father, to him be glory and dominion for ever and ever.' For a

For the church has been appointed by Christ to be 'a royal house of priests' (i. 6; v. 10), to mediate his royal and priestly authority to the whole world. Through the church he is to exercise his sovereignty over the nations, smashing their resistance to his rule and releasing their subjects for a new and better loyalty (i. 5; ii. 26f.; xi. 15ff.; xii. 5; xv. 3–4; xvii. 14; xix. 11ff.). Through the church he is to mediate God's forgiveness and lead the world to repentance (iii. 7–9; xi. 13; xiv. 6–7; xx. 1–6). And all this they may achieve only by following the Lamb wherever he goes (xiv. 4).[37]

One day this present age will give way to another, when the earth will be rejuvenated and the sovereignty of God will finally become an undisputed reality in the New Jerusalem. Until then, we are taught by Jesus to pray:

> Our Father in heaven,
> hallowed be your name.
> Your kingdom come,
> your will be done,
>   on earth as it is in heaven.
> (Matt. 6:9–10)

But the time will arrive when we shall no longer need to pray this. As the final vision of Revelation 21 – 22 reveals, at the climax of history the divine kingdom will be established in all its glory and the citizens of the New Jerusalem will live in complete conformity to God's will on a transformed earth. At that time Zechariah's prediction will be fulfilled: 'the LORD will be king over all the earth' (Zech. 14:9).

---

helpful discussion of both these passages, see A. J. Bandstra, '"A Kingship and Priests": Inaugurated Eschatology in the Apocalypse', *Calvin Theological Journal* 27 (1992), pp. 10–25. Bandstra notes that the future-orientated translation 'they will reign on the earth' reflects one of two textual traditions found in the manuscripts. The alternative reading, which he prefers, is present tense: 'they reign on the earth'.

37. G. B. Caird, *A Commentary on the Revelation of St. John the Divine*, Black's New Testament Commentaries (London: A. & C. Black, 1966), p. 297.

4. DEALING WITH THE DEVIL: DESTROYING THE SOURCE OF EVIL

John's vision in the final chapters of Revelation focuses on God's creation of a new heaven and earth, to replace the present ones. Here a gigantic golden city, which descends fully constructed from heaven, becomes the dwelling place of God. A perfect cube in shape, it is the authentic Holy of Holies, the reality to which the Old Testament models of the tabernacle and temple pointed. At the centre of this holy garden-city stands the throne of God, for throughout the New Jerusalem God's sovereign rule is unassailed and every citizen lives in complete harmony with the divine will.

Although John's vision gives us a window into the future, the origins of the New Jerusalem go back to the opening chapters of Genesis, which describe how God created the earth with the specific intention that it should be his dwelling place. To bring his project to completion, God initially bestowed on humanity a holy and royal status. As they filled the earth, human beings were to extend God's temple and kingdom throughout the world. However, the successful completion of this divine project was tragically endangered when Adam and Eve, in an act of wilful arrogance, heeded the serpent rather that the divine Creator. Adam and Eve's disobedience introduced major obstacles to the fulfilment of God's plan for the earth. Rather than extending the temple of God throughout the earth through holy service, humanity defiled the world through their unrighteous behaviour. Having been delegated authority to rule, they now use this authority inappropriately; unrestrained human dominion brings violence to the earth, rather than peace.

Before exploring in chapter 5 how Jesus Christ stands at the heart of God's plan to redeem humanity and restore creation to its divinely intended order, we shall focus our attention on the being who plays a major role in opposing God's purposes.

The dragon who is the devil and Satan

In Revelation, before he has his final vision of the New Jerusalem coming down out of heaven, John's attention is directed to what happens to 'the dragon, that ancient serpent, who is the devil and Satan' (Rev. 20:2). We read of this in Revelation 20:

> Then I saw an angel coming down from heaven, holding in his hand the key to the bottomless pit and a great chain. And he seized the dragon, that ancient serpent, who is the devil and Satan, and bound him for a thousand years, and threw him into the pit, and shut it and sealed it over him, so that he might not deceive the nations any longer, until the thousand years were ended. After that he must be released for a little while. . . .
>
> And when the thousand years are ended, Satan will be released from his prison and will come out to deceive the nations that are at the four corners of the earth, Gog and Magog, to gather them for battle; their number is like the sand of the sea. And they marched up over the broad plain of the earth and surrounded the camp of the saints and the beloved city, but fire came down from heaven and consumed them, and the devil who had deceived them was thrown into the lake of fire and sulphur where the beast and the false prophet were, and they will be tormented day and night for ever and ever. (Rev. 20:1–3, 7–10)

In verse 2 various terms are used to denote God's arch-enemy. He is called 'the dragon, that ancient serpent, who is the devil and

Satan'. While he is undoubtedly a most influential figure in the biblical meta-story, Scripture does not provide us with a detailed and comprehensive picture of him. We catch but occasional glimpses of this shadowy opponent. This should not surprise us. As divine revelation, the Bible exists to give us a deeper understanding of God. It is not designed to promote knowledge of the enemy, beyond what is necessary for comprehending the world in which we live and our own experience of it. Consequently, many questions remain unanswered when we collate what the Bible says about the devil or Satan. Although much is unknown, the Bible provides a relatively clear and consistent picture regarding his control of the earth. This is important to note, especially in the light of what we observed in chapter 2 regarding the sovereignty of God. While the Bible affirms beyond all doubt that God alone is all-powerful and his authority exceeds every other authority, it also indicates that Satan has dominion over the world in which we live, although that control is gradually being wrested from him.

Ruler of this world

Three New Testament passages in particular go some way towards establishing that the devil exercises authority over this present world.

First, in the final chapter of the apostle John's first epistle, we read:

> We know that everyone who has been born of God does not keep on sinning, but he who was born of God protects him, and the evil one does not touch him. We know that we are from God, and the whole world lies in the power of the evil one. (1 John 5:18–19)

Here John, as part of a fuller discussion, alludes to the fact that this world is in the grip of the evil one. John affirms, however, that those who now belong to the family of God have been delivered from the power of the evil one. As F. F. Bruce observes:

> As this ruler, on Jesus' own testimony, has no authority over Him, so he has none over those who by faith share in Jesus' victory over the world.

But those who are still dominated by the standards of the world organized without reference to God are enslaved by its ruler and cannot share in the victory which has overcome him. This passing world order and its ruler are on their way out, to be superseded by the eternal order and *its* Ruler; the subjects of the latter will abide for ever (cf. 2.17).[1]

While John naturally wants to reassure his readers that Christ has overcome the evil one and that their future is secure because of this, he nevertheless states unambiguously that this world presently lies in the power of the evil one.

Secondly, on three occasions in John's Gospel Jesus himself refers to Satan as 'the ruler [or 'prince'] of this world' (John 12:31; 14:30; 16:11). Each time Jesus declares that he has come in order to overthrow him. Again, this points to the authority the evil one has over the present world. Ephesians 2:2 provides a somewhat similar image with its reference to 'the prince of the power of the air, the spirit that is now at work in the sons of disobedience'.

Thirdly, when Jesus is tempted in three different ways by the devil or Satan (Matthew uses both terms), one of these involves Satan offering Christ 'all the kingdoms of the world and their glory'. Here is how Matthew records it:

Again, the devil took him to a very high mountain and showed him all the kingdoms of the world and their glory. And he said to him, 'All these I will give you, if you will fall down and worship me.' Then Jesus said to him, 'Be gone, Satan! For it is written,

"You shall worship the Lord your God
and him only shall you serve."'
(Matt. 4:8–10)

Implicit in Satan's temptation is the understanding that he possesses all of the world's kingdoms. Particular emphasis is given to the term 'all', for Satan does not merely offer Jesus some

1. F. F. Bruce, *The Epistles of John: Introduction, Exposition and Notes* (London: Pickering & Inglis, 1978), p. 127.

kingdoms. At stake are all the kingdoms of the earth. For this temptation to be genuine, Satan must possess these kingdoms; they are his to give. If in reality he did not control all of these kingdoms, Jesus could simply have replied, 'How can you give these to me? They don't belong to you!'

In the light of these observations, all drawn from the New Testament, there is every reason to believe that Satan is the 'ruler of this world'.[2] When we turn to the Old Testament, the concept of Satan or the devil having dominion over this world is present also, although in a much more disguised manner.

The ancient serpent

Previously, we observed that when Adam and Eve obey the serpent, they concede to it the authority delegated to them by God. Having been appointed by God as his viceroys to rule the earth, the human couple disown God. In doing so they elevate the serpent's authority over God's. Consequently, they become subject to it. Through the serpent's cunning approach to Adam and Eve, it usurps God's sovereignty over the earth.

The events of Genesis 3 are exceptionally important for understanding the biblical meta-story. However, the brevity of the passage means that many points are not explicated in detail. This is especially so regarding the nature and identity of the serpent.

The way in which the serpent is introduced is highly intriguing, despite what appears to be a rather straightforward statement of fact: 'Now the serpent was more crafty than any other beast of the field that the LORD God had made' (Gen. 3:1). No explanation is given for the craftiness of this wild animal. It is not even clear at the outset whether this should be taken as a positive or negative quality. While the reader is left in the dark as to why the serpent is 'more crafty', this brief remark undoubtedly sets the serpent above other animals.

The serpent is elevated above every other 'beast of the field', that is, the wild animals. This comment is likely to have had a neg-

---

2. In 2 Cor. 4:4 Paul refers to Satan as the 'god of this world'.

ative connotation in the minds of the first readers or listeners to this story. Wild animals presented a threat to human beings. Ezekiel 34:8 describes, for example, how a flock of sheep without a shepherd could become 'meat to every beast of the field'. For this reason, the introduction of the serpent as the craftiest of the wild animals has an ominous ring to it.

The peculiar nature of the serpent is confirmed when it speaks, for animals do not normally talk. Moreover, the serpent's words, reflecting its crafty nature, seek to persuade the human couple to disregard God's instructions. Subtly the serpent implies that it knows better than God.

These features make this serpent unique. The closest parallel to the serpent talking comes in the account of Balaam and his donkey. In Numbers 22 we read:

> So Balaam rose in the morning and saddled his donkey and went with the princes of Moab.
>
> But God's anger was kindled because he went, and the angel of the LORD took his stand in the way as his adversary. . . . When the donkey saw the angel of the LORD, she lay down under Balaam. And Balaam's anger was kindled, and he struck the donkey with his staff. Then the LORD opened the mouth of the donkey, and she said to Balaam, 'What have I done to you, that you have struck me these three times?' And Balaam said to the donkey, 'Because you have made a fool of me. I wish I had a sword in my hand, for then I would kill you.' And the donkey said to Balaam, 'Am I not your donkey, on which you have ridden all your life long to this day? Is it my habit to treat you this way?' And he said, 'No.' Then the LORD opened the eyes of Balaam, and he saw the angel of the LORD standing in the way, with his drawn sword in his hand. (Num. 22:21–22, 27–31)

The extraordinary event of the donkey speaking to Balaam is clearly ascribed to the Lord God opening the animal's mouth.[3] If such an explanation is required here, then it follows

---

3. The incident contains an interesting wordplay involving the Lord opening the mouth of the donkey (v. 28) and opening the eyes of Balaam (v. 31).

that something exceptionally unusual lies behind the speaking serpent.

While the author of Genesis stops well short of identifying the serpent as Satan, it is clear that the serpent acts against God. Given the earth-shattering consequences of the serpent's actions and the peculiar nature of the punishment meted out to it, a case can be marshalled in favour of the claim in Revelation 20:2 that the 'ancient serpent' is Satan or the devil. While many Old Testament scholars have shied away from this interpretation, the traditional New Testament understanding of the serpent has much to commend it.[4] The serpent is more than an ordinary snake.

The mystery that surrounds the serpent continues when we observe what God says regarding its punishment:

The LORD God said to the serpent,

> 'Because you have done this,
>   cursed are you above all livestock

---

4. G. J. Wenham, *Genesis 1–15*, Word Biblical Commentary 1 (Waco: Word, 1987), p. 73, observes that the serpent would have been an 'obvious candidate for an anti-God symbol': 'it may be noted that according to the classification of animals found in Lev 11 and Deut 14, the snake must count as an archetypal unclean animal. Its swarming, writhing locomotion puts it at the farthest point from those pure animals that can be offered in sacrifice. Within the world of Old Testament animal symbolism a snake is an obvious candidate for an anti-God symbol, notwithstanding its creation by God. In one way, a dead animal, which is even more unclean than any living creature, would be a better anti-God symbol, yet it would be quite absurd to have a corpse talk. So for any Israelite familiar with the symbolic values of different animals, a creature more likely than a serpent to lead man away from his creator could not be imagined.'

It should also be noted that aspects to this story are unique and place it outside the normal realm of human experience. For example, we are told that prior to eating from the tree of the knowledge of good and evil the human couple were naked but had no sense of embarrassment about this. This reinforces the idea that the speaking serpent is no ordinary snake.

and above all beasts of the field;
on your belly you shall go,
    and dust you shall eat
    all the days of your life.
I will put enmity between you and the woman,
    and between your offspring and her offspring;
he shall bruise your head,
    and you shall bruise his heel.'
(Gen. 3:14–15)

God's pronouncement contains an element of poetic justice, for the seed of the woman will be responsible for punishing the serpent. Yet, this punishment will not be achieved without both parties being injured. However, the distinction between 'head' and 'heel' may be significant in terms of the impact of the bruising.

The identity of the woman's offspring has divided biblical scholarship. While many modern scholars take 'offspring' to refer to all of the woman's descendants, some continue to support the long-standing interpretation that the 'offspring' denotes one descendant, as suggested by the remark 'he shall bruise your head'.[5]

---

5. There is a very long tradition supporting a messianic reading of Gen. 3:15. The first indication of such an interpretation comes in the Septuagint translation of this verse, dating from the third century BC; see R. A. Martin, 'The Earliest Messianic Interpretation of Genesis 3:15', *Journal of Biblical Literature* 84 (1965), pp. 425–427. A similar understanding appears in the earliest Aramaic translations of Genesis, as revealed in the Jewish Targums *Pseudo-Jonathan*, *Neofiti* and *Fragmentary*, and possibly also *Onqelos*. These works interpret this verse as referring to a victory over Satan in the days of King Messiah. Various New Testament allusions to Gen. 3:15 also possibly reflect a messianic interpretation of this verse (1 Cor. 15:22–28; Heb. 2:14; Rev. 12:1 – 13:1). A similar trend is found in the writings of some of the early church fathers, the earliest known examples appearing in the works of Justin (c. AD 160) and Irenaeus (c. AD 180). Gen. 3:15 is considered to be the first announcement of the gospel, a view that led to its designation Protevangelium. Although Rom. 16:20 alludes to

Without unpacking all of the arguments for and against these two possibilities, I want to side firmly with those who think that one descendant is in view here.[6] This reading is supported by the fact that the whole of Genesis is interested in highlighting a single line of descendants that begins with Seth, whom Eve describes as being 'another offspring' in place of Abel (Gen. 4:25). In Genesis the members of this distinctive lineage include Noah, Abraham, Isaac and Jacob, all of whom play a central role in the outworking of God's purposes for the world.[7] Beyond Genesis this line is traced to King David and eventually to Jesus Christ, who overthrows Satan, although not without suffering himself.

The intervention of the serpent in the Garden of Eden has tragic consequences for Adam and Eve. Expelled from God's

----

Footnote 5 (*continued*)

Gen. 3:15, T. Longman III and D. G. Reid, *God Is a Warrior*, Studies in Old Testament Biblical Theology (Grand Rapids: Zondervan, 1995), pp. 143–144, rightly observe that this passage speaks of God restoring 'to the children of the Last Adam their role of dominion and eschatological *shalom*'.

6. For a fuller discussion of this issue, see T. D. Alexander, 'Messianic Ideology in the Book of Genesis', in P. E. Satterthwaite, R. S. Hess and G. J. Wenham (eds.), *The Lord's Anointed: Interpretation of Old Testament Messianic Texts* (Grand Rapids: Baker; Carlisle: Paternoster, 1995), pp. 19–39; C. J. Collins, 'A Syntactical Note (Genesis 3:15): Is the Woman's Seed Singular or Plural?', *Tyndale Bulletin* 48 (1997), pp. 139–148; F. Ninow, *Indicators of Typology within the Old Testament: The Exodus Motif*, Friedensauer Schriftenreihe A4 (Frankfurt am Main: Lang, 2001), pp. 103–109. In Gal. 3:16 the apostle Paul underlines that the promises were made to Abraham and his 'offspring/seed', the latter being an individual person. In making this observation, Paul reflects accurately what the text of Genesis claims. See C. J. Collins, 'Galatians 3:16: What Kind of an Exegete Was Paul?', *Tyndale Bulletin* 54 (2003), pp. 75–86.

7. T. D. Alexander, 'Genealogies, Seed and the Compositional Unity of Genesis', *Tyndale Bulletin* 44 (1993), pp. 255–270; *From Paradise to the Promised Land: An Introduction to the Pentateuch*, 2nd ed. (Carlisle: Paternoster; Grand Rapids: Baker, 2002), pp. 101–113.

presence, they lose their holy and royal status and are unable to fulfil the commission God gave them to extend his temple and kingdom throughout the earth. By obeying the serpent, Adam and Eve take on his image and defile the earth.

While Adam and Eve's actions have terrible consequences, all is not lost, for God introduces the idea that the serpent will be overcome through an offspring of the woman. From Genesis 4 onwards the reader's attention is directed to this offspring. Initially, this is achieved by contrasting two lines of offspring that descend from Eve. Genesis 4 introduces the line of Cain, and then, in chapter 5, we have the line of Seth. These two lines are very different in nature. Cain's is marked by death, with both Cain and his future descendant Lamech being murderers. In marked contrast, the line of Seth contains, among others, Enoch, who enjoyed an exceptionally close relationship with God (Gen. 5:22–24).[8]

The contrast between the lines of Cain and Seth is striking.[9] Here we encounter the idea that human beings may by their actions be perceived as belonging either to the unrighteous 'offspring of the serpent' or to the righteous 'offspring of the woman'. This distinction is clearly reflected in two New Testament passages. John 8:39–44 records part of a protracted discussion involving Jesus and some Pharisees:

> Jesus said to them, 'If you were Abraham's children, you would be doing what Abraham did, but now you seek to kill me, a man who has told you the truth that I heard from God. This is not what Abraham did. You are doing what your father did.' They said to him, 'We were not born of

---

8. In Genesis the idiom 'walked with God' is also linked to Noah (Gen. 6:9) and Abraham (17:1), having been used first in Gen. 3:8 to refer to God walking in the garden with Adam and Eve.

9. R. S. Hess, *Studies in the Personal Names of Genesis 1–11*, Alter Orient und Altes Testament 234 (Kevelaer: Butzon & Bercker, 1993), pp. 111–162; cf. P. E. Satterthwaite, 'Genealogy in the Old Testament', in W. A. VanGemeren (ed.), *New International Dictionary of Old Testament Theology and Exegesis*, vol. 4 (Carlisle: Paternoster; Grand Rapids: Zondervan, 1996), pp. 660–661.

sexual immorality. We have one Father – even God.' Jesus said to them,
'If God were your Father, you would love me, for I came from God and
I am here. I came not of my own accord, but he sent me. Why do you
not understand what I say? It is because you cannot bear to hear my
word. You are of your father the devil, and your will is to do your
father's desires. He was a murderer from the beginning, and has nothing
to do with the truth, because there is no truth in him. When he lies, he
speaks out of his own character, for he is a liar and the father of lies.'

Jesus contradicts the Pharisees' claim that they are sons of
Abraham by stating that their actions identify them as sons of the
devil. The apostle John applies a similar line of reasoning in his
first epistle:

> By this it is evident who are the children of God, and who are the
> children of the devil: whoever does not practice righteousness is not
> of God, nor is the one who does not love his brother.
>
> For this is the message that you have heard from the beginning,
> that we should love one another. We should not be like Cain, who was
> of the evil one and murdered his brother. And why did he murder him?
> Because his own deeds were evil and his brother's righteous. (1 John
> 3:10–12)

In both of these passages the point is made that the children of
God will resemble him by how they live; the same is true regarding
the children of the devil.

Having observed that Genesis contrasts the family lines of Cain
and Seth, we should also observe that the righteous line of Seth
plays a central role in the outworking of God's purposes for the
redemption of humanity. As members of this lineage, Noah and
Abraham are especially significant. Whereas the righteousness of
the former prevents the whole human race from being extermi-
nated in the flood, through Abraham and his offspring all the
nations of the earth will be blessed. This divine blessing, guaranteed by oath on account of Abraham's obedience, will come
through a future royal descendant (Gen. 22:16–18). Although
Genesis concludes by associating future royalty with Joseph and
the line of Ephraim, the expectation is introduced that in time

kingship will come through the tribe of Judah and the descendants of David.[10]

The kings of the earth

Within the biblical meta-story the royal house of David becomes the focus of attention as regards the fulfilment of God's creation blueprint. One element of this expectation is the anticipation of a conflict involving kings who are at one with Satan in opposing God's sovereignty on the earth. This is perhaps best illustrated by Psalm 2:

> Why do the nations rage
> and the peoples plot in vain?
> The kings of the earth set themselves,
> and the rulers take counsel together,
> against the LORD and against his anointed, saying,
> 'Let us burst their bonds apart
> and cast away their cords from us.'
>
> He who sits in the heavens laughs;
> the Lord holds them in derision.
> Then he will speak to them in his wrath,
> and terrify them in his fury, saying,
> 'As for me, I have set my King
> on Zion, my holy hill.'

10. See T. D. Alexander, 'Royal Expectations in Genesis to Kings: Their Importance for Biblical Theology', *Tyndale Bulletin* 49 (1998), pp. 191–212; 'The Regal Dimension of the *tŏlĕdôt ya`ăqob*: Recovering the Literary Context of Genesis 37–50', in J. G. McConville and K. Möller (eds.), *Reading the Law: Studies in Honour of Gordon J. Wenham*, Library of Hebrew Bible / Old Testament Studies 461 (Edinburgh: T. & T. Clark, 2007); J. M. Hamilton, 'The Seed of the Woman and the Blessing of Abraham', *Tyndale Bulletin* 58 (2007), pp. 253–273.

I will tell of the decree:
The LORD said to me, 'You are my Son;
    today I have begotten you.
Ask of me, and I will make the nations your heritage,
    and the ends of the earth your possession.
You shall break them with a rod of iron
    and dash them in pieces like a potter's vessel.'

Now therefore, O kings, be wise;
    be warned, O rulers of the earth.
Serve the LORD with fear,
    and rejoice with trembling.
Kiss the Son,
    lest he be angry, and you perish in the way,
    for his wrath is quickly kindled.
Blessed are all who take refuge in him.

Although considerable hostility is directed against God and his anointed, the King, the psalmist anticipates that God's authority will eventually be extended over the earth. The choice set out in this psalm is between embracing God's chosen King or opposing him, between knowing God's blessing or his wrath. As Psalm 2 illustrates, a significant and recurring theme in the Old Testament is the establishment of God's kingdom on the earth in the face of sustained and violent opposition (e.g. Joel 3:1–21; Mic. 4:11–13; Zech. 12:2–9; 14:1–3, 12–19).[11]

The conflict between divine and human kingship is perhaps most evident in the remarkable stories and visions that comprise the book of Daniel. Interestingly, the opening four chapters of Daniel are constructed around the figure of Nebuchadnezzar, the king of Babylon from 605 to 562 BC, who was responsible for the destruction of Jerusalem and its temple in 586 BC.

In Daniel 2, Nebuchadnezzar has a strange dream in which he witnesses the destruction of a large statue made up of different sub-

---

11. See D. E. Gowan, *Eschatology in the Old Testament* (Philadelphia: Fortress, 1986), pp. 45–54.

stances (gold, silver, bronze, iron and clay) that represent different types of human kingship. Daniel describes what the king saw:

> As you looked, a stone was cut out by no human hand, and it struck the image on its feet of iron and clay, and broke them in pieces. Then the iron, the clay, the bronze, the silver, and the gold, all together were broken in pieces, and became like the chaff of the summer threshing floors; and the wind carried them away, so that not a trace of them could be found. But the stone that struck the image became a great mountain and filled the whole earth. (Dan. 2:34–35)

A little later Daniel interprets the meaning of this to Nebuchadnezzar:

> And in the days of those kings the God of heaven will set up a kingdom that shall never be destroyed, nor shall the kingdom be left to another people. It shall break in pieces all these kingdoms and bring them to an end, and it shall stand for ever, just as you saw that a stone was cut from a mountain by no human hand, and that it broke in pieces the iron, the bronze, the clay, the silver, and the gold. (Dan. 2:44–45)

Daniel foresees an eternal kingdom that will bring to an end various kingdoms associated with human rulers. Furthermore, the picture of this stone becoming a mountain that fills the whole earth echoes other Old Testament passages that associate the temple of God with a mountain.[12] This vision is consistent with the expectation that God's temple will fill the earth.

Satan defeated

Whereas the Old Testament looks forward to the defeat of God's enemies and the establishment of his reign upon the earth, the

---

12. See G. K. Beale, *The Temple and the Church's Mission: A Biblical Theology of the Dwelling Place of God*, New Studies in Biblical Theology 17 (Leicester: Apollos, 2004), pp. 144–153.

New Testament presents Jesus Christ as the one who overthrows Satan. In doing so, considerable use is made of the divine-warrior tradition, drawing especially on the Exodus account of God's defeat of Pharaoh in order to free the enslaved Israelites.[13] Focusing primarily on the Gospel of Mark, Tremper Longman and Dan Reid outline in detail how allusions to the divine warrior tradition have been woven into the narrative. Without reproducing their detailed discussion, the significance of Jesus' conflict with demonic forces is reflected in the prominence given to Jesus' rebuttal of Satan's temptations (Mark 1:13; cf. Matt. 4:1–11; Luke 4:1–13) and the recurring references to Jesus driving out 'unclean spirits' (Mark 1:23, 26; 3:30; 5:2, 8; 7:25; 9:25) and 'demons' (Mark 1:32, 34, 39; 3:15, 22; 5:18; 6:13; 9:38).

While Mark's account of the temptations is by far the shortest in the Synoptic Gospels, the conflict between Jesus and demonic powers reappears soon afterwards in Mark 1:23–27. In a synagogue on the Sabbath, a man, possessed by an unclean spirit, cries out, 'What have you to do with us, Jesus of Nazareth? Have you come to destroy us? I know who you are – the Holy One of God' (Mark 1:24). The spirit's unusual outburst draws attention to the purpose of Jesus' coming. He has come as a divine warrior to overthrow the evil one.[14] In the light of this, the location (a syna-

---

13. The discussion that follows is largely dependent upon Longman and Reid, *God Is a Warrior*, pp. 91–192; cf. R. E. Watts, *Isaiah's New Exodus and Mark*, Biblical Studies Library (Grand Rapids: Baker, 2000). T. Holland, *Contours of Pauline Theology: A Radical New Survey of the Influences on Paul's Biblical Writings* (Fearn: Mentor, 2004), argues in detail that the exodus theme is a central component of Paul's theology.

14. D. G. McCartney, '*Ecce Homo*: The Coming of the Kingdom as the Restoration of Human Vicegerency', *Westminster Theological Journal* 56 (1994), pp. 9–10, writes, 'Throughout the Galilean ministry in the synoptic Gospels, Jesus casts demons out by the Spirit of God, and this is a sign that "the kingdom of God has come upon you" (Matt 12:28; Luke 11:20). This is one of the clearest statements by Jesus that the kingdom has already arrived (*ephthasen* rather than the more usual *ēngiken*). When Jesus as man, empowered by the Spirit, exercises authority over the

gogue) and the timing (on the Sabbath) underline the extent of the enemy's control.

The theme of Jesus' conflict with Satan, evident through the many exorcisms Mark includes in his Gospel, comes to the fore when scribes from Jerusalem accuse Jesus of being possessed by Beelzebul, the prince of demons. Mark records Jesus' response:

> And he called them to him and said to them in parables, 'How can Satan cast out Satan? If a kingdom is divided against itself, that kingdom cannot stand. And if a house is divided against itself, that house will not be able to stand. And if Satan has risen up against himself and is divided, he cannot stand, but is coming to an end. But no one can enter a strong man's house and plunder his goods, unless he first binds the strong man. Then indeed he may plunder his house. (Mark 3:23–27)

Implicit in Jesus' remarks is the idea that he has come to bind the strong man, Satan, and plunder his house.[15] To establish the reign of God on the earth it is necessary for the Evil One and those siding with him to be defeated.[16] Since the Son of God has come to bind Satan, it is no surprise that Mark gives particular attention to how Jesus exorcizes demonic spirits. Such spirits are naturally associated with Satan.[17] However, they are not alone in siding with

---

demons, the proper viceregency of man under God is restored. Jesus did what Adam should have done; he cast the serpent out of the garden.'

15. Since Mark's Gospel associates the religious authorities in Jerusalem with Satan, Jesus may be implying here that the temple itself has become part of Satan's house. If this is so, his later cleansing of the temple takes on additional significance.

16. As Longman and Reid, *God Is a Warrior*, p. 109, observe, 'From an eschatological perspective, Jesus was carrying out a new Exodus and Conquest, routing the enemy that had occupied the land and held individuals in his thrall.' In line with this, it is interesting to observe that the Gospels associate John's baptism of people in the Jordan with the coming of a 'Joshua' who looks to repossess the land for God.

17. We see this connection in Luke 10:17–20: 'The seventy-two returned with joy, saying, "Lord, even the demons are subject to us in your name!" And

Satan against Jesus, for Mark indicates that the religious authorities, who are associated with the temple in Jerusalem, are at one
with Satan in opposing Jesus, as are, to a lesser extent, Jesus' own
disciples.

As regards the latter, it is noteworthy that Peter, following his
all-important confession of Jesus as the Christ, is linked to Satan
when he rebukes Jesus for claiming that 'the Son of Man must
suffer many things and be rejected by the elders and the chief
priests and the scribes and be killed' (Mark 8:31). Jesus reproves
Peter, 'Get behind me, Satan! For you are not setting your mind on
the things of God, but on the things of man' (Mark 8:33).[18]

While Satan's influence occasionally extends even to Jesus' own
disciples,[19] it is associated more significantly with the religious
leaders who fail to recognize Jesus as the Son of God. Whereas in
chapters 1–9 Mark mainly associates hostility against Jesus with
demonic spirits, when Jesus moves from Galilee to Judea at the
start of Mark 10, resistance to Jesus comes chiefly from the religious leaders. Three times the religious authorities 'test/tempt'

Footnote 17 (*continued*)

he said to them, "I saw Satan fall like lightning from heaven. Behold, I
have given you authority to tread on serpents and scorpions, and over
all the power of the enemy, and nothing shall hurt you. Nevertheless, do
not rejoice in this, that the spirits are subject to you, but rejoice that your
names are written in heaven.'" Since Gen. 3 links God's arch-enemy with a
serpent, it is noteworthy that Jesus' comment about treading on 'serpents
and scorpions' is set in the context of overcoming demons and Satan.

18. In the light of this, it is worth recalling what Jesus says to Peter in Luke
22:31–34: '"Simon, Simon, behold, Satan demanded to have you, that he
might sift you like wheat, but I have prayed for you that your faith may not
fail. And when you have turned again, strengthen your brothers." Peter
said to him, "Lord, I am ready to go with you both to prison and to
death." Jesus said, "I tell you, Peter, the rooster will not crow this day, until
you deny three times that you know me."'

19. Although Mark does not specifically associate Judas' betrayal of Jesus
with Satan, this link is unambiguously made in the Gospels of Luke and
John (Luke 22:3, 31; John 13:27).

Jesus (Mark 8:11; 10:2; 12:15), echoing Satan's testing/tempting of Jesus in Mark 1:13.

The intensity of the religious leaders' opposition to Jesus eventually results in his death.[20] Undoubtedly, in the light of Mark's Gospel as a whole, Christ's death on the cross appears to be a decisive victory for Satan over the Son of God. Yet, although Christ's crucifixion has every appearance of being a triumph for Satan – the Son of God is overcome by death – the Gospel account does not end there. Apparent defeat is dramatically turned into victory with the resurrection of Jesus. For this reason, Jesus can subsequently proclaim to his disciples, 'All authority in heaven and on earth has been given to me' (Matt. 28:18).

While the theme of Jesus' conflict with Satan is a major component in the Gospels, especially in Mark, it also lies at the heart of the apostle Paul's writings. As Longman and Reid rightly observe, underlying the rhetoric of Paul's letters is a story of Christ that, drawing upon the Old Testament story of God, Israel and the nations, displays 'the progressive pattern of warfare, victory, kingship, temple building, and celebration'.[21] Longman and Reid helpfully summarize this story of Christ as follows:

> The contours of the story are of one sent from heaven to subject the cosmos to its Creator and Lord. Born of a woman (Gal 4:4) and taking

---

20. The theme of conflict between Jesus and the religious authorities is prominent in the Gospel of Matthew. J. D. Kingsbury, 'The Plot of Matthew's Story', *Interpretation* 46 (1992), pp. 347–356, suggests that this conflict is at the very heart of the plot of Matthew's Gospel. Interestingly, Kingsbury notes that in Matt. 21 – 22 the intensity of the conflict between the religious leaders and Jesus is underlined by the setting: the temple is both the seat of authority for the religious leaders and the place of God's presence. At the very heart of the conflict is the issue of power. Jesus' authority as the Son of God is rejected by the religious leaders linked to the temple. Implicit in this is the idea that the temple itself has come under the control of Satan. For this reason, its future destruction is presented in Mark 13 as an act of divine judgment.

21. Longman and Reid, *God Is a Warrior*, p. 136.

human form (Php 2:7), he engaged the enemy, was victorious in an epochal battle (Col 2:15; cf. 1:12–14), and was exalted to God's right hand, where he now reigns as cosmic Lord (1Co 15:24–26; Eph 1:20–22; Php 2:9; Col 3:1; 1Ti 3:16), building his new temple (1Co 3:16–17; 2Co 6:16; Eph 2:19–22), and receiving praise and obeisance (Php 2:10–11). He will come again at the end of the age and conclude his defeat of the enemy, who will have waged a final revolt (2Th 2:8). In the end, death, the final enemy, will stand defeated along with every other hostile power, and Christ will hand over the kingdom to God (1Co 15:24–28). But in the meantime, the people of the Messiah stand between two episodes – climax and resolution – in the eschatological warfare, enjoying the benefits and advantage of Christ's defeat of the enemy at the cross (Ro 8:37). Yet, as they await their Lord to descend from heaven on the final day (1Th 4:16–17), they are still beset by a hostile foe (Eph 6:10–17).[22]

This overview of Paul's understanding of the story of Christ is very much in keeping with that found in the Gospels. Like the Gospel writers, Paul too underscores the centrality of the cross as the means by which Satan is defeated. As the author of Hebrews observes, it is 'through death' that Jesus destroys 'the one who has the power of death, that is, the devil' (Heb. 2:14).[23]

---

22. Ibid., pp. 136–137. Additional evidence for this pattern is provided by T. G. Gombis, 'Ephesians 2 as a Narrative of Divine Warfare', *Journal for the Study of the New Testament* 26 (2004), pp. 403–418; 'Cosmic Lordship and Divine Gift-Giving: Psalm 68 in Ephesians 4:8', *Novum Testamentum* 47 (2005), pp. 367–380; 'The Triumph of God in Christ: Divine Warfare in The Argument of Ephesians' (PhD thesis, University of St Andrews, St Andrews, 2005).

23. Longman and Reid, *God Is a Warrior*, p. 150 write, 'Christ in his death as the obedient second Adam turned the tables on the powers of evil and defeated their purposes, publicly displaying *(edeigmatisen en parrēssia,* Col 2:15) their true and shameful nature. Just as a criminal justice system is exposed in its short-comings when it executes an innocent person, so much more were the cosmic powers exposed and defeated when they crucified the sinless Lord of glory. The victory celebrated is, at its heart, not the victory of a more powerful being over less powerful beings (as if

Satan's reign ended

As noted earlier, Revelation 20 describes how Satan, 'the dragon, that ancient serpent', is bound for a thousand years so that he might not deceive the nations any longer. After that, Satan is released and gathers for battle nations from the four corners of the earth. However, his army is destroyed and he is thrown into the lake of fire and sulphur to be tormented day and night for ever.

Over the centuries, Christians have understood the events described in this chapter in various ways. There are three broad approaches, known as 'premillennialism', 'postmillennialism' and 'amillennialism'.

In general terms, premillennialism teaches that Christ will return in glory to reign on the earth for a period of 1,000 years. He comes 'pre' (before) the millennium. Such an understanding underlies dispensationalist readings of the Bible, associated with J. N. Darby (1800–82) and later the Scofield Bible (1909).

Postmillennialism maintains that Christ comes after the period of 1,000 years. Before Christ's return, there will be 1,000 years of spiritual prosperity and peace for the church on earth. Such thinking was especially popular in the eighteenth century and played an important role in developing missionary thinking.

The third approach, amillennialism, is strictly speaking an inaccurate designation because it implies *no* millennium (the prefix 'a' being the negative 'no'). Amillennialism usually takes the 1,000 years as symbolic, like many of the numbers in Revelation, and sees it as referring to the age of the church, that is, the period from the resurrection of Christ to his return.

---

it were a cosmic struggle of strength against strength in which salvation was achieved by a tour de force); it is the victory of holy, righteous, and creative love over the destructive forces of evil.'

As a perfect viceroy, Jesus demonstrates his trust in God the Father through being a righteous sufferer. As the book of Job reveals, Satan is permitted to inflict terrrible suffering upon Job in order to demonstrate that his commitment to God is not prompted by purely selfish motives. Jesus' suffering, in part at least, fulfils a similar purpose.

The differences between these three approaches are considerable and should not be underestimated. Yet, all three views agree about the ultimate fate of the devil or Satan. Stripped of his power, he will no longer, as 'ruler of this world', be able to champion the cause of evil. Every vestige of Satan's influence will be destroyed.

While Revelation focuses on the defeat of Satan, it also reveals that those who are at one with him in opposing God will share a similar fate. John sees this in his final vision:

> But as for the cowardly, the faithless, the detestable, as for murderers, the sexually immoral, sorcerers, idolaters, and all liars, their portion will be in the lake that burns with fire and sulphur, which is the second death. (Rev. 21:8)

Since our hope is for a holy garden-city untarnished by evil, it naturally follows that the children of the evil one will be barred from God's dwelling place. As we shall observe in more detail later, only the holy may live in God's presence.

Resisting the devil

A number of important implications arise out of these observations regarding Satan and his dominion over this present earth.

First, Satan's greatest deception is to persuade us that we do not need to acknowledge the sovereignty of God. As with Adam and Eve, he continues to deceive human beings regarding God's authority. Not surprisingly, he is particularly keen to have people ignore or reject the biblical meta-story. By doing so Satan bolsters his own position as ruler of this world.

Secondly, we need to be conscious that until he is finally thrown into the lake of fire, Satan's evil influence continues to make its horrific presence felt in our world. It is all around us. Evil is one of the terrible realities of life, although we rarely fully acknowledge its existence. When we witness the terrible atrocities people can commit against one another, we need to recall that these things occur because Satan is, among other things, a liar and a murderer (John 8:44).

Thirdly, as Christians we are involved in a spiritual battle. The ruler of this world refuses to admit defeat. He continues to do all in his power to undermine the purposes of God, and directs his attacks most strongly at the followers of Christ.[24] As the apostle Peter puts it, 'Be sober-minded; be watchful. Your adversary the devil prowls around like a roaring lion, seeking someone to devour' (1 Pet. 5:8).

Fourthly, in this spiritual battle God has given us armour for protection. Paul highlights this in writing to the Christians at Ephesus:

> For we do not wrestle against flesh and blood, but against the rulers, against the authorities, against the cosmic powers over this present darkness, against the spiritual forces of evil in the heavenly places. Therefore take up the whole armour of God, that you may be able to withstand in the evil day, and having done all, to stand firm. Stand therefore, having fastened on the belt of truth, and having put on the breastplate of righteousness, and, as shoes for your feet, having put on the readiness given by the gospel of peace. In all circumstances take up the shield of faith, with which you can extinguish all the flaming darts of the evil one . . . (Eph. 6:12–16)

Fifthly, as Christians we are called upon to persevere in this spiritual battle. To those who stand fast in the face of evil, God promises a wonderful inheritance. Revelation 21 highlights this, although this theme runs throughout the book of Revelation:

> And he who was seated on the throne said, 'Behold, I am making all things new.' Also he said, 'Write this down, for these words are trustworthy and true.' And he said to me, 'It is done! I am the Alpha

---

24. We see this reflected in Rev. 2:12–13: 'And to the angel of the church in Pergamum write: "The words of him who has the sharp two-edged sword.

'I know where you dwell, where Satan's throne is. Yet you hold fast my name, and you did not deny my faith even in the days of Antipas my faithful witness, who was killed among you, where Satan dwells."'

and the Omega, the beginning and the end. To the thirsty I will give from the spring of the water of life without payment. The one who conquers will have this heritage, and I will be his God and he will be my son. (Rev. 21:5–7)

Difficult as it may be to envisage now, one day those who conquer will live in God's presence, in a new world liberated from every trace of evil.

5. THE SLAUGHTER OF THE LAMB: ACCOMPLISHING THE REDEMPTION OF CREATION

Our study of John's final vision in the book of Revelation has revealed that the New Jerusalem brings to completion a project that God initiated when he created the present earth and commissioned Adam and Eve as his viceroys. However, by disobeying God and siding with his enemy, Adam and Eve jeopardized the divine plan that they and their descendants should rule over the earth and make it God's dwelling place. Under satanic influence, the human couple betrayed their Creator and consequently lost their status as priestly monarchs. Although the enemy, 'the dragon, that ancient serpent, who is the devil and Satan', is presently 'ruler of this world', his days are numbered and he will ultimately be vanquished. Crucial to the demise of Satan is Jesus Christ, for he is the one who overcomes the devil.

The Lamb

Remarkably, John's description of the New Jerusalem in Revelation 21 – 22 contains no specific reference to the name of Jesus Christ.

This is not to say that the Son of God is absent from the New Jerusalem. On the contrary, he is very much at the centre of it. However, each time he is mentioned, he is designated by the title 'the Lamb'. In all, Revelation 21 – 22 has five references to the Lamb:

> And the wall of the city had twelve foundations, and on them were the twelve names of the twelve apostles of the Lamb. (Rev. 21:14)

> And I saw no temple in the city, for its temple is the Lord God the Almighty and the Lamb. (Rev. 21:22)

> And the city has no need of sun or moon to shine on it, for the glory of God gives it light, and its lamp is the Lamb. (Rev. 21:23)

> Then the angel showed me the river of the water of life, bright as crystal, flowing from the throne of God and of the Lamb. (Rev. 22:1)

> No longer will there be anything accursed, but the throne of God and of the Lamb will be in it, and his servants will worship him. (Rev. 22:3)

The image of Christ as a Lamb is highly significant in Revelation. Throughout the book the term 'Lamb' denotes Christ twenty-eight times. On seven of these occasions, the Lamb is coupled with God, drawing attention to the special relationship that exists between them.[1]

Central to understanding this image is Revelation 5, where Christ is first introduced as the Lamb. The chapter begins by describing a sealed scroll. When no one appears to be able to open it, John weeps. Then one of the elders speaks to him:

> 'Weep no more; behold, the Lion of the tribe of Judah, the Root of David, has conquered, so that he can open the scroll and its seven seals.'

---

1. We see this three times in Rev. 21 – 22, twice with reference to their sharing a throne and once with reference to their being a temple; we might even want to include Rev. 21:23, which associates both God and the Lamb with light.

And between the throne and the four living creatures and among the elders I saw a Lamb standing, as though it had been slain, with seven horns and with seven eyes, which are the seven spirits of God sent out into all the earth. And he went and took the scroll from the right hand of him who was seated on the throne. And when he had taken the scroll, the four living creatures and the twenty-four elders fell down before the Lamb, each holding a harp, and golden bowls full of incense, which are the prayers of the saints. And they sang a new song, saying,

'Worthy are you to take the scroll
   and to open its seals,
for you were slain, and by your blood you ransomed people for God
   from every tribe and language and people and nation,
and you have made them a kingdom and priests to our God,
   and they shall reign on the earth.' (Rev. 5:5–10)

The apocalyptic nature of John's vision permits two contrasting images of Jesus Christ to be set side by side. In verse 5, one of the elders speaks to John about the Lion of the tribe of Judah, who 'has conquered, so that he can open the scroll and its seven seals'. However, when John looks, he sees not a lion, but a lamb 'standing, as though it had been slain'. An obvious contrast exists between what John hears and what he sees: he hears of a lion, but sees a lamb.

In Revelation it is common for John both to 'hear' and 'see' certain things in close proximity. When this happens, a link is established between what is heard and what is seen, even when this may at first not seem obvious. This is what occurs in Revelation 5:5–6. The lion and the lamb refer to the same person, Jesus Christ. However, the two images could hardly be more different. We normally associate a lion with power and aggression, but a lamb with weakness and vulnerability.

While this distinction is present in Revelation 5, both images convey much more. The expression 'Lion of Judah' draws attention to the kingly dimension of Jesus as the Messiah or anointed one, who comes to establish the kingdom of God. As the 'Root of David' he brings to fulfilment the divine promises given to King David and his descendants. Here the emphasis is upon the victory of the promised Davidic king in overcoming all who are opposed to God.[2]

Although John is told that the Lion of Judah has conquered and can open the scroll, when he looks he sees a lamb. This lamb, while now clearly alive, has in the past been slaughtered as a sacrificial offering. Two features strongly associate the lamb with a Passover sacrifice.

First, the phrase 'by your blood you ransomed people for God' is reminiscent of the divine deliverance of the Israelites from bondage in Egypt. On several occasions the language of ransom or redemption is used to describe God's release of the people. Exodus 6:6 states:

> Say therefore to the people of Israel, 'I am the LORD, and I will bring you out from under the burdens of the Egyptians, and I will deliver you from slavery to them, and I will redeem you with an outstretched arm and with great acts of judgment.' (Exod. 6:6; cf. Deut. 7:8)

The motif of redemption is later incorporated into the victory song of Exodus 15:

> You have led in your steadfast love the people whom you have redeemed;
> you have guided them by your strength to your holy abode.
> (Exod. 15:13)

As these passages reveal, redemption is one of the important theological ideas of the exodus.[3]

---

2. E.g. Ps. 2:1–12.

3. While we might be inclined to think that the Israelites are redeemed or ransomed from slavery to Pharaoh, this is hardly the case. On the contrary, when a payment passes between the Israelites and the Egyptians, it is the latter who give to the former. Nothing is given to Pharaoh or his people. Rather, they give jewellery and clothing to the Israelites. In the light of this, it would seem likely that the Israelites are redeemed from death. This interpretation rests on the assumption that death is under-

Secondly, not only has the Lamb ransomed people for God, but he has also 'made them a kingdom and priests to our God, and they shall reign on the earth'. This is clearly an allusion to Exodus 19:5–6, where, as we saw previously, the expression 'kingdom of priests' is used of Israel.[4]

When we put these two observations together, the Lamb of Revelation 5 is undoubtedly associated with the Old Testament exodus story. However, whereas the first exodus was principally about rescuing the Israelites from slavery, John has in view a new exodus that brings about the deliverance of people 'from every nation, from all tribes and peoples and languages' (Rev. 7:9).

Christ, our Passover Lamb

Without unpacking all of the details, the Gospel writers clearly understood the death of Jesus as having an 'exodus' significance. All four Gospels link the timing of Jesus' death to the annual celebration of the Passover, which marked the start of the Feast of Unleavened Bread. John's Gospel, in particular, highlights this connection by observing that when Jesus was put to death on the cross not one of his bones was broken. John indicates that this 'took place that the Scripture might be fulfilled: "Not one of his bones will be broken"' (John 19:36). By drawing attention to this, John observes a typological link between Jesus' death and the Passover sacrifice (Exod. 12:46).[5]

---

stood to be a hostile power opposed to Yahweh, the God of life. This would explain why the Israelites have to take special actions to prevent the death of their firstborn. It also accounts for the special emphasis given to redeeming the firstborn males whenever the Israelites enter the land of Canaan (see Exod. 13:11–16).

4. See page 84.

5. Other major features of John's Gospel also support the idea of Jesus' death being part of a new exodus. Three are worthy of particular note: (1) The signs that dominate the first half of the Gospel recall the signs performed by God in Egypt. However, whereas the latter are signs of

The concept of Jesus being a Passover sacrifice is also picked up by the apostle Paul when he comments to the Christians in Corinth, 'Cleanse out the old leaven that you may be a new lump, as you really are unleavened. For Christ, our Passover lamb, has been sacrificed' (1 Cor. 5:7).[6]

The idea of Christ's death being a ransom is perhaps most clearly expressed in Mark 10:45: 'For even the Son of Man came not to be served but to serve, and to give his life as a ransom for many.'[7] The apostle Peter also picks up the same concept in his first epistle when he writes:

Footnote 5 (*continued*)

   judgment (water into blood; death of firstborn), the signs associated with Jesus bring hope (water into wine; resurrection of Lazarus). See S. V. McCasland, 'Signs and Wonders', *Journal of Biblical Literature* 76 (1957), pp. 149–152. (2) John is especially interested in highlighting Jesus' activities at the time of feasts, almost all of which commemorate the exodus. (3) The 'I am' sayings recall God's revelation of his name 'I am' to Moses in Exod. 3:14.

6. The Greek text does not use the term 'lamb'; it merely states, 'For Christ, our Passover, has been sacrificed.' For a fuller discussion of paschal imagery in Paul's letters, see T. Holland, *Contours of Pauline Theology: A Radical New Survey of the Influences on Paul's Biblical Writings* (Fearn: Mentor, 2004), pp. 85–291.

7. Holland (ibid., pp. 172–173) notes that the concept of ransom is linked to the Passover through the substitution of the Levites for the firstborn males of Israel. He writes (p. 173), 'The Levites, man for man, were to be substituted for the firstborn of Israel who had been spared by the Lord. Because they had been spared, the Lord claimed them as his own. Strictly speaking, that meant as a sacrificial offering, but that would have defeated the purpose of the protection of the blood of the lamb. Instead, the Lord claimed them as living sacrifices, as priests, to serve him. But in order to allow them to remain with their families, the Lord arranged for the tribe of Levi to become priests in their place. They were the ransom. We see that Jesus uses language taken from the very heart of the Passover/Exodus event to explain the significance of his death. Indeed, the parallel Lucan text places the saying at the heart of the Last Supper with its immediate Paschal celebration.'

you were ransomed from the futile ways inherited from your forefathers, not with perishable things such as silver or gold, but with the precious blood of Christ, like that of a lamb without blemish or spot. (1 Pet. 1:18–19)

While the identity of the lamb in 1 Peter 1:18–19 as a Passover sacrifice is less clear, the context in which it appears favours this interpretation.[8]

The Passover in Exodus

To understand the significance of Jesus Christ's portrayal as a Passover sacrifice, we must return to the original Passover account in Exodus. We have already observed that the exodus from Egypt led to the creation of Israel as a theocracy and the construction of the tabernacle. These events, which include the Israelites becoming priest-kings, are both a partial fulfilment of the creation blueprint and an anticipation of its ultimate fulfilment. The movement from being slaves of Pharaoh to servants of the Lord involves the divine redemption of the Israelites from Pharaoh's control. Furthermore, in order for the people to become priest-kings of the Lord, an additional process of consecration must take place. Central both to the redemption and consecration of the Israelites is the Passover.

According to Exodus 12, the Passover ritual consists of three distinctive parts: (1) the slaying of a lamb or young goat as a sacrifice, (2) the smearing of its blood on the doorposts and (3) the eating of its meat (Exod. 12:6–11, 21–22).[9] The first part of the Passover ritual was clearly a sacrifice, as Exodus 12:27 confirms: 'It is the sacrifice of the LORD's Passover.' Yet, while

---

8. See S. Jeffery, M. Ovey and A. Sach, *Pierced for our Transgressions: Rediscovering the Glory of Penal Substitution* (Nottingham: IVP, 2007), p. 41.

9. A fuller discussion of the Passover is available in T. D. Alexander, 'The Passover Sacrifice', in R. T. Beckwith and M. Selman (eds.), *Sacrifice in the Bible* (Carlisle: Paternoster; Grand Rapids: Baker, 1995), pp. 1–21.

resembling other sacrifices, the Passover ceremony is unique, reflecting its historical setting. Since it takes place before the appointment and consecration of the Aaronic priesthood (Lev. 8:1 – 9:24), Moses commands 'all the elders of Israel' to slaughter the Passover animals (Exod. 12:21). In line with this, there is no reference to the central sanctuary first instituted at Mount Sinai (Exod. 27:1–8). Whereas other sacrifices were normally offered up during daylight, the Passover is sacrificed at 'twilight' (Exod. 12:6), as this was the only convenient time due to the exploitation of the Israelites by the Egyptians.

Special attention is focused on the use made of the sacrificial animal's blood, which is smeared on the sides and tops of the door frame of the house (Exod. 12:7, 22). Some scholars emphasize the apotropaic (warding off) purpose of this action, designed to protect those within from hostile powers without (cf. Exod. 12:13, 23). Others suggest that the blood was used to purify the Israelite houses, a proposal strongly supported by the mention of hyssop (Exod. 12:22), elsewhere associated with ritual purification (e.g. Lev. 14:4, 6, 49, 51, 52; Num. 19:6, 18). Both aspects may be relevant.

An equally important element of the Passover rite is the eating of the animal. Everyone in the Israelite community is to participate (Exod. 12:47), and for each animal slaughtered there has to be an adequate number of people to eat all of the meat. Any meat not consumed by the morning must be burnt (Exod. 12:10). To underline the importance of this part of the ritual, special instructions are given concerning the cooking and eating of the meat: the entire animal is roasted, not boiled (Exod. 12:9); the meat must be eaten indoors; the animal's bones must not be broken (Exod. 12:46).

The three elements that make up the Passover ritual are also found in the account of the consecration of the Aaronic priests in Exodus 29 and Leviticus 8. Here the sacrifice of a ram, the sprinkling of its blood and the eating of its meat constitute a consecration ritual that sets Aaron and his sons apart from the rest of the people. This special ritual enables them to serve as priests in the tabernacle.

Although some differences in the details exist, there is good reason to believe that the Passover ritual is about consecrating the people as 'priests'. The sacrifice of the animal atones for the sin of the people, the blood smeared on the doorposts purifies those within the house, and the sacrificial meat sanctifies or makes holy all who eat it. Understood in this way, the Passover ritual enables all of the Israelites to obtain a holy status, an important requisite for becoming a royal priesthood (Exod. 19:6).[10] All of this comes about through the sacrificed lambs or young goats. Without the sacrificial offerings there could be no atonement, purification or sanctification.

The process of transferring the Israelites from the satanic power of the king of Egypt to the kingdom of God requires more than merely rescuing them from Egypt. If they are to live in the presence of God, they must regain the holy status humanity had prior to the disobedience of Adam and Eve. The Passover ritual performs this function in the historical context of the Israelites coming out of Egypt and becoming God's people at Mount Sinai.[11]

The Passover sacrifice contributes in a highly significant way to the divine redemption of the Israelites from Egypt. Such was the importance of this occasion that God instructed the Israelites to remember it annually with special celebrations. Later generations were to commemorate this unique event, which was a vital part of the process by which God established Israel as his holy people, his royal priesthood. Not surprisingly, therefore, the Passover became a central component of a larger paradigm or model of God's redemptive activity. In order to restore the holy or priestly status

---

10. The priestly dimension of the Passover is also reflected in the substitution of the Levites for the firstborn Israelite males. Those redeemed from death by the blood of the Passover sacrifices are bound to serve God in a special way. See n. 7 above (p. 126).

11. Later, because there was a recurring need to restore this holy status, a range of sacrifices was instituted by the Lord in Lev. 1 – 7. The Day of Atonement ritual performs a complementary function by annually purifying the ark of the covenant from defilement caused by Israelite wrongdoings.

of human beings, there had to be atonement, purification and sanctification. When we turn to the New Testament these same three elements are associated with the death of Jesus Christ at Passover.

Atonement

The original Passover took place in the context of God punishing all of the firstborn males of Egypt by death. Without the sacrificial ritual, the firstborn Israelites would also have been put to death. What distinguished the Israelites from the Egyptians was not that the former were inherently more righteous than the latter. Judged by God, the Israelites and the Egyptians all deserved to die. However, the Passover lambs became a substitute for the Israelite firstborn. The lambs died in the place of the Israelite firstborn males and atoned for human sin or wrongdoing. These sacrifices made God and human beings 'at one'. They addressed the righteous anger God has towards evil human beings.

To appreciate the necessity of atonement, we must grasp clearly that God is not indifferent to our immoral thoughts and behaviour. On the contrary, his holy nature is deeply offended by such things. As a perfect God, he cannot ignore anything evil. The smallest lie is offensive to the One who is truth. The tiniest feeling of animosity towards another person is repulsive to the One who is love. Due to his holy and perfect nature God cannot turn a blind eye to perverse human behaviour as if it does not matter.

We also need to appreciate that due to our own perversity, we do not realize fully how objectionable our imperfections are to God. If we contemplate our shortcomings and failures at all, we merely dismiss them as something natural; this is part of our human nature – we are all like this.

Yet, in truth, our imperfections are anything but natural. C. S. Lewis alludes to this idea profoundly in his science fiction novel *Out of the Silent Planet*. The hero of the story, Ransom, has been kidnapped by two men and taken to the foreign planet Malacandra. There he comes into contact with strange creatures known as *hrossa*. In the process of getting to know one of these alien beings, he discovers that they are naturally monogamous. Ransom ponders this:

> Among the *hrossa*, anyway, it was obvious that unlimited breeding and promiscuity were as rare as the rarest perversions. At last it dawned upon him that it was not they, but his own species, that were the puzzle. That the *hrossa* should have such instincts was mildly surprising; but how came it that the instincts of the *hrossa* so closely resembled the unattained ideals of that far-divided species Man whose instincts were so deplorably different? What was the history of Man?[12]

From God's perspective human nature is anything but natural. Unfortunately, we are far too blind to see this. When judged according to divine standards, it is no surprise that we deserve to be punished by death.

Moreover, behind all our perverse behaviour lies a far more scandalous and sinister crime: the dethroning of God. As already noted, human beings have betrayed God and sided with his enemy. We are evil, like Satan himself. As traitors we deserve to die. No lesser a punishment is appropriate.

Yet, may God not turn a blind eye to our wrongdoing and treachery? Is it not possible for him as a God of love to overlook our human wrongdoing. Never! As Satan, the accuser,[13] would quickly remind him, to do so is unjust. If God is to be true to his own righteous nature, all wrongdoing must be punished. In addition, if God is to condemn and punish Satan, then he must be consistent in condemning and punishing all who are like Satan. For God to deal justly with the prince of evil, he must punish every other creature that has rebelled against his divine authority.

---

12. C. S. Lewis, *Out of the Silent Planet* (London: Pan, 1968), pp. 85–86.

13. One of the roles associated with Satan in the Bible is that of accuser; see B. Baloian, '*śāṭān*', in W. A. VanGemeren (ed.), *New International Dictionary of Old Testament Theology and Exegesis*, vol. 3 (Carlisle: Paternoster; Grand Rapids: Zondervan, 1996), pp. 1231–1232.

In the light of this, atonement is necessary. We need to be made 'at one' with God. However, the justice of God requires that a death must occur. As the author of Hebrews succinctly puts it, 'without the shedding of blood there is no forgiveness of sins' (Heb. 9:22). Only in this way may God's righteous wrath be appeased and justice be done.

While the Old Testament sacrifices rely upon the offering of animals, these merely foreshadow the sacrifice of Christ. As the author of Hebrews correctly observes, 'it is impossible for the blood of bulls and goats to take away sins' (Heb. 10:4). However, he proceeds to affirm the total effectiveness of Christ's death:

> But when Christ had offered for all time a single sacrifice for sins, he sat down at the right hand of God, waiting from that time until his enemies should be made a footstool for his feet. For by a single offering he has perfected for all time those who are being sanctified. (Heb. 10:12–14)

As this passage reveals, the Passover sacrifices, as with many other things in the Old Testament, point forward to a greater reality. They prepare for the authentic Lamb of God, Jesus Christ (see John 1:29, 36).

Purification

While the sacrificial death of the lamb atones for human sin, the sprinkling of its blood purifies those within the house. Here another major aspect of human wrongdoing is addressed. Although atonement secures peace with God, it does not remove the stain of sin. Sin taints and defiles: it takes away our innocence and tarnishes our purity. We see this in Genesis 3. Prior to the fall, Adam and Eve were innocent and pure; they were naked, but unashamed. After disobeying God, they hid because their consciences condemned them; no longer were they clean.

The need to be cleansed because of sin's defilement is a recurring motif within the Bible. It underlines God's comment in Isaiah 1:18:

> Come now, let us reason together, says the LORD:
> though your sins are like scarlet,
>> they shall be as white as snow; though they are red like
>> crimson,
>> they shall become like wool.

Cleansing is vital if we are to become holy. With good reason the Bible develops this theme at length (e.g. Num. 19:1–9; Ezek. 36:17–19, 25–29; Heb. 9:16–24; 1 John 1:7).

Perhaps one of the best illustrations of how sin stains us comes in Shakespeare's play *Macbeth*. After Macbeth murders Duncan and discovers the king's blood on his hand, he comments:

> Will all great Neptune's ocean wash this blood
> Clean from my hand? No, this my hand will rather
> The multitudinous seas incarnadine,
> Making the green one red.
> (Act II, Scene i, lines 58–61)

While Macbeth is painfully conscious of how Duncan's murder has stained him, Lady Macbeth is initially far less troubled. In time, however, her bloodstained hands return to haunt her. Later in the play, she is witnessed rubbing them together in a vain attempt to remove the stain of sin. Her guilty conscience constantly torments her. Unsurprisingly, the Doctor comments:

> Foul whisperings are abroad. Unnatural deeds
> Do breed unnatural troubles; infected minds
> To their deaf pillows will discharge their secrets.
> More needs she the divine than the physician.
> (Act V, Scene i, lines 79–82)

Shakespeare tellingly captures that the stain of sin cannot easily be washed away. He understands that it is not easy to cleanse a guilty conscience. No matter how much we may wish to forget past actions, our consciences do not let us rest in peace. Sin's mark needs something special to remove it. To this end, the blood of the Lamb cleanses us from the pollution of sin. Of necessity, purification must accompany atonement.[14]

Sanctification

Beyond atonement and purification, the Israelites still need to be sanctified in order to obtain a holy status. This happens when they eat the sacrificial meat. By consuming holy meat the people also become holy. The sacred nature of the meat explains why the Israelites are to burn any that is left over, after first ensuring that they roast only as much as they can eat.

If eating holy meat sanctifies the ancient Israelites, the New Testament equivalent is the Lord's Supper. Instituted by Jesus when celebrating the Passover meal with his disciples, the bread and wine represent the body and blood of Christ, the Passover Lamb. Given the obvious links between the Passover meal and the Lord's Supper, it seems reasonable to conclude that both fulfil the same purpose of sanctification. Since Christ's body and blood are sacred, Paul cautions those who participate in the Lord's Supper – to eat holy food inappropriately is to invite divine condemnation (1 Cor. 11:23–28).

Each of the three elements of the Passover ritual contributes in a different way towards making people holy. As already noted, the same elements are reflected in the comparable process by which the Levitical priests are set apart from the other Israelites in order to serve in the tabernacle (Exod. 29; Lev. 8).

By linking the crucifixion of Jesus to the Passover, the New Testament writers draw attention to the redemptive nature of

---

14. The same point is made by the author of Hebrews: 'Therefore, brothers, since we have confidence to enter the holy places by the blood of Jesus, by the new and living way that he opened for us through the curtain, that is, through his flesh, and since we have a great priest over the house of God, let us draw near with a true heart in full assurance of faith, with our hearts sprinkled clean from an evil conscience and our bodies washed with pure water' (Heb. 10:19–22).

Jesus' death. Like the original Passover sacrifice, his death atones for the sin of the people, his blood purifies and cleanses, and those who eat his body at the Lord's Supper share in his holy nature. In this way, the followers of Jesus become 'holy ones' or 'saints'.

The New Testament frequently uses the term 'saints' to designate the followers of Jesus.[15] Paul introduces his letter to the Christians at Corinth with these words:

> To the church of God that is in Corinth, to those sanctified in Christ Jesus, called to be saints together with all those who in every place call upon the name of our Lord Jesus Christ, both their Lord and ours . . . (1 Cor. 1:2)

Undoubtedly, Paul has in view all of the Christians at Corinth, not just some who are exceptionally holy. All believers are saints, because each has been made holy by Christ. They are sanctified by Christ. As Hebrews 10:10 expresses it, 'And by that will we have been sanctified through the offering of the body of Jesus Christ once for all.' Significantly, as David Peterson argues in detail, the New Testament writers present sanctification not as a process that occurs after justification but as something that coincides with justification.[16] This view of sanctification is very much in keeping with the idea that the followers of Jesus form the temple of God. If they are corporately to be the dwelling place of God, they need to be holy. We shall return to the concept of holiness in chapter 6, for it has important ethical implications for the lifestyle Christians are to adopt.

The Passover sacrifice provides an important paradigm for the process by which the holy status of human beings is restored. Only those who have been sanctified through the sacrificial death of the Lamb, Jesus Christ, can expect to enter the New Jerusalem to live in the presence of God on a transformed earth.

---

15. There are thirty-three occasions in the New Testament (excluding Revelation) where believers are designated as 'saints' or 'holy ones' (e.g. Acts 9:13, 32; 26:10; Rom. 1:7; 8:27; 15:25, 26, 31; 16:2, 15).

16. D. Peterson, *Possessed by God: A New Testament Theology of Sanctification and Holiness* (Leicester: Apollos, 1995).

Christians have always been very conscious of the importance of Christ's death on the cross. Reflecting on his own Christian experience, Charles Wesley writes:

> And can it be that I should gain
> An interest in the Saviour's blood?
> Died He for me, who caused His pain?
> For me, who Him to death pursued?
> Amazing love! How can it be
> That Thou, my God, shouldst die for me!
>
> He left His father's throne above,
> So free, so infinite His grace;
> Emptied Himself of all but love,
> And bled for Adam's helpless race;
> 'Tis mercy all, immense and free;
> For, O my God, it found out me!
>
> Long my imprisoned spirit lay
> Fast bound in sin and nature's night;
> Thine eye diffused a quickening ray,
> I woke, the dungeon flamed with light;
> My chains fell off, my heart was free;
> I rose, went forth, and followed Thee.
>
> No condemnation now I dread;
> Jesus, and all in Him, is mine!
> Alive in Him, my living Head,
> And clothed in righteousness divine,
> Bold I approach the eternal throne,
> And claim the crown, through Christ, my own.

Charles Wesley understands passionately the transforming power of the cross. By grace, through the death of Christ, he is set free to be a priest-king. With him, we too share in the hope of reigning with Christ, the Lamb of God, in the New Jerusalem. Our hope rests not on what we can do to please God, but rather on what the Lamb has done for us. Little wonder that in Revelation 5 John both sees and hears

the voice of many angels, numbering myriads of myriads and thousands of thousands, saying with a loud voice, 'Worthy is the Lamb who was slain, to receive power and wealth and wisdom and might and honour and glory and blessing!' (Rev. 5:11–12)

6. FEASTING FROM THE TREE OF LIFE: REINVIGORATING THE LIVES OF PEOPLE FROM EVERY NATION

John's vision of the New Jerusalem has revealed a number of significant themes that run throughout the whole of Scripture. As we have unpacked these it has become clear that God's original blueprint for the earth envisaged a temple-city, filled with people who have both a priestly and a royal status. However, the divine plan for the world was disrupted early on when Adam and Eve rejected God's ordering of creation and transferred their allegiance to Satan. Consequently, this earth and its inhabitants came under the devil's dominion.

In the light of these events, we have traced how God has acted to reclaim the earth as his own and build a temple-city by gradually establishing his presence and sovereignty through the theocracy of Israel and the church. Central to the redemptive activity of God is the cross of Christ, for through it Satan is defeated and human beings are enabled to regain the holy, royal status Adam and Eve lost.

Building on these observations, this chapter explores how John's vision of the New Jerusalem anticipates human existence as we have never known it. The life to come will be truly abundant and fully satisfying. This hope is reflected in themes found in Revelation 21 – 22 that reappear throughout the entire biblical meta-story, in particular, the concepts of 'holy people', 'tree of life' and 'nations'.

Holy people in the New Jerusalem

The New Jerusalem, as a golden cube, resembles the inner sanctum or Holy of Holies of the Old Testament temple. As noted earlier, the latter, as a microcosm, foreshadows the new earth. What is true of the model will be equally true of the reality to which it points. Consequently, the practices and rituals of the Old Testament tabernacle/temple shed light on the New Jerusalem. Drawing on this, it is significant that only the high priest could go into the inner sanctum, and even he was permitted to enter but once per year, on the Day of Atonement. Since the high priest has to be holy to enter the Holy of Holies, those who enter the New Jerusalem will also have to be holy.[1]

The concept of holiness is exceptionally important within the biblical meta-story, especially for understanding the fulfilment of God's creation blueprint that the entire earth should become his temple-city. Holiness is closely associated with God, for he alone is innately holy. As the seraphim announce in the hearing of Isaiah, 'Holy, holy, holy is the LORD of hosts' (Isa. 6:3). Throughout Scripture, holiness is one of God's distinctive characteristics. Indeed, God is the supreme manifestation of holiness.

Closely associated to God's holy nature is the idea that holiness emanates from him. Anything that comes into contact with God becomes holy. Moses discovers this when he encounters the Lord at the burning bush. He is instructed to remove his sandals

---

1. The holiness of the New Jerusalem is reflected in Zech. 14:20. As E. P. Clowney, 'The Final Temple', *Westminster Theological Journal* 35 (1973), p. 164, notes, 'So holy will the city become that the inscription of the high priest's tiarra [*sic*] will be on the bells of the horses and the wash pots will be as temple vessels (Zech. 14:20).'

because the divine presence has made the ground holy (Exod. 3:5). Later, when the Israelites accompany Moses to Mount Sinai, the upper regions of the mountain become holy due to the theophany.[2] On account of this, Moses is instructed to consecrate or sanctify the people (Exod. 19:9–15).

Since the Lord radiates holiness to everything near to him, the inner sanctum of the tabernacle is the holiest part of the tabernacle. However, the further one moves away from the Holy of Holies, the less holy everything becomes. By way of reflecting this, the book of Leviticus draws attention to three related categories: *holy*, *clean/pure* and *unclean/impure*. The existence of these three distinct categories is reflected in the layout of the Israelite camp. At the heart of the camp stands the tabernacle courtyard, a holy area. The rest of the camp is viewed as clean, and everywhere outside the camp is unclean.[3] This same threefold pattern is mirrored in the status of the people linked to each region. The priests are holy, the Israelites clean, and the non-Israelites unclean.

An appreciation of these categories is vital for our understanding of the structure of the tabernacle and its rituals. For this reason the book of Leviticus, which is largely devoted to explicating these three categories, comes immediately after the account of the tabernacle's construction. The frequent occurrence of the terms 'holy', 'clean' and 'unclean' throughout Leviticus underlines the importance of these concepts. Words based on the Hebrew root *qādaš* (e.g. 'holy', 'holiness', 'sanctify') come 152 times in Leviticus, representing about one-fifth of all occurrences in the Old Testament. The adjective *ṭāhor*, 'clean', and associated words

---

2. This theophany is linked to the burning-bush incident, for both occur at the same location. However, because it involves the whole nation of Israel, God manifests his presence in a much grander way. For a detailed discussion of theophanies, see J. J. Niehaus, *God at Sinai* (Grand Rapids: Zondervan, 1995).

3. The entire area outside the camp was considered unclean, apart from selected places set apart as clean for the disposal of the ashes from the altar situated in the tabernacle courtyard (Lev. 4:12, 21; 6:11; cf. the burning of the bull of the purification offering [Lev. 16:27]).

occur 74 times, representing more than one-third of all Old Testament occurrences. The adjective *ṭāmē'*, 'unclean', and cognate terms come 132 times, representing more than half of the total occurrences in the Old Testament.

Within these main categories exist subdivisions. Differing degrees of holiness are evident within the priesthood and laity. The high priest, for example, is distinguished from the other priests by his clothes, title, access to the Holy of Holies and much stricter rules regarding marriage, purity and mourning. Just below the priests in holiness are the Levites (Num. 3:17). While they are not permitted to offer sacrifices, they undertake other duties linked to the tabernacle, especially its transportation and erection (Num. 4:1–49). Whereas the priests and Levites have different degrees of holiness due to their ancestry and divine appointment, non-priestly Israelites are given the opportunity to enjoy a special holy status by becoming Nazirites. This requires an individual to take a vow 'to separate himself to the LORD', which entails (1) abstaining from the produce of the vine, and (2) not cutting the hair (Num. 6:1–21).[4]

These observations demonstrate that the book of Leviticus envisages a world in which people and places have differing degrees of holiness. These categories also embrace objects[5] and

---

4. These subdivisions of people surface in different contexts within Leviticus. For example, whereas ordinary Israelites might touch any corpse, regular priests were permitted to touch only the corpse of a close relative (Lev. 21:1–4), and the high priest was prohibited from touching any corpse (Lev. 10:1–7).

5. The tabernacle furnishings have different degrees of holiness depending upon (1) their location, (2) the materials used in their manufacture, (3) their accessibility to human beings, and (4) their use in religious rituals. Whereas the holiest furniture, made of pure gold, was placed within the tent, the altar and laver, made of bronze, were located in the courtyard. Although ordinary Israelites were permitted to view the bronze altar and laver, only priests could look upon the gold furnishings in the Holy Place with immunity (Num. 4:18–20). Within the tent, the ark of the covenant was set apart from the other items of furniture by being placed in the

periods of time.[6] And, just as there are varying degrees of holiness, so too with uncleanness. We see this reflected in a variety of ways: pollution of the sanctuary; processes for the rectification of uncleanness; imparting uncleanness to other items.

The existence of different levels of uncleanness is shown by the level to which human wrongdoing pollutes tabernacle furnishings. Deliberate or intentional sins pollute the ark of the covenant in the Holy of Holies (cf. Lev. 16:16); unintentional or inadvertent sins by the high priest or the community pollute the incense altar in the Holy Place (Lev. 4:2–21); lesser sins or impurities pollute the bronze altar in the courtyard (Lev. 4:22–35). In each case the location of the pollution determines where the blood of the purification offering is placed.

Leviticus also distinguishes between impurities that can be rectified and those that cannot. In chapters 12–15 instructions are given for the rectification of uncleanness arising from skin diseases and various bodily discharges. In marked contrast, among those impurities that cannot be rectified are sexual sins (Lev. 18:20, 23–25, 27–30), idolatry (Lev. 20:2–5), murder (Num. 35:16–21, 31) and profaning the sacred (e.g. Lev. 7:19–21; 22:3, 9). In these cases

---

Footnote 5 (*continued*)

Holy of Holies. It was so holy that only the high priest could approach it, and even then he possibly used smoke from incense to conceal the top of the ark from view (Lev. 16:12–13). These distinctions between the items of furniture are also reflected in the instruction given in Num. 4:5–33 regarding the activities of the Kohathites, Gershonites and Merarites in helping the priests transport the tabernacle.

6. Particular days of the week and year exhibited differing degrees of holiness. The weekly Sabbath and the annual Day of Atonement were marked as especially holy by the prohibition of all work (Lev. 23:3, 28). The pilgrimage festivals of Unleavened Bread, Weeks and Tabernacles and certain other days were considered less holy and therefore required abstinence from regular work only (Lev. 23:7, 21, 25, 35). Finally, while the Israelites were expected to make special offerings on the first day of each month, they were permitted to work on these days, indicating that they were the least holy of all special days.

only the death of the guilty party can remove the pollution caused by his or her sin. However, according to Jacob Milgrom, when an individual expressed remorse regarding a deliberate sin, this had the effect of lessening the resulting pollution and thereby reducing the amount of rectification required.[7]

When rectification is possible, the process of purification varies, depending upon the seriousness of the uncleanness. Normally, a person or object is purified by (1) the passage of time and (2) washing and/or laundering.[8] For minor impurities the length of time required for purification is one day (e.g. for touching the carcass of an animal, Lev. 11:39). More serious impurities require the passing of seven days (e.g. touching a human corpse, Num. 19:11). As regards the washing of the body and the laundering of clothes, requirements again differ depending upon the seriousness of the impurity. For example, whoever *touches* an animal carcass is unclean for a day; whoever *carries* an animal carcass sustains greater impurity and is required to wash his or her clothes (Lev. 11:24–25, 27–28).

The strength or weakness of an impurity is also seen in its ability to communicate uncleanness to other objects or persons. Only more serious forms of uncleanness can pollute other people or objects. For example, if a man lies with a woman during her monthly period, she causes him to become unclean for seven days, and, in turn, any bed upon which he lies also becomes unclean (Lev. 15:24). Anyone who touches this bed becomes unclean. However, this latter uncleanness lasts only for one day and cannot be transferred to other people or objects.

From these observations, it is apparent that holiness and uncleanness form a spectrum of closely associated categories. On the one side is *holiness*, in the middle *cleanness* and on the other side *uncleanness* (see the figure below). The further one moves from the middle of this spectrum the greater the intensity of either holiness

---

7. J. Milgrom, *Cult and Conscience: The ASHAM and the Priestly Doctrine of Repentance* (Leiden: Brill, 1976), pp. 108–121.

8. Those objects that could not be washed were disposed of by burial, burning or some other method.

or uncleanness. For the ancient Israelites every person, object, place and period of time could be located somewhere on this holiness-to-uncleanness spectrum.

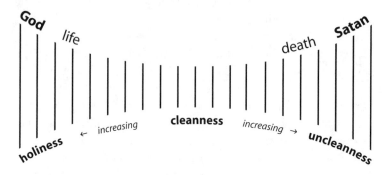

The regulations in Leviticus reveal that holiness and uncleanness are incompatible. Not only is it impossible for anyone or anything to be holy and unclean at the same time, but, more importantly, no holy object or person is normally permitted to come into contact with anything unclean.[9] This incompatibility between holiness and uncleanness accounts for the complex sacrificial system, outlined in Leviticus 1 – 7, which enables the unclean to become pure and holy. Without these sacrifices, it would have been impossible for the Israelites to live in close contact with the Lord their God.

The evidence from Leviticus indicates that holiness and uncleanness are dynamic in nature: they have the ability to transmit their nature to other people or objects. In this regard they differ significantly from the state of cleanness/purity, which is merely neutral and unable to make anything else clean or pure. Consequently, any clean person or object is constantly in the middle of a struggle between the powers of holiness and uncleanness. Since the status of an individual may change, Leviticus consistently underlines the danger posed by uncleanness to those who are holy or pure. This danger is greatest for the priests who work within the

---

9. When such contact occurs, it has either a purifying or a defiling effect, depending on the circumstances.

tabernacle, a holy area, and handle the tabernacle furniture, holy objects. For a priest to serve in the tabernacle, he must remain holy. If he becomes unclean, he can no longer carry out his duties; to do so without being cleansed and sanctified means death.[10]

Holiness comes through sanctification, the process by which someone or something is made holy. Holiness is the result of divine activity: it is God who sanctifies. This is reflected in the refrain 'I am the LORD who sanctifies you' (Lev. 20:8; 21:8, 15, 23; 22:9, 16, 32). Yet, while Leviticus notes the divine side of sanctification, it also emphasizes the human side. Those made holy by God are expected to remain holy by doing nothing that will compromise their special status (cf. Lev. 11:44). The Israelites are also to keep holy anything sanctified by God. This applies, for example, to the Sabbath day. Because God has sanctified it, the Israelites are commanded to maintain its sanctity by refraining from all work (Exod. 20:8–11).

While holiness comes from God, uncleanness emanates from the powers diametrically opposed to God. Relatively little is said about these powers in Scripture; their presence is assumed rather than explicated.[11]

Uncleanness is associated with human beings in two ways. First, certain forms of uncleanness or impurity arise as a natural consequence of being human. These include specific skin diseases and certain bodily discharges. These and related forms of uncleanness are linked in one way or another to death. By associating some bodily conditions with death, the regulations of Leviticus indicate that death dominates human existence. Only by becoming holy can an individual escape the domain of death and experience the life-giving power of God.[12]

---

10. A fear of becoming unclean explains why the priest and the Levite are reluctant to touch the man who has been left for dead in Jesus' parable of the Good Samaritan (Luke 10:30–35).

11. The Synoptic Gospels draw attention to 'unclean' spirits. While they are designated 'unclean', using the Greek term *akathartos*, most English versions refer to them as 'evil' spirits.

12. The idea of death being a power is picked up by Paul in the New Testament (e.g. 1 Cor. 15:50–56).

Secondly, there are other forms of uncleanness that human beings have the power to control. These occur when individuals by their actions transgress a boundary established by God. People who wilfully ignore God's commands, decrees, or laws are a source of uncleanness and defile all they touch. Their actions both distance them from God and bring them further into the domain of death.

If uncleanness comes through immoral human deeds and thoughts, holiness is associated with perfect moral behaviour (cf. Lev. 20:7; 22:32–33). For this reason, in the context of imperatives governing the people's behaviour, God commands the Israelites, 'You shall be holy, for I the LORD your God am holy' (Lev. 19:2). Their actions and attitudes are to reflect God's perfect nature. This is underlined especially in Leviticus 19 (but compare also chapters 18 and 20), which contains a long list of commands governing personal conduct. Interestingly, the material in this chapter echoes closely the Decalogue or Ten Commandments (Exod. 20:2–17) and the collection of moral instructions found within the Book of the Covenant (Exod. 22:21 – 23:9). To be holy is to live in a way that reflects the moral perfection of God; it is to live a life marked by love, purity and righteousness, these being the three most important hallmarks of perfect behaviour.

In line with this, it is worth observing that the obligations of the Sinai covenant are placed in the ark of the covenant, the footstool of the heavenly throne (e.g. Deut. 10:1–5).[13] An intimate connection exists between divine presence and moral order.[14] As Psalm 24:3–4 states:

---

13. See chapter 2, n. 45.

14. As J. D. Levenson, *Sinai and Zion: An Entry into the Jewish Bible* (Minneapolis: Winston, 1985), p. 172, observes, 'The cosmic center is also the moral center.' A similar point is made by C. L. Meyers, 'Temple, Jerusalem', in D. N. Freedman (ed.), *Anchor Bible Dictionary*, vol. 6 (New York: Doubleday, 1992), p. 360: 'The purity of the sacred center involved physical cleanliness. But it also involved the moral perfection associated with the nature of Yahweh. . . . God's presence in the inner sanctum, in the last analysis, is symbolized by the covenant document, the "two tables of stone"

Who shall ascend the hill of the LORD?
And who shall stand in his holy place?
He who has clean hands and a pure heart,
who does not lift up his soul to what is false
and does not swear deceitfully.

Holiness, reflected in moral perfection, is a prerequisite for entering the divine sanctuary. Since the Holy of Holies is a microcosm of the cosmos, the presence of the Decalogue within the ark underlines that God is the one who determines the moral order of the universe.[15]

Although the holiness of the tabernacle and temple is intimately linked to the concept of moral order, the Old Testament repeatedly draws attention to the failure of the Israelites to live according to these standards. From the golden calf incident in Exodus through to the book of Malachi, the record of the Israelites' relationship with God bears witness to their repeated inability to live according to the principles contained in the Decalogue. In the light of this, the book of Ezekiel looks forward to a time when God will put his Spirit within his people, transforming their hearts and enabling them to live by God's statues:

I will sprinkle clean water on you, and you shall be clean from all your uncleannesses, and from all your idols I will cleanse you. And I will give

---

contained in the ark that was placed under the protective wings of the cherubim and that represented the moral imperatives of the Israelite pact with Yahweh, according to the Deuteronomistic record of the Temple dedication (1 Kgs 8:9). As important as the ideas of cosmic center and divine accessibility are for understanding the role of the Temple, so too is the association of sanctuary with covenant and the concomitant establishment of social order through law.'

15. While the stone tablets of the Decalogue were placed inside the ark of the covenant, the Book of the Law was placed beside the ark. As Deut. 31:25–26 records, 'Moses commanded the Levites who carried the ark of the covenant of the LORD, "Take this Book of the Law and put it by the side of the ark of the covenant of the LORD your God, that it may be there for a witness against you."'

you a new heart, and a new spirit I will put within you. And I will
remove the heart of stone from your flesh and give you a heart of flesh.
And I will put my Spirit within you, and cause you to walk in my statutes
and be careful to obey my rules. You shall dwell in the land that I gave to
your fathers, and you shall be my people, and I will be your God. (Ezek.
36:25–28)

In a similar fashion the prophet Jeremiah anticipates a future
when the law will be inscribed on human hearts:

But this is the covenant that I will make with the house of Israel after
those days, declares the LORD: I will put my law within them, and I will
write it on their hearts. And I will be their God, and they shall be my
people. (Jer. 31:33).

Jeremiah, like Ezekiel, foresees a time when the moral order
centred on God himself will decisively influence human behaviour.

The concepts of holiness and uncleanness are frequently mentioned in the New Testament and reflect closely what we observe
in Leviticus. As regards uncleanness, Jesus focuses attention on
those actions or attitudes that make a person unclean:

What comes out of a person is what defiles him. For from within, out of
the heart of man, come evil thoughts, sexual immorality, theft, murder,
adultery, coveting, wickedness, deceit, sensuality, envy, slander, pride,
foolishness. All these evil things come from within, and they defile a
person. (Mark 7:20–23; cf. Matt. 15:17–20)

In saying this, Jesus is highly critical of the Pharisees and teachers
of the law who neglect these causes of uncleanness while concen-
trating on relatively minor aspects of ritual purity (cf. Matt.
23:23–28; Luke 11:37–41). Paul, likewise, associates impurity with
wickedness and immorality (e.g. Rom. 1:24; 6:19; 2 Cor. 12:21;
Eph. 4:19; 5:3, 5). According to Paul, believers are to shun such
sinful behaviour, 'For God has not called us for impurity, but in
holiness', or, as the New International Version (NIV) expresses it,
'for God did not call us to be impure, but to live a holy life' (1
Thess. 4:7; cf. 1 Cor. 1:2; 2 Tim. 2:8).

The New Testament references to purification highlight two complementary aspects. On the one hand, they underline that it is God who purifies those who are unclean (cf. Acts 15:9). More specifically, it is emphasized that purification is achieved through the sacrificial death of Jesus Christ: 'But if we walk in the light, as he is in the light, we have fellowship with one another, and the blood of Jesus his Son cleanses us from all sin' (1 John 1:7; cf. John 15:3; Tit. 2:14; Heb. 1:3; 1 John 1:9). On the other hand, believers are exhorted to purify themselves: 'Since we have these promises, beloved, let us cleanse ourselves from every defilement of body and spirit, bringing holiness to completion in the fear of God' (2 Cor. 7:1; cf. Jas 4:8).

The concept of holiness features prominently in all of the New Testament epistles. Holiness of life is to be the ambition of every believer. Peter expresses this most clearly, quoting in the process Leviticus: 'but as he who called you is holy, you also be holy in all your conduct, since it is written, "You shall be holy, for I am holy"' (1 Pet. 1:15–16; cf. Rom. 6:19, 22; 2 Cor. 1:12; Eph. 4:24; Col. 3:12; 1 Thess. 2:10; 3:13; 1 Tim. 2:15; Tit. 1:8; Heb. 12:14; 2 Pet. 3:11). The author of Hebrews underlines the importance of holiness: 'Strive for peace with everyone, and for the holiness without which no one will see the Lord' (Heb. 12:14). Such holiness is clearly linked to morally exemplary behaviour. For this reason, Jesus tells his followers to have a righteousness that exceeds that of the scribes and Pharisees (Matt. 5:20). Indeed, he goes further and instructs them, 'You therefore must be perfect, as your heavenly Father is perfect' (Matt. 5:48).

Although believers are constantly exhorted to be holy, God's role in the process of sanctification is also recognized (1 Thess. 5:23). In Hebrews he is pictured as a father disciplining his children in order to produce holiness of character: 'but he disciplines us for our good, that we may share his holiness' (Heb. 12:10). Most attention, however, tends to be focused on the role Jesus Christ and the Holy Spirit play. On three occasions both are mentioned together in connection with the sanctification of believers (1 Cor. 6:11; Heb. 10:29; 1 Pet. 1:2). 2 Thessalonians 2:13 refers specifically to 'sanctification by the Spirit' (cf. Rom. 15:16). This is obviously linked to the belief that the Holy Spirit dwells within believers: 'Or do you not know that your body is a temple of the Holy Spirit within you, whom you have from God' (1 Cor. 6:19)? As God's presence made the tabernacle holy, so too the presence of the Holy Spirit sanctifies believers as they become part of the temple of God.

Elsewhere, the sanctifying work of Jesus Christ is highlighted; he is the one 'who sanctifies' (Heb. 2:11; cf. Acts 26:18; 1 Cor. 1:2). Significantly, this is linked to Christ's death: 'we have been sanctified through the offering of the body of Jesus Christ once for all' (Heb. 10:10; cf. Col. 1:22; Heb. 10:14; 13:12). As noted in chapter 5, the sanctifying work of Christ is accomplished through his death as a paschal sacrifice.

While the moral order associated with the Old Testament tabernacle and temple continues unaltered into the New Testament temple, regulations associated with the Levitical priesthood become redundant. The author of Hebrews alludes to this briefly, when he observes that the coming of Jesus Christ establishes a priesthood 'after the order of Melchizedek':

> Now if perfection had been attainable through the Levitical priesthood (for under it the people received the law), what further need would there have been for another priest to arise after the order of Melchizedek, rather than one named after the order of Aaron? For when there is a change in the priesthood, there is necessarily a change in the law as well. (Heb. 7:11–12)

The reference here to 'a change in the law' indicates that the regulations associated with the Levitical priesthood were no longer in force once the church became the new temple of God. This development is hardly surprising, given that the Jerusalem temple was replaced by a very different type of divine dwelling. Moreover, given the sufficiency of Christ's death as a sacrifice, there is now no need to maintain the complex sacrificial rituals integral to the operation of the tabernacle and Jerusalem temple as divine abodes.

Among the various 'Levitical' regulations no longer applicable to the new temple, the food laws of Leviticus 11:1–47 and Deuteronomy 14:3–20 are especially noteworthy. As Peter's vision

in Acts 10:9–16 indicates, the clean and unclean foods were
intended to distinguish Jews from Gentiles. With the coming of
Christ and the establishment of the church as the temple of God,
this distinction was no longer necessary.[16] The apostle Paul develops this theme in Ephesians 2:14–15 when he writes that Christ
'has broken down in his flesh the dividing wall of hostility by abol-
ishing the law of commandments and ordinances'. As Beale
observes:

> Christ has abolished that part of the Law which divided Jew from
> Gentile, so that they could become one. Gentiles no longer need to
> adapt the signs and customs of national Israel to become true Israelites:
> they do not need to move to geographical Israel to become Israelites, but
> they need only move to Jesus, the true Israel; they do not need to be
> circumcised in flesh, but in the heart by Christ's death, which is their true
> circumcision, since it cuts them off from the old world and sets them
> apart to the new (*cf.* Col. 2:10–14; Gal. 6:14–15); Gentiles do not need
> to make pilgrimage to Israel's temple to get near to God, but they merely
> need to make pilgrimage to Jesus, the true temple, of which the Ephesian
> Christians were a part (see Eph. 2:20–22).[17]

Holiness and wholeness

A natural extension of the belief that God is holy is the idea that
holiness means wholeness or perfection. To be holy is to be

---

16. For a fuller discussion of the food laws, see T. D. Alexander, *From Paradise
    to the Promised Land: An Introduction to the Pentateuch*, 2nd ed. (Carlisle:
    Paternoster; Grand Rapids: Baker, 2002), pp. 227–234.
17. G. K. Beale, 'The Eschatological Conception of New Testament
    Theology', in K. E. Brower and M. W. Elliott (eds.), *'The Reader Must
    Understand': Eschatology in Bible and Theology* (Leicester: Apollos, 1997),
    pp. 36–37. Beale goes on to say (p. 37), 'The parallel passage to Ephesians
    2:13–18 in Colossians 2 defines the "decrees" (*dogma*) of Ephesians 2:15
    which Christ abolished as the external nationalistic expressions of the Law:
    food, drink festivals, new moons, or Sabbaths (see Col. 2:15–17, 20–21).'

unblemished or unmarred; it is to be complete, perfect, whole. This point is illustrated in Leviticus 21:16–23. At first sight this passage may appear somewhat repulsive because it seems to run totally counter to modern thinking regarding equality of treatment for those with a disability:

> And the LORD spoke to Moses, saying, 'Speak to Aaron, saying, None of your offspring throughout their generations who has a blemish may approach to offer the bread of his God. For no one who has a blemish shall draw near, a man blind or lame, or one who has a mutilated face or a limb too long, or a man who has an injured foot or an injured hand, or a hunchback or a dwarf or a man with a defect in his sight or an itching disease or scabs or crushed testicles. No man of the offspring of Aaron the priest who has a blemish shall come near to offer the LORD's food offerings; since he has a blemish, he shall not come near to offer the bread of his God. He may eat the bread of his God, both of the most holy and of the holy things, but he shall not go through the veil or approach the altar, because he has a blemish, that he may not profane my sanctuaries, for I am the LORD who sanctifies them.'

These regulations apply to ordinary priests. Those for the high priest are much stricter, for he is required to avoid anything that might be perceived as making him less than perfect (see Lev. 21:10–15). This even includes his choice of wife.

Viewed from a modern human-rights perspective, these instructions discriminate cruelly against men with some kind of physical deformity. Why should priests with these imperfections be excluded from approaching the altar? Is this not blatant discrimination? Would we not legislate against such an outlook today?

Before we judge these instructions too harshly, we need to consider them from another perspective, for this passage is part of a much larger collection of instructions designed to teach the Israelites about the nature of holiness.[18] Everything associated with the tabernacle is part of a grand visual illustration. The

---

18. Interestingly, the defects that disqualified both priests and sacrificial animals correspond closely (21:18–20 and 22:22–24).

Israelites viewed the Holy of Holies as a mini-cosmos. As a model of the earth the arrangements for the tabernacle reflect what the earth will be like as God's dwelling place. This is true regarding the instructions for the priesthood. Those who would dwell in God's presence must be perfect, without defects of any kind.

Implicit in all of this is the expectation that the future restoration of human beings to a holy state on a renewed earth will be accompanied by a restoration of our bodies to full capacity and strength. We shall be made whole physically, as well as morally. These instructions regarding the priests remind us that holiness and wholeness go together. To be holy is to be whole.

The issue of bodily wholeness explains why the Gospels have such an interest in the ability of Jesus both to restore those who are disabled and to bring to life those who are dead. When Jesus heals, it is not just simply about showing off his divine power, like a magician, in order to impress and win converts. Rather, it is about restoring people to the holy status Adam and Eve enjoyed before sinning.[19]

The Gospels make much of Jesus' authority to heal others. When John's disciples come to Jesus looking for reassurance that he is the promised Messiah, Jesus answers them thus:

> Go and tell John what you hear and see: the blind receive their sight and the lame walk, lepers are cleansed and the deaf hear, and the dead are raised up, and the poor have good news preached to them. And blessed is the one who is not offended by me. (Matt. 11:4–6)

---

19. D. G. McCartney, '*Ecce Homo*: The Coming of the Kingdom as the Restoration of Human Vicegerency', *Westminster Theological Journal* 56 (1994), p. 10, writes, 'Healing too is associated with the reign of God (Luke 9:1–6; Matt 9:35; 10:1, 9–11; Mark 6:6–12), because disease, like demon possession, was a disruption of the proper order of creation with man over creation. "Healing thus implied the victory of the Divine King in the cosmic conflict and Creation as an aspect of the imposition of His government." The proper order of man over creation was being restored.' The quotation in this passage is from J. Gray, *The Biblical Doctrine of the Reign of God* (Edinburgh: T. & T. Clark, 1979), p. 1, n. 1.

By way of preparing for this statement, Matthew has in chapters 8–9 already recorded how Jesus did all of these things.[20] By bringing healing, wholeness and life to others, Jesus confirms that he has the power to make others holy. To signal this to his readers, Matthew deliberately begins his collection of life-restoring incidents with Jesus healing a man with a skin disease (Matt. 8:1–4). By making him clean, Jesus enables the man to worship at the temple.[21] Interestingly, Matthew's report of Jesus entering and cleansing the temple includes a brief reference to Jesus healing the blind and the lame.[22] Holiness and wholeness go together.

---

20. There are strong echoes here of Isa. 35:5–6.

21. The issue of uncleanness features prominently in the closely related incidents of Jesus raising Jarius' daughter and healing the woman with an issue of blood. Both events illustrate Jesus' power over uncleanness. Contrary to normal expectations, Jesus himself is not made unclean through contact with the child's corpse and the unclean woman.

22. In Isa. 35:4–6 the healing of the blind and lame is associated with God's coming: 'Say to those who have an anxious heart, / "Be strong; fear not! / Behold, your God / will come with vengeance, / with the recompense of God. / He will come and save you." / Then the eyes of the blind shall be opened, / and the ears of the deaf unstopped; / then shall the lame man leap like a deer, / and the tongue of the mute sing for joy.'

It is also noteworthy that in 2 Sam. 5:6–8, the motif of the blind and the lame being excluded from 'the house' is introduced: 'And the king and his men went to Jerusalem against the Jebusites, the inhabitants of the land, who said to David, "You will not come in here, but the blind and the lame will ward you off" – thinking, "David cannot come in here." Nevertheless, David took the stronghold of Zion, that is, the city of David. And David said on that day, "Whoever would strike the Jebusites, let him get up the water shaft to attack 'the lame and the blind,' who are hated by David's soul." Therefore it is said, "The blind and the lame shall not come into the house"' (2 Sam. 5:6–8). As this passage reveals, the expression 'the lame and the blind' denotes those who oppose the establishment of Jerusalem as the temple-city of God. By healing the blind and the lame in the temple, David's greater son enables them to enter the 'house'. In addition, these healings could be inter-

In the Gospels the life-restoring activities of Jesus and the exorcisms of unclean or evil spirits are both associated with the coming of God's presence to the earth. Jesus' actions anticipate what will happen when the New Jerusalem is eventually established on earth. Here we have a glimpse of what the coming age will be like.

In the light of this, it is possible for Jesus' followers also to experience in the present something of the eschatological age in terms of healings and exorcisms. However, this will always be less than what awaits us. God may heal, here and now, but not on every occasion. There may be occasions, here and now, when evil powers are defeated, but not always. This should not surprise us. The present evil age will eventually give way to the next. If we all received from God complete holiness and wholeness now, there would be no need for the new earth. As it is, however, we live on an earth presently controlled by the evil one. Only when Satan is finally defeated shall we know life as God intended it.

The tree of life

Closely linked to the concepts of holiness and wholeness is the 'tree of life', introduced in Revelation 22:1–3 when John's eyes focus on a river that flows from the centre of the New Jerusalem.

> Then the angel showed me the river of the water of life, bright as crystal, flowing from the throne of God and of the Lamb through the middle of the street of the city; also, on either side of the river, the tree of life with its twelve kinds of fruit, yielding its fruit each month. The leaves of the tree were for the healing of the nations. No longer will there be anything accursed, but the throne of God and of the Lamb will be in it, and his servants will worship him. (Rev. 22:1–3)

This tree of life is undoubtedly related to the tree of the same name mentioned in Genesis 2:9. While initially little is said about

---

preted as symbolizing the recapture of Mount Zion from those opposed to God's reign.

the 'tree of life' in Genesis 2, its location at the centre of the garden points to its significance, as does its name. This is reinforced when we encounter it next in Genesis 3:

> Then the LORD God said, 'Behold, the man has become like one of us in knowing good and evil. Now, lest he reach out his hand and take also of the tree of life and eat, and live for ever –' therefore the LORD God sent him out from the garden of Eden to work the ground from which he was taken. He drove out the man, and at the east of the garden of Eden he placed the cherubim and a flaming sword that turned every way to guard the way to the tree of life. (Gen. 3:22–24)

In keeping with its designation, the tree of life produces fruit that gives immortality. After betraying God, Adam and Eve are expelled from the garden in order to ensure that they cannot eat from the tree – and live for ever.

Whereas Genesis 3 highlights the negative impact of being excluded from the tree of life, John's vision of the New Jerusalem in Revelation 22 includes a description of the tree, echoing an earlier passage in Ezekiel 47:12. Revelation 22 underlines the tree's life-giving power by describing how it produces twelve kinds of fruit every month. The context implies that the tree's leaves renew those who eat them. The concept of rejuvenation predates cosmetic companies! God patented it when he created the tree of life. No one will grow frail by becoming old in the New Jerusalem. Citizens of the new earth will experience and enjoy both wholeness of body and longevity of life. They will have a quality of life unrestricted by disability or disease. To live in the New Jerusalem is to experience life in all its fullness and vitality. It is to live as one has never lived before. It is to be in the prime of life, for the whole of one's life.[23]

John's vision of the new earth is refreshingly attractive. We live in a world constantly struggling to overcome sickness, disease and death. We look to medical doctors to prolong our lives and ensure that we have a meaningful quality of life. We pour vast sums of

---

23. Isa. 35:5–6 and 65:20 also point forward to human beings experiencing bodily wholeness and long life.

money into the prevention and treatment of diseases, with limited success. In spite of this, few of us expect to live longer than eighty or ninety years, and, if we should, we probably anticipate that our capacity to enjoy life fully will be severely restricted. Few ninety-year-olds skip around like newborn lambs. How different life will be in the New Jerusalem!

Alongside a personal or individual perspective, John's vision of the future new earth also points to both ecological and social transformations.

Ecological transformation

The expectation that the coming of the New Jerusalem will herald significant changes for the natural world is reflected in a very brief comment made in Revelation 22:3: 'No longer will there be any-thing accursed,' or, as the NIV has it, 'No longer will there be any curse.' Behind this remark is the idea that the present earth is under the disfavour of God. This explains the present hostility of nature towards human beings. We live in a global environment weighted against us because God has cursed this world.

We first encounter this idea in Genesis 3 when the Lord God punishes Adam for betraying the trust placed in him:

And to Adam he said,

'Because you have listened to the voice of your wife
    and have eaten of the tree
of which I commanded you,
    "You shall not eat of it,"
cursed is the ground because of you;
    in pain you shall eat of it all the days of your life;
thorns and thistles it shall bring forth for you;
    and you shall eat the plants of the field.'
(Gen. 3:17–18)

Adam's punishment involves the ground being cursed. Consequently, the earth no longer produces edible plants in abundance, and of necessity humanity must toil laboriously in order to have sufficient food.

Other passages in Scripture present a similar picture of people being punished for wrongdoing through natural phenomena. In Deuteronomy 28:15–45 Moses lists various curses involving nature by way of warning the Israelites to remain faithful to God:

> But if you will not obey the voice of the LORD your God or be careful to do all his commandments and his statutes that I command you today, then all these curses shall come upon you and overtake you. Cursed shall you be in the city, and cursed shall you be in the field. . . .
>
> The LORD will strike you with wasting disease and with fever, inflammation and fiery heat, and with drought and with blight and with mildew. They shall pursue you until you perish. (Deut. 28:15–16, 22)

Moses makes clear that various curses will come upon the Israelites if they disobey God. As this passage illustrates, natural phenomena, such as droughts, may be a form of punishment. The same is true of diseases. All of these things may be sent by God to punish wayward human beings.[24]

In the light of these observations, it seems reasonable to conclude that hostile natural phenomena exist upon the present earth due to human wrongdoing in general.[25] They were never intended by God to be part of the natural order of creation. Their ongoing existence is an expression of God's righteous anger at how human beings have overturned his ordering of creation.

While every inhabitant of the present earth is subject to the effects of an environment cursed by God, the Bible contains various passages that anticipate a time when the natural order will be wonderfully transformed. The eighth century BC prophet Amos

---

24. This is not to say that those who suffer from natural catastrophes or diseases are directly responsible for their own affliction.

25. It is also possible that because human wrongdoing pollutes the earth, thereby defiling it, God of necessity must distance himself from that which is unclean. The chaos of the natural world may be a consequence of God's withdrawal.

reports the divine announcement of a world in which agricultural abundance will transform people's lives:

> 'Behold, the days are coming,' declares the LORD,
>   'when the plowman shall overtake the reaper
>   and the treader of grapes him who sows the seed;
> the mountains shall drip sweet wine,
>   and all the hills shall flow with it.
> I will restore the fortunes of my people Israel,
>   and they shall rebuild the ruined cities and inhabit them;
> they shall plant vineyards and drink their wine,
>   and they shall make gardens and eat their fruit.
> I will plant them on their land,
>   and they shall never again be uprooted
>   out of the land that I have given them,' says the LORD your God.
> (Amos 9:13–15)

The fertility of the land is underscored by the fact that the periods of planting and harvesting merge together. A similar picture of plentiful harvests, as well as verdant pastures, is found in Isaiah 30:23–25:

> And he will give rain for the seed with which you sow the ground, and bread, the produce of the ground, which will be rich and plenteous. In that day your livestock will graze in large pastures, and the oxen and the donkeys that work the ground will eat seasoned fodder, which has been winnowed with shovel and fork. And on every lofty mountain and every high hill there will be brooks running with water, in the day of the great slaughter, when the towers fall.

As in Amos 9, this description of agricultural prosperity is clearly associated with a transformed environment that comes after events of cosmic significance. Complementary pictures of an abundantly fertile and divinely renewed earth are also found in Isaiah 32:15 and 35:1–2.

Centuries later, in the shadow of the Babylonian exile, the prophet Ezekiel expresses similar hopes of the land being fruitful in the future due to divine blessing. Desolation and ruin will give way to people living and prospering on the land. Addressing initially the mountains of Israel, the Lord says:

> But you, O mountains of Israel, shall shoot forth your branches and yield your fruit to my people Israel, for they will soon come home. For behold, I am for you, and I will turn to you, and you shall be tilled and sown. And I will multiply people on you, the whole house of Israel, all of it. The cities shall be inhabited and the waste places rebuilt. And I will multiply on you man and beast, and they shall multiply and be fruitful. And I will cause you to be inhabited as in your former times, and will do more good to you than ever before. Then you will know that I am the LORD. (Ezek. 36:8–11)

Some verses later, the theme of agricultural abundance is picked up when God subsequently speaks to the people:

> You shall dwell in the land that I gave to your fathers, and you shall be my people, and I will be your God. And I will deliver you from all your uncleannesses. And I will summon the grain and make it abundant and lay no famine upon you. I will make the fruit of the tree and the increase of the field abundant, that you may never again suffer the disgrace of famine among the nations. . . . And the land that was desolate shall be tilled, instead of being the desolation that it was in the sight of all who passed by. And they will say, 'This land that was desolate has become like the garden of Eden, and the waste and desolate and ruined cities are now fortified and inhabited.' (Ezek. 36:28–35)

The future hope expressed here by God is of the land becoming 'like the garden of Eden'. In line with this, recalling the rivers that emanated from Eden, Ezekiel's vision of an ideal, restored temple in chapters 40–48 also alludes to a transformation of the natural environment. The river flowing out from the temple gives new life to the land through which it passes, resulting in an ample provision of food:

> And on the banks, on both sides of the river, there will grow all kinds of trees for food. Their leaves will not wither, nor their fruit fail, but they will bear fresh fruit every month, because the water for them flows from

the sanctuary. Their fruit will be for food, and their leaves for healing. (Ezek. 47:12)[26]

While these descriptions of future abundance are relatively brief, they nevertheless display a consistent pattern in terms of the elements found within them. We see this repeated in two short passages in Joel 3 and Jeremiah 31, both of which associate agricultural and pastoral fruitfulness with the Lord's temple on Zion:

> And in that day
> the mountains shall drip sweet wine,
>   and the hills shall flow with milk,
> and all the stream beds of Judah
>   shall flow with water;
> and a fountain shall come forth from the house of the LORD
>   and water the Valley of Shittim.
> (Joel 3:18)

> They shall come and sing aloud on the height of Zion,
>   and they shall be radiant over the goodness of the LORD,
> over the grain, the wine, and the oil,
>   and over the young of the flock and the herd;
> their life shall be like a watered garden,
>   and they shall languish no more.
> (Jer. 31:12)

In these passages, and additionally in Joel 2:24–26 and Zechariah 8:12, the emphasis is upon the rich provision of food for people.

There is, however, another interesting aspect to the ecological transformation anticipated by the Old Testament prophets. This concerns animals that are normally predatory. No longer will they be a threat to other animals or people. Isaiah 11:6–9 provides the clearest description of how predatory animals will be changed:

---

26. As already noted, this description is incorporated into John's vision of the New Jerusalem in Rev. 22:2. There, however, it is applied to the 'tree of life'.

The wolf shall dwell with the lamb,
    and the leopard shall lie down with the young goat,
and the calf and the lion and the fattened calf together;
    and a little child shall lead them.
The cow and the bear shall graze;
    their young shall lie down together;
    and the lion shall eat straw like the ox.
The nursing child shall play over the hole of the cobra,
    and the weaned child shall put his hand on the adder's den.
They shall not hurt or destroy
    in all my holy mountain;
for the earth shall be full of the knowledge of the LORD
    as the waters cover the sea.

In the context of Isaiah 11, this transformed animal world is closely linked to the coming of a remarkable Davidic king. Later, Isaiah 65:25 echoes this expectation:

'The wolf and the lamb shall graze together;
    the lion shall eat straw like the ox,
    and dust shall be the serpent's food.
They shall not hurt or destroy
    in all my holy mountain,' says the LORD.

This latter description of harmony concludes a short passage that begins by referring to the divine creation of a new heavens and a new earth, which is equated with a new Jerusalem that fills God with joy:

For behold, I create new heavens
    and a new earth,
and the former things shall not be remembered
    or come into mind.
But be glad and rejoice for ever
    in that which I create;
for behold, I create Jerusalem to be a joy,
    and her people to be a gladness.
(Isa. 65:17–18)

All of these passages describing a transformed environment look forward to a time when nature and humanity will be in harmony as God originally intended. When this happens, the earth will be very different, for God's disfavour and curses will be removed. Conscious that nature itself has been enslaved as a result of human wrongdoing, Paul looks forward to the time when it too will be 'set free':

> For the creation waits with eager longing for the revealing of the sons of God. For the creation was subjected to futility, not willingly, but because of him who subjected it, in hope that the creation itself will be set free from its bondage to decay and obtain the freedom of the glory of the children of God. For we know that the whole creation has been groaning together in the pains of childbirth until now. (Rom. 8:19–22)

Social transformation

Alongside the ecological transformation of the earth, John's vision of the New Jerusalem introduces an important international dimension. This is reflected in three references to the 'nations'. In Revelation 21:24 we read, 'By its light will the nations walk, and the kings of the earth will bring their glory into it.' Two verses later, we are informed, 'They will bring into it the glory and the honour of the nations' (Rev. 21:26). Finally, Revelation 22:2 states that the leaves of the tree of life are 'for the healing of the nations'.

These references to nations underline the international dimension of life in the New Jerusalem. Those who are citizens of the new earth will be drawn from all the ethnic groups of this earth. This theme echoes the words of the 'new song' in Revelation 5:9 concerning those who are ransomed by the blood of the Lamb:

> Worthy are you to take the scroll
> > and to open its seals,
> for you were slain, and by your blood you ransomed people for God
> > from every tribe and language and people and nation.
> (Rev. 5:9)

Like so many other things in Revelation, the participation of all the nations of the earth in the New Jerusalem finds its roots in the book of Genesis. It comes, for example, in the divine oath that brings the divine testing of Abraham to a significant conclusion. After Abraham has shown his willingness to sacrifice his beloved son, Isaac, God swears to him:

> By myself I have sworn, declares the LORD, because you have done this and have not withheld your son, your only son, I will surely bless you, and I will surely multiply your offspring as the stars of heaven and as the sand that is on the seashore. And your offspring shall possess the gate of his enemies, and in your offspring shall all the nations of the earth be blessed, because you have obeyed my voice. (Gen. 22:16–18)

Echoing earlier divine promises to Abraham (Gen. 12:1–3; 15:5; 17:4–6; cf. 18:18), this oath states, among other things, that all the nations of the earth will be blessed through one of Abraham's descendants.[27] Many of the English versions assume that the final sentence of the oath refers to Abraham's descendants in the plural. Thus, for example, the NIV reads, 'Your descendants will take possession of the cities of their enemies, and through your offspring all nations on earth will be blessed, because you have obeyed me.' Such translations, however, fail to recognize the disjunction that exists in the Hebrew text between the reference to many offspring in the first part of the oath and the mention of a particular offspring in the second half. While the interpretation of the oath is complicated by the use of the Hebrew term *zera'*, 'offspring/seed', which can denote either singular or plural (like the English term 'sheep'), the associated verbs and pronouns in the second half of the oath all favour a singular translation.[28]

---

27. Alexander, *From Paradise*, pp. 143–156; P. R. Williamson, *Sealed with an Oath: Covenant in God's Unfolding Purpose*, New Studies in Biblical Theology 23 (Downers Grove: IVP; Leicester: Apollos, 2007), pp. 77–93.

28. T. D. Alexander, 'Further Observations on the Term "Seed" in Genesis', *Tyndale Bulletin* 48 (1997), pp. 363–368. The divine oath in Gen. 22:16–18 highlights two distinctive ways in which the motif of Abraham's offspring

Viewed in this way, the divine oath contributes to the larger narrative in Genesis that anticipates a future king who will play a central role in establishing God's blueprint for the earth. This king will mediate God's blessing to the nations of the earth.

The promise of divine blessing being mediated to the nations is echoed in Psalm 72:17. The psalm, which speaks about an exceptional, future king of Jerusalem, begins with these words:

> Give the king your justice, O God,
>> and your righteousness to the royal son!
> May he judge your people with righteousness,
>> and your poor with justice!
> Let the mountains bear prosperity for the people,
>> and the hills, in righteousness!
> May he defend the cause of the poor of the people,
>> give deliverance to the children of the needy,
>> and crush the oppressor!
> (Ps. 72:1–4)

The author then goes on to speak of the universal reign of this king:

> In his days may the righteous flourish,
>> and peace abound, till the moon be no more!
>
> May he have dominion from sea to sea,
>> and from the River to the ends of the earth! . . .
> May all kings fall down before him,

---

is developed in Genesis. The first part of the oath focuses on multiplication, a necessary development in order for the earth to be filled with priest-kings. The second part of the oath concentrates on a single offspring. Paul picks up both elements in Gal. 3. Whereas in v. 16 he focuses on the single offspring, in v. 29 he refers to his many offspring. See F. Ninow, *Indicators of Typology within the Old Testament: The Exodus Motif*, Friedensauer Schriftenreihe A4 (Frankfurt am Main: Lang, 2001), pp. 103–109.

all nations serve him!
(Ps. 72:7–8, 11)

Finally, after describing how this king will rescue the poor and the needy and usher in an age of fruitfulness and prosperity, the psalmist concludes with these words:

May his name endure for ever,
    his fame continue as long as the sun!
May people be blessed in him,
    all nations call him blessed!
(Ps. 72:17)

Without going into a detailed discussion of the whole psalm, it anticipates a time when a future Davidic king will bring blessing to the nations by overthrowing all those who resist his God-given authority. This righteous king will be at one with God in all he does.

The promises contained within this psalm are fulfilled in Jesus Christ. However, the universal reign mentioned here does not relate to Christ's first coming, but to his second. The expectations highlighted in this psalm become a reality only when the New Jerusalem is established on the new earth. Only then will the whole earth be filled with God's glory (see Ps. 72:19).

Other passages in the Old Testament contribute to this picture of people from every nation submitting to the kingship of God and his anointed one, the Davidic king. For example, Isaiah 2 looks forward to a time when Zion will stand at the heart of international peacemaking, dispensing justice to the nations:

It shall come to pass in the latter days
    that the mountain of the house of the LORD
shall be established as the highest of the mountains,
    and shall be lifted up above the hills;
and all the nations shall flow to it,
    and many peoples shall come, and say:
'Come, let us go up to the mountain of the LORD,
    to the house of the God of Jacob,

that he may teach us his ways
    and that we may walk in his paths.'
For out of Zion shall go the law,
    and the word of the LORD from Jerusalem.
He shall judge between the nations,
    and shall decide disputes for many peoples;
and they shall beat their swords into ploughshares,
    and their spears into pruning hooks;
nation shall not lift up sword against nation,
    neither shall they learn war anymore.
O house of Jacob, come, let us walk in the light of the LORD.
(Isa. 2:2–5)[29]

Isaiah here clearly contemplates future developments, for the passage begins with an unambiguous reference to 'the latter days'. In marked contrast, the Jerusalem of his day rightly deserves divine condemnation. As Isaiah has already revealed, the city of Jerusalem and especially its leadership in the eighth century BC falls far short of God's ambitions for it:

How the faithful city
    has become a whore,
    she who was full of justice!
Righteousness lodged in her,
    but now murderers.
Your silver has become dross,
    your best wine mixed with water.
Your princes are rebels
    and companions of thieves.
Everyone loves a bribe
    and runs after gifts.
They do not bring justice to the fatherless,
    and the widow's cause does not come to them.
(Isa. 1:21–23)

---

29. The contents of this passage were viewed as especially important; it is repeated almost word for word in Mic. 4:1–3.

These criticisms are especially damning because Jerusalem is meant to be the 'city of God' and its king the one who will mediate God's blessing to all the nations of the earth. What hope can there be for the fulfilment of God's plans, if his city and king are corrupt and faithless? Against this background, to summon the Jerusalemites to 'walk in the light of the LORD' Isaiah uses the picture of the nations flowing into Jerusalem in obedience to the Lord. By portraying the nations as obeying God, he hopes to shame the citizens of Jerusalem into being obedient.

In line with God's promises to the patriarchs regarding the blessing of the nations of the earth, Isaiah 2 highlights their inclusion in God's plans. They will be found within a transformed Jerusalem, having committed themselves to obeying God wholeheartedly. Something of this international dimension is captured by Köstenberger and O'Brien when they write:

> In the last days, the nations will flock to Jerusalem to learn about Yahweh and his ways (Is. 2:2–3; cf. Zech. 8:20–23; Mic. 4:1–2). As they come, they bring the scattered children of Israel with them (Is. 60:2–9). In an amazing reversal, the nations submit to Israel (v. 14), bring their wealth into the city (vv. 11–22) and join in the worship of Yahweh, whose people they have now become. Thus the prophet's admonition, 'Turn to me and be saved, all you ends of the earth' (Is. 45:22), is fulfilled. Significantly, this ingathering of Gentiles is depicted as an eschatological event, effected by God, not Israel.[30]

The theme of God's temple-city being filled with different nations and peoples continues through into the New Testament. It underlies the commission Jesus gives his disciples in Matthew 28, when he tells them to go and make disciples of all nations (Matt. 28:19). It also features in the book of Acts where the church, as God's new temple, expands to include Samaritans and Gentiles, alongside Jews. In anticipation of this, Acts 2 records how the dis-

---

30. A. J. Köstenberger and P. T. O'Brien, *Salvation to the Ends of the Earth: A Biblical Theology of Mission*, New Studies in Biblical Theology 11 (Downers Grove: IVP; Leicester: Apollos, 2001), pp. 252–253.

ciples, when they are filled with the Holy Spirit, speak in different languages:[31]

> Now there were dwelling in Jerusalem Jews, devout men from every nation under heaven. And at this sound the multitude came together, and they were bewildered, because each one was hearing them speak in his own language. And they were amazed and astonished, saying, 'Are not all these who are speaking Galileans? And how is it that we hear, each of us in his own native language? Parthians and Medes and Elamites and residents of Mesopotamia, Judea and Cappadocia, Pontus and Asia, Phrygia and Pamphylia, Egypt and the parts of Libya belonging to Cyrene, and visitors from Rome, both Jews and proselytes, Cretans and Arabians – we hear them telling in our own tongues the mighty works of God.' (Acts 2:5–11)

At Pentecost the believers become the new temple of God and, as the rest of Acts goes on to illustrate, the church expands to include people from many different nations. As a result, the international dimension of the church foreshadows and prepares for the New Jerusalem.

If our Christian hope involves sharing the New Jerusalem with people from every nation, this should have a profound influence on how we view people from other nations and races. We ought to respect foreigners and distance ourselves from xenophobic

---

31. See G. K. Beale, 'The Descent of the Eschatological Temple in the Form of the Spirit at Pentecost: Part 2: Corroborating Evidence', *Tyndale Bulletin* 56.2 (2005), pp. 64–66. In the first part, 'The Descent of the Eschatological Temple in the Form of the Spirit at Pentecost: Part 1: The Clearest Evidence', *Tyndale Bulletin* 56.1 (2005), pp. 73–102, Beale explores the relationship between the tongues of Babel and Pentecost. Given my earlier observation that the Babel incident is presented in Genesis as the antithesis of God's creation blueprint, it is noteworthy that the coming of the Spirit to create God's new temple results in language barriers being broken down. As previously noted, the coming of the Holy Spirit in Acts 2 resembles what happened when God came and filled the tabernacle in Exod. 40:34–35 and the temple in 1 Kgs 8:10–11 (cf. 2 Chr. 7:1–2).

attitudes. Racism should have no place in the Christian church. In line with this, the aspirations of the church should never be equated with those of a political cause or party that promotes national self-interest. Whatever sense of patriotism we may have, it must never cause us to despise or hate those from other nations. Unfortunately, we live in a world where national or racial arrogance is all too often exploited for evil purposes. On God's new earth people from all nationalities and races will coexist.

Life in the New Jerusalem will be very different from how we experience it now. As holy and whole people, we shall inherit a perfect world where everything is in harmony. Little wonder that John hears a loud voice from the throne saying:

> Behold, the dwelling place of God is with man. He will dwell with them, and they will be his people, and God himself will be with them as their God. He will wipe away every tear from their eyes, and death shall be no more, neither shall there be mourning nor crying nor pain anymore, for the former things have passed away. (Rev. 21:3–4)

Given all of the aches and pains, all of the grief and turmoil we experience in this life, this is a wonderfully reassuring hope to embrace.

7. STRONG FOUNDATIONS AND SOLID WALLS: LIVING SECURELY AMONG THE PEOPLE OF GOD

We have already considered how the New Jerusalem, using imagery that highlights its holy and royal aspects, is described in Revelation 21 – 22. As a golden cube it resembles the Holy of Holies, signalling the city's primary function as God's dwelling place. In addition, references to 'the throne of God and of the Lamb' emphasize that the divine kingdom is a reality on the new earth. God is the sole and supreme sovereign of the arboreal temple-city that is the New Jerusalem.

Alongside these images of temple and throne, John provides a detailed and intriguing description of the city's foundations and walls:

> And he carried me away in the Spirit to a great, high mountain, and showed me the holy city Jerusalem coming down out of heaven from God, having the glory of God, its radiance like a most rare jewel, like a jasper, clear as crystal. It had a great, high wall, with twelve gates, and at the gates twelve angels, and on the gates the names of the twelve tribes of the sons of Israel were inscribed – on the east three gates, on the north three gates, on the south three gates, and on the west three gates.

And the wall of the city had twelve foundations, and on them were the twelve names of the twelve apostles of the Lamb. (Rev. 21:10–14)

By drawing attention to the twelve tribes of Israel and the twelve apostles of Jesus Christ, John's vision of the New Jerusalem emphasizes the intimate relationship and continuity that exist between them. Both Old Testament tribes and New Testament apostles contribute to the construction of the New Jerusalem.

Old and New Testaments united

This theme of continuity is important because there is a tendency to separate Old Testament religion from what the New Testament teaches. However, as we have seen, although the New Testament introduces important new developments, these build upon what is revealed in the Old Testament. We cannot understand the New Testament church, founded by the apostles of Jesus, without seeing how it links to the beliefs and practices of Old Testament Israel.

The continuity between the Old and New Testaments is also important because it provides a greater basis for believing in the reality of the future New Jerusalem. The new earth and the new heaven is merely a vision. It does not presently exist, and we certainly cannot go and visit it. Is it, therefore, just a figment of the apostle John's imagination? How can we have any confidence regarding it?

As our study has revealed, the New Jerusalem is a natural extension of all that has been revealed in the rest of the Bible. We have traced its origins back to the opening chapters of Genesis. At that stage God created human beings in his image in order that they would fill the earth and extend the boundaries of Eden to encompass the whole earth. Although Adam and Eve's rebellion endangered this project, God has graciously sought to rescue human beings from Satan's control in order to bring to completion his plan for the world. The New Jerusalem marks the triumphal conclusion of this process. As we have noted, the Old Testament tabernacle and Jerusalem temple point forward to it, as does the church established by Jesus' twelve apostles. Consequently, the whole of Scripture, and not just its final two chapters, provides us with a solid reason to believe in the future reality of the New Jerusalem. Our hope rests upon all that God has revealed, throughout the entire Bible, not just one small part at the end.

John's vision of the twelve tribes and the twelve apostles contributing to the building of the New Jerusalem is reminiscent of something that comes towards the conclusion of the apostle Peter's second epistle. 2 Peter 3 echoes what we have been considering and adds a further dimension to it. The chapter begins with these comments:

> This is now the second letter that I am writing to you, beloved. In both of them I am stirring up your sincere mind by way of reminder, that you should remember the predictions of the holy prophets and the commandment of the Lord and Saviour through your apostles, knowing this first of all, that scoffers will come in the last days with scoffing, following their own sinful desires. They will say, 'Where is the promise of his coming? For ever since the fathers fell asleep, all things are continuing as they were from the beginning of creation.' (2 Pet. 3:1–4)

Peter addresses here a difficult issue. Some people were mocking the Christians to whom he was writing. They were being ridiculed because of their belief that Jesus Christ will return to establish a new earth.

By way of response, Peter reminds his readers of the flood and how God had previously destroyed the world (see 2 Pet. 3:5–6). In the light of this event, Peter goes on to speak of a future judgment:

> But by the same word the heavens and earth that now exist are stored up for fire, being kept until the day of judgment and destruction of the ungodly. But do not overlook this one fact, beloved, that with the Lord one day is as a thousand years, and a thousand years as one day. The Lord is not slow to fulfil his promise as some count slowness, but is patient toward you, not wishing that any should perish, but that all should reach repentance. (2 Pet. 3:7–9)

Peter emphasizes that the delay in divine judgment is due to the patience of God, for he wants people to repent rather than perish. Peter then comments:

> But the day of the Lord will come like a thief, and then the heavens will pass away with a roar, and the heavenly bodies will be burned up and dissolved, and the earth and the works that are done on it will be exposed.
>
> Since all these things are thus to be dissolved, what sort of people ought you to be in lives of holiness and godliness, waiting for and hastening the coming of the day of God, because of which the heavens will be set on fire and dissolved, and the heavenly bodies will melt as they burn! But according to his promise we are waiting for new heavens and a new earth in which righteousness dwells. (2 Pet. 3:10–13)

As this passage makes clear, one day God will intervene and bring this present, corrupt world to an end. Note especially the final sentence in this quotation. Anticipating a new earth where righteousness rather than evil will dominate, Peter sees this as the fulfilment of God's promise.

Genuine hope

As we have noted, the whole of the Bible provides a basis for believing that after death we shall eventually dwell in the New Jerusalem. This hope is vital. It brings us comfort and reassurance in the face of death. It helps us deal with the trauma of losing a loved one. It is a rock to cling to in the midst of life's severest storms.

However, we need to distinguish carefully true Christian hope from the wishy-washy expectation many people have regarding life after death. Many harbour a vague hope that when they die they will go to heaven. You often hear people say things that reflect this. Here are four examples I came upon following the death of a well-known Northern Irish footballer:

> Dear George, Gone to the 'Big Match' in heaven.

George will be missed by all. He was the perfect gentleman and a great man to know. What a game they will be having in heaven.

Georgie Best Superstar*, how many goals have you scored so far? Now playing for the Heaven Eleven. RIP

I am sure you are now in heaven – and if its half as good as they say – you'll have a glass in your hand and a woman on your knee – but the ball at your feet! nothing can hurt you now. R.I.P.xx

Such remarks reflect a sorely misguided view of the afterlife! However well meaning these comments are intended to be, there is nothing remotely Christian here. This kind of hope is certainly not what the Bible has in view.

A tale of two cities

To understand why this is so, we need to observe that the book of Revelation as a whole provides visions of not one city, but two. John's vision of the New Jerusalem in 21:9 – 22:9 stands alongside the vision of another city that is very different. This other city is called Babylon.

Whereas the New Jerusalem lies in the future and will be a city built by God,[1] Babylon already exists. It is here and now, for it is the great human city built by people who live in defiance of God. As we shall see, the book of Revelation presents us with an important choice. We have to choose between being a citizen of this world's godless Babylon or a citizen of God's future New Jerusalem.

Babylon and the New Jerusalem represent contrasting worlds.[2]

---

1. In John's vision the New Jerusalem descends from heaven fully formed. This may indicate that it is already in the process of being constructed.

2. R. Bauckham, *The Theology of the Book of Revelation*, New Testament Theology (Cambridge: Cambridge University Press, 1993), pp. 131–132, lists some of the ways in which the New Jerusalem is presented as an

This is even reflected in how the visions of the two cities are introduced. Compare what is said in Revelation 17:3 and 21:10 about the locations of the two visions:

And he carried me away in the Spirit into a wilderness . . . (Rev. 17:3)

And he carried me away in the Spirit to a great, high mountain . . . (Rev. 21:10)

As we move between the wilderness and the great, high mountain, the visions of the two cities are full of fascinating contrasts. Perhaps the most striking of these, and the most telling, is the way in which they are both pictured as women.[3] In Revelation 21:9 the New Jerusalem is briefly portrayed as 'the Bride, the wife of

---

Footnote 2 (*continued*)

alternative to Babylon: '(1) The chaste bride, the wife of the Lamb (21:2, 9) v. the harlot with whom the kings of the earth fornicate (17:2) (2) Her splendour is the glory of God (21:11–21) v. Babylon's splendour from exploiting her empire (17:4; 18:12–13, 16) (3) The nations walk by her light, which is the glory of God (21:24) v. Babylon's corruption and deception of the nations (17:2; 18:3, 23; 19:2) (4) The kings of the earth bring their glory into her (i.e. their worship and submission to God: 21:24) v. Babylon rules over the kings of the earth (17:18) (5) They bring the glory and honour of the nations into her (i.e. glory to God: 21:26) v. Babylon's luxurious wealth extorted from all the world (18:12–17) (6) Uncleanness, abomination and falsehood are excluded (21:27) v. Babylon's abominations, impurities, deceptions (17:4, 5; 18:23) (7) The water of life and the tree of life for the healing of the nations (21:6; 22:1–2) v. Babylon's wine which makes the nations drunk (14:8; 17:2; 18:3) (8) Life and healing (22: 1–2) v. the blood of slaughter (17:6; 18:24) (9) God's people are called to enter the New Jerusalem (22:14) v. God's people are called to come out of Babylon (18:4).'

3. A much fuller discussion of woman-city imagery in Revelation is provided by G. Campbell, 'Antithetical Feminine-Urban Imagery and a Tale of Two Women-Cities in the Book of Revelation', *Tyndale Bulletin* 55 (2004), pp. 81–108.

the Lamb'. While this image is not developed in any detail in Revelation 21 – 22, Revelation 19:6–8 provides further clarification:

Then I heard what seemed to be the voice of a great multitude, like the roar of many waters and like the sound of mighty peals of thunder, crying out,

'Hallelujah!
For the Lord our God
 the Almighty reigns.
Let us rejoice and exult
 and give him the glory,
for the marriage of the Lamb has come,
 and his Bride has made herself ready;
it was granted her to clothe herself
 with fine linen, bright and pure' –

for the fine linen is the righteous deeds of the saints.

This picture of the bride in fine linen contrasts sharply with how Babylon is presented. She is the 'great prostitute'. Revelation 17 describes her as follows:

Then one of the seven angels who had the seven bowls came and said to me, 'Come, I will show you the judgment of the great prostitute who is seated on many waters, with whom the kings of the earth have committed sexual immorality, and with the wine of whose sexual immorality the dwellers on earth have become drunk.' And he carried me away in the Spirit into a wilderness, and I saw a woman sitting on a scarlet beast that was full of blasphemous names, and it had seven heads and ten horns. The woman was arrayed in purple and scarlet, and adorned with gold and jewels and pearls, holding in her hand a golden cup full of abominations and the impurities of her sexual immorality. And on her forehead was written a name of mystery: 'Babylon the great, mother of prostitutes and of earth's abominations.' And I saw the woman, drunk with the blood of the saints, the blood of the martyrs of Jesus.

When I saw her, I marvelled greatly. (Rev. 17:1–6)

The two women could hardly be more different. Even their style of dress emphasizes how dissimilar they are. The prostitute's purple and scarlet clothing, along with her glittering jewellery, is contrasted with the, presumably white, linen dress of the bride, which speaks of purity.

By placing the visions of the prostitute, Babylon, and the Bride of the Lamb, New Jerusalem, side by side, John vividly contrasts the *faithlessness* of the former with the *faithfulness* of the latter. Babylon represents those who have deserted God and replaced him with another lover. As a prostitute Babylon has used her alluring charm to deceive and control the 'peoples, multitudes, nations and languages' (Rev. 17:15). To underline her power over those who have been enticed by her charms, she has made the nations drunk with wine. Drunkenness and sexual immorality combine here to accentuate the truly evil nature of Babylon.

The imagery used here to describe Babylon is chosen carefully. This is not the first time in the Bible that the metaphor of a prostitute/adulteress is used, for no other image conveys better the seductiveness of evil. This is captured vividly in Proverbs 7, as the father graphically illustrates for his son the deceptive charm of the brazen adulteress:

> For at the window of my house
>   I have looked out through my lattice,
> and I have seen among the simple,
>   I have perceived among the youths,
>   a young man lacking sense,
> passing along the street near her corner,
>   taking the road to her house
> in the twilight, in the evening,
>   at the time of night and darkness.
>
>
> And behold, the woman meets him,
>   dressed as a prostitute, wily of heart.
> She is loud and wayward;
>   her feet do not stay at home;
> now in the street, now in the market,
>   and at every corner she lies in wait.

She seizes him and kisses him,
  and with bold face she says to him,
'I had to offer sacrifices,
  and today I have paid my vows;
so now I have come out to meet you,
  to seek you eagerly, and I have found you.
I have spread my couch with coverings,
  coloured linens from Egyptian linen;
I have perfumed my bed with myrrh,
  aloes, and cinnamon.
Come, let us take our fill of love till morning;
  let us delight ourselves with love.
For my husband is not at home;
  he has gone on a long journey;
he took a bag of money with him;
  at full moon he will come home.'

With much seductive speech she persuades him;
  with her smooth talk she compels him.
All at once he follows her,
  as an ox goes to the slaughter,
or as a stag is caught fast
  till an arrow pierces its liver;
as a bird rushes into a snare;
  he does not know that it will cost him his life.
(Prov. 7:6–23)

While the father is acutely aware of the danger posed by an actual adulteress, he astutely uses the image of this enticing female as a metaphor for folly. The son must flee the fatal attraction of the 'temptress folly' and choose instead as a companion 'sister wisdom':

Say to wisdom, 'You are my sister,'
  and call insight your intimate friend,
to keep you from the forbidden woman,
  from the adulteress with her smooth words.
(Prov. 7:4–5)

Elsewhere in the Old Testament, the motif of the prostitute/ adulteress is commonly applied to the Israelites when they abandon the Lord for other gods. The prophetic books of Hosea, Jeremiah and Ezekiel, and to a lesser extent Isaiah and Micah, develop the theme of Israel as an unfaithful wife.[4]

The portrait of Babylon as a prostitute, who entices men to commit adultery, clearly builds on these Old Testament passages that associate the attraction of evil with faithlessness towards God.

As John's vision of Babylon unfolds, one of the most striking features of Babylon is its *wealth*. As a prostitute, Babylon has clearly prospered. She is pictured in expensive clothes, 'glittering with gold, precious stones and pearls' (Rev. 17:4), and holding a golden cup in her hand. The theme of Babylon's wealth reappears frequently throughout Revelation 18. The city is obsessed with acquiring material goods and overflows with excessive luxuries.[5] For this reason, she describes her entrepreneurs as 'the great ones of the earth' (Rev. 18:23). This obsession with wealth is also exposed as we read of the city's merchants weeping over her eventual destruction:

> And the merchants of the earth weep and mourn for her, since no one buys their cargo anymore, cargo of gold, silver, jewels, pearls, fine linen, purple cloth, silk, scarlet cloth, all kinds of scented wood, all kinds of articles of ivory, all kinds of articles of costly wood, bronze, iron and marble, cinnamon, spice, incense, myrrh, frankincense, wine, oil, fine flour, wheat, cattle and sheep, horses and chariots, and slaves, that is, human souls. (Rev. 18:11–13)

---

4. For a fuller discussion, see R. C. Ortlund, Jr., *God's Unfaithful Wife: A Biblical Theology of Spiritual Adultery*, New Studies in Biblical Theology 2 (Downers Grove: IVP; Leicester: Apollos, 1996), pp. 47–136.

5. There is a certain irony to this given that the New Jerusalem is made of gold. While Babylon's wealth is created by the *exploitation* of other nations and the stripping away of their wealth and people, Rev. 21:26 draws attention to how the nations willingly *bring* their glory and honour into the New Jerusalem.

The rest of the chapter goes on to speak of how those who use the sea for trade, shipmasters and sailors, also mourn over the city's destruction. With Babylon's demise there will no longer be any trade for them.

The Babylon of Revelation is often taken to be a cipher for Rome, the greatest 'city' in the first century AD.[6] There is no doubt that Rome is included within the image of Babylon. However, Babylon as a symbol should not be restricted to the capital of the Roman Empire, because it represents and embodies what human beings strive after when separated from God. Babylon is the antithesis of the city that God himself desires to construct upon the earth.

While the Babylon of John's vision is clearly symbolic, it shares many of the characteristics found in the real city of Babylon, which used its military might to amass wealth to itself. Even the city of Jerusalem, including the temple, was plundered for this purpose in the early sixth century BC. In the light of this, the book of Habakkuk provides an interesting commentary on the king of Babylon around 600 BC:

> He gathers for himself all nations
>   and collects as his own all peoples.

> Shall not all these take up their taunt against him, with scoffing and riddles for him, and say,

---

6. T. Holland, *Contours of Pauline Theology: A Radical New Survey of the Influences on Paul's Biblical Writings* (Fearn: Mentor, 2004), pp. 129–132, provides a helpful outline of five distinctive ways in which the harlot of Rev. 17 has been understood. He quotes T. F. Torrance, *The Apocalypse Today* (London: James Clarke, 1960), p. 140, as saying, 'Babylon is, in fact, an imitation Kingdom of God; based on the demonic trinity. Ostensibly Babylon is a world-wide civilisation and culture, magnificent in her science and arts and commerce, but it is drugged with pride and intoxicated with its enormous success – Babylon is the worship of this world, the deification of economic power and worldly security. There is no doubt but that our world is in the grip of this wicked Babylon today – Babylon represents human collectivity.'

'Woe to him who heaps up what is not his own –
  for how long? –
  and loads himself with pledges!'
Will not your debtors suddenly arise,
  and those awake who will make you tremble?
  Then you will be spoil for them.
Because you have plundered many nations,
  all the remnant of the peoples shall plunder you,
for the blood of man and violence to the earth,
  to cities and all who dwell in them.

'Woe to him who gets evil gain for his house,
  to set his nest on high,
  to be safe from the reach of harm!
You have devised shame for your house
  by cutting off many peoples;
  you have forfeited your life.
For the stone will cry out from the wall,
  and the beam from the woodwork respond.

'Woe to him who builds a town with blood
  and founds a city on iniquity!
Behold, is it not from the LORD of hosts
  that peoples labour merely for fire,
  and nations weary themselves for nothing?
For the earth will be filled
  with the knowledge of the glory of the LORD
  as the waters cover the sea.'
(Hab. 2:5–14)

Tellingly, Habakkuk's comments highlight the futility of building Babylon through the oppression of others, for ultimately, when the New Jerusalem comes, the earth will be filled with God's glory.

In Revelation, the city of Babylon symbolizes humanity's obsession with wealth and power, which become a substitute for knowing God. History witnesses to the ongoing existence of Babylon, as one nation after another has used its power to grow rich at the expense of others. We live in a world where economic power dominates national and international politics.

Throughout the latter half of the twentieth century the two great superpowers of the world, the USSR and the US, represented the opposing ideologies of communism and capitalism respectively. For many Christians it was unquestioningly assumed that communism was the great enemy of the church. Given its openly atheistic philosophy, it clearly opposed what Christians believed. However, in resisting communism Christians may have been deceived into thinking that capitalism is the church's ally. Yet, if we want to identify the greatest enemy of the Christian faith, we must look closely at Babylon and observe its obsession with consumerism. There is nothing that stands more effectively as a barrier to people knowing God than the desire for wealth that comes through capitalism.

There is something deceptive about the acquisition of wealth, and those who draw attention to this are never popular. Politicians know they get votes by promising more and more, not less and less. This, in part at least, explains why Jimmy Carter failed to get re-elected as President of the US in 1979.

After a two-week retreat at Camp David, where he had spent time reflecting on the state of the nation, Carter gave a major televised speech on 18 July 1979. In a sermon-like address, he drew attention to what he saw as the moral crisis facing the USA. He summarized the problem in these words:

> In a nation that was proud of hard work, strong families, close-knit communities and our faith in God, too many of us now worship self-indulgence and consumption. Human identity is no longer defined by what one does, but by what one owns.

To underline the seriousness of this he added, 'This is not a message of happiness or reassurance, but it is the truth and it is a warning.'

Unsurprisingly, many Americans did not take well to this message. As the historian David Shi has observed, President Carter 'totally ignored the fact that the country's dominant institutions – corporations, advertising, popular culture – were instrumental in promoting and sustaining the hedonistic ethic'.[7] Although Carter's analysis was correct, when election time came, Ronald Reagan won by a landslide.

The seductiveness of wealth is all around us. We can never escape from it. Wealth may bring security, and perhaps even a measure of happiness. But the desire to be rich comes at a price, for it relies heavily on competition and encourages greed. In the world of business, we are told that competition is good for consumers. Yet, while competition may have some positive effects, there are also negative aspects. It encourages cheating and there have to be losers. Competition is about doing better than others and there is nothing very Christian in this. The only competition that should exist among Christians is outdoing others in love.

As far as greed is concerned, according to a 2006 report on the distribution of household wealth, the top 1% of adults own 40% of global wealth, whereas the bottom 50% of adults have barely 1%.[8] According to Forbes.com, in 2007 the combined wealth of the world's 587 billionaires was $1.9 trillion. How can it be morally acceptable that so much of the planet's wealth should be in the hands of so few? Who needs billions of dollars to live? This reflects the ethos of Babylon, not that of New Jerusalem. People captivated by wealth and power are divorced from God.

Such is the influence of Babylon's spell that it has bred a new malaise in Western society: 'affluenza'. This term was popularized in the US in 1997 through a one-hour documentary that explored 'the high social and environmental costs of materialism and over-consumption'.[9] The issues raised in the programme have obviously resonated with others, both inside and outside the US. In a recent book, *Affluenza: When Too Much Is Never Enough*, Clive Hamilton

---

7. See <http://www.pbs.org/kcts/affluenza/diag/hist13.html>, accessed 10 Jan. 2008.

8. J. B. Davies, S. Sandstrom, A. Shorrocks and E. N. Wolff, 'The World Distribution of Household Wealth' (2006), <http://www.iariw.org/papers/2006/davies.pdf>, p. 26, accessed 8 Jan. 2008.

9. See <http://www.pbs.org/kcts/affluenza/>, accessed 10 Jan. 2008.

and Richard Denniss explore this issue in the context of Australia. They conclude:

> Since the early 1990s, Australia has been infected by affluenza, a growing and unhealthy preoccupation with money and material things. This illness is constantly reinforcing itself at both the individual and the social levels, constraining us to derive our identities and sense of place in the world through our consumption activity.[10]

They go on to argue that affluenza causes overconsumption, 'luxury fever', consumer debt, overwork, waste, and harm to the environment. This leads to 'psychological disorders, alienation and distress',[11] causing people to 'self-medicate with mood-altering drugs and excessive alcohol consumption'.[12]

Affluenza may not be a genuine class of illness, but we all recognize the symptoms. This is what living in Babylon does to some people. Little wonder that the Bible affirms two things crystal clearly: 'You cannot serve both God and money' (Matt. 6:24); and, 'the love of money is a root of all kinds of evils' (1 Tim. 6:10).

In marked contrast to the opulent prostitute Babylon, the image of the New Jerusalem as a bride highlights different qualities. The bridal metaphor has already been anticipated elsewhere in the Bible. Perhaps the most obvious passage is Ephesians 5:25–33.[13] In the context of giving instructions about submitting to one another in love, Paul writes:

> Husbands, love your wives, as Christ loved the church and gave himself up for her, that he might sanctify her, having cleansed her by the

---

10. C. Hamilton and R. Denniss, *Affluenza: When Too Much Is Never Enough* (Crows Nest, N. S. W.: [Northam: Allen & Unwin; Roundhouse distributor], 2006), p. 178.

11. Ibid., p. 179.

12. Ibid., p. 180.

13. Paul also introduces briefly wife/husband imagery in 2 Cor. 11:2: 'I feel a divine jealousy for you, for I betrothed you to one husband, to present you as a pure virgin to Christ.'

washing of water with the word, so that he might present the church to himself in splendour, without spot or wrinkle or any such thing, that she might be holy and without blemish. In the same way husbands should love their wives as their own bodies. He who loves his wife loves himself. For no one ever hated his own flesh, but nourishes and cherishes it, just as Christ does the church, because we are members of his body. 'Therefore a man shall leave his father and mother and hold fast to his wife, and the two shall become one flesh.' This mystery is profound, and I am saying that it refers to Christ and the church. However, let each one of you love his wife as himself, and let the wife see that she respects her husband. (Eph. 5:25–33)

Paul observes an interesting parallel between Christ's love for the church and the love a man should have for his wife. This link is noteworthy, for it conveys something of the intensity of the love we shall experience in the New Jerusalem. Without wishing to be irreverent, there will be a passion to the love God has for us and we for him. The love we shall receive and give will resemble the love experienced between a man and a woman when they commit themselves to each other in a relationship marked by exclusive allegiance to one another. Marriage is special, in spite of the fact that it is often marred because of our fallen nature. The intimate love a man and a woman share, founded on a deep commitment to each other, can hardly be surpassed. This is the kind of love that will bind us to God in the New Jerusalem. As Robert W. Jenson comments, 'The deepest reason why God is concerned with monogamy and faithfulness is that our arrangements here must shape the form and intensity of our relation to him.'[14]

In comparing Christ's love for the church to that of a man for a woman, Paul was probably influenced by the Song of Songs. The lovers in the Song are portrayed as making love in a garden, which has links to both Eden and the temple. To quote Jenson again:

---

14. R. W. Jenson, 'Male and Female He Created Them', in C. E. Braaten and C. R. Seitz (eds.), *I Am the Lord Your God: Christian Reflections on the Ten Commandments* (Grand Rapids: Eerdmans, 2005), pp. 184–185.

The Song's poesy of sheer bodily delight, invoked in order to speak
of the Lord and his people joined passionately in the temple, simultaneously evokes human love as it would be, were we lovers in Eden
or in the garden the temple depicted: it would be the joyous image of
God's love for Israel.[15]

With good reason, the New Jerusalem is portrayed as a bride,
whereas Babylon is a prostitute. Genuine passionate love will be
found only in God's presence; what the prostitute offers is but a
fleeting, deceitful shadow of the real thing.

The New Jerusalem promises holiness, wholeness and love in
the presence of God. While our inheritance still lies in the future,
we must claim our citizenship now. For this reason, the book of
Revelation warns us to come out of Babylon and encourages us to
take our stand with Christ (see Rev. 18:4). However, being a citizen
of God's kingdom in this present evil world is not easy. For this
reason, we need to take to heart the promise of Christ: 'To him
who overcomes, I will give the right to sit with me on my throne,
just as I overcame and sat down with my Father on his throne'
(Rev. 3:21, NIV).

---

15. Ibid., p. 185; cf. E. F. Davis, *Proverbs, Ecclesiastes, and the Song of Songs*,
Westminster Bible Companion (Louisville: Westminster John Knox,
2000).

8. CONCLUSION

In drawing to a conclusion this study of the biblical meta-story, it may be helpful to summarize briefly our main findings.[1] As we move from Genesis to Revelation, a consistent and coherent pattern emerges, centred on the idea that God created this earth with the intention of constructing an arboreal temple-city. This unique metropolis, as God's abode, will be inhabited by people who display the holy nature of God himself.

While the opening chapters of Genesis allude briefly to God's

---

1. I am aware that other themes could have been added to those explored in the preceding chapters. For example, the related concepts of rest and peace are closely coupled with temple-building. Moreover, much more could have been said about the intimate link that exists within the biblical meta-story between the Davidic dynasty and the divine temple. However, to do justice to this latter subject would have expanded this study considerably and moved it well beyond the paramaters initially chosen to determine what should and should not be included. This is a subject I hope to explore in a subsequent volume.

blueprint for the earth, his plans are almost immediately over-turned – for Adam and Eve betray their Creator and give their allegiance to his enemy. Expelled from God's presence, they forfeit their unique status as viceroys of the divine king.

Against this tragic background, the rest of the biblical meta-story describes how God acts to reclaim the earth, and especially its people, from Satan's control. In the process of denouncing the serpent, God indicates that his eventual punishment will come fittingly through 'the woman's seed'. Thereafter Genesis traces a unique line of descendants that moves initially from Adam to Noah, and then from Noah to Abraham, Isaac and Jacob. Beyond Genesis, this line is linked centuries later to the royal house of David and ultimately to Jesus Christ. As we have noted, through Christ's death, resurrection and ascension to the right hand of God the Father, Satan is defeated, preparing the way for the future establishment of God's uncontested reign in the New Jerusalem.

In Genesis the unique family line, which anticipates the defeat of the serpent, is intimately associated with the special divine promises given to the patriarchs. While these promises are intro-duced with the call of Abraham in Genesis 12:1–3, they are later guaranteed by two distinct covenants.[2] At the heart of these promises/covenants are two important expectations. First, God's relationship with Abraham will result in the creation of a unique nation that will inherit the region of Canaan. Secondly, blessing will be mediated by one of Abraham's descendants to the

---

2. P. R. Williamson, *Abraham, Israel and the Nations: The Patriarchal Promise and Its Covenantal Development in Genesis*, Journal for the Study of the Old Testament, Supplement Series 315 (Sheffield: Sheffield Academic Press, 2000); cf. T. D. Alexander, 'Abraham Re-Assessed Theologically: The Abraham Narrative and the New Testament Understanding of Justification by Faith', in R. S. Hess, P. E. Satterthwaite and G. J. Wenham (eds.), *He Swore an Oath: Biblical Themes from Genesis*, 2nd ed. (Grand Rapids: Baker; Carlisle: Paternoster, 1994), pp. 7–28; P. R. Williamson, *Sealed with an Oath: Covenant in God's Unfolding Purpose*, New Studies in Biblical Theology 23 (Downers Grove: IVP; Leicester: Apollos, 2007), pp. 77–93.

members of other nations. God's command to Abraham in Genesis 12:3 underlines, however, that this blessing will extend only to those who have a positive attitude towards Abraham; those who make light of him will be cursed by God.

While the book of Genesis does not contain a lengthy discussion of the purpose behind the divine promises/covenants given to the patriarchs, there is good reason to interpret them in the light of God's blueprint for the earth. Thus, for example, the repeated promise that Abraham's descendants will be fruitful echoes Genesis 1:28 and implies that they will play a noteworthy part in fulfilling the mandate originally given to the first human couple (see Gen. 12:2–3; 17:2, 6, 8, 20; 22:17–18; 26:3–4, 24; 28:3–4; 35:11–12; cf. 41:52; 47:27; 48:4; 49:22). In fulfilment of this, the subsequent history of the Israelites reveals that they are responsible for establishing the temple-city of Jerusalem. While this development is significant, it is only a part of God's plan for the completion of his creation blueprint. Tied closely to Abraham's descendants becoming a great nation is the blessing of the nations. This international dimension looks beyond the merely national dimension associated with Israel/Judah in the Old Testament and anticipates something that will have universal significance: the creation of the church and ultimately the New Jerusalem.

The outworking of the patriarchal promises/covenants proceeds via the divine rescue of the Israelites from slavery in Egypt. Through this paradigmatic event, God bestows upon the Israelites the special status of a holy nation and comes to dwell in their midst. With the construction of the tabernacle, God's creation blueprint moves closer to being fulfilled, although there is still much more to be done. By living among the Israelites, God makes a significant advance towards accomplishing his ultimate purpose for the earth. Although there is external opposition and internal failure, the Israelites eventually settle in the land of Canaan, in time establishing Jerusalem as the temple-city of God.

By way of anticipating future developments, the tabernacle and Jerusalem temple function as microcosms. They point forward to the reality that will come to fulfilment in the New Jerusalem. Each structure underlines the holy nature of God's abode and is intimately connected to the heavenly temple. Thus, the footstool of the heavenly throne (the ark of the covenant) is located on the earth within the tabernacle and Jerusalem temple.[3]

While the developments described within the Old Testament are an important part of the divine redemptive process, the coming of Jesus Christ is vital for the ultimate restoration of the earth as God's abode. Bringing to fulfilment a series of interlocking expectations that link to the royal line of David, Jesus Christ, as the perfect man, overcomes Satan through his death, resurrection and ascension. As a result of his sacrificial death upon the cross, Christ brings about a new exodus that delivers people from Satan's control, and bestows on them a holy and royal status. By repenting of their sin and acknowledging Christ's kingship, human beings are enabled by the Holy Spirit to become citizens of the kingdom of God. However, while this kingdom continues to grow, its members must endure considerable hostility, for the ultimate banishment of Satan awaits the return of Jesus Christ. For the present, human beings, who have been deceived and enslaved by Satan, are called to abandon the way of evil and embrace Jesus Christ as their king and saviour.

The significance of Christ's contribution, the divine redemption of humanity, is emphasized further by the intimate link that exists between him and believers. Just as his earthly body was the temple of God, by extension those who comprise his spiritual body also become the temple of God. Through the work of the Holy Spirit those in Christ form a new temple. By becoming part of the living temple of God, the church, they are expected to live here and now as citizens of the New Jerusalem, reflecting in their lifestyle the values that set God's future dwelling place apart from the counterfeit city of 'Babylon'.

Although this present earth has much in common with the new

---

3. It is worth observing that the earthly structures are patterned after the heavenly temple, further emphasizing both the link between heaven and earth, and God's intention that the earth should be an integral part of the heavenly sphere. Heaven and earth are meant to be a unity, rather than two separate spheres of existence.

earth described in Revelation 21 – 22, the biblical meta-story anti-cipates the eventual replacement of this world by another. While Christians are to be active here and now in promoting the kingdom of God, ultimately God's throne will be set up only on an earth devoid of everything evil. When this occurs through the return of Christ, all those who have throughout the history of this earth acknowledged the sovereignty of the Lord God and rejected the reign of Satan will be resurrected to live in the New Jerusalem.

While the Bible does not give a detailed picture of our existence beyond this life, the final chapters of Revelation open a window into this new world. Through his vision of the new heaven and the new earth the apostle John provides an extraordinary insight into what the future holds after death. This revelation focuses on a transformed earth, filled by an enormous, holy city.

John's vision of the New Jerusalem reveals that life's ultimate experience is closely linked to this present world. The new earth is portrayed using concepts that go back to the opening chapters of Genesis. The life to come brings to fulfilment expectations charted throughout the whole of the Bible. For this reason, we can begin to appreciate our future hope only by understanding how human history moves from the first creation of the earth to its future recreation.

Although our future experience of life will have something in common with the present, it will also be radically different. Everything that detracts from experiencing life to the full will one day be totally eradicated. Then, and only then, shall we know life as God intends it to be. Then, and only then, shall we truly grasp the immensity of the grace of God, whose love for rebellious and errant human beings was demonstrated through the gift of his own unique Son. Then, and only then, shall we know God fully in all his majestic glory and splendour. With such a prospect in view, what more could we possibly desire?

SELECT BIBLIOGRAPHY

ALEXANDER, T. D., 'Abraham Re-Assessed Theologically: The Abraham Narrative and the New Testament Understanding of Justification by Faith', in R. S. Hess, P. E. Satterthwaite and G. J. Wenham (eds.), *He Swore an Oath: Biblical Themes from Genesis*, 2nd ed. (Grand Rapids: Baker; Carlisle: Paternoster, 1994), pp. 7–28.

——, *From Paradise to the Promised Land: An Introduction to the Pentateuch*, 2nd ed. (Carlisle: Paternoster; Grand Rapids: Baker, 2002).

——, 'Further Observations on the Term "Seed" in Genesis', *Tyndale Bulletin* 48 (1997), pp. 363–368.

——, 'Genealogies, Seed and the Compositional Unity of Genesis', *Tyndale Bulletin* 44 (1993), pp. 255–270.

——, 'Messianic Ideology in the Book of Genesis', in P. E. Satterthwaite, R. S. Hess and G. J. Wenham (eds.), *The Lord's Anointed: Interpretation of Old Testament Messianic Texts* (Grand Rapids: Baker; Carlisle: Paternoster, 1995), pp. 19–39.

——, 'The Passover Sacrifice', in R. T. Beckwith and M. Selman (eds.), *Sacrifice in the Bible* (Carlisle: Paternoster; Grand Rapids: Baker, 1995), pp. 1–24.

——, 'The Regal Dimension of the *tolĕdôt yaʿăqob*: Recovering the Literary Context of Genesis 37–50', in J. G. McConville and K. Möller (eds.), *Reading the Law: Studies in Honour of Gordon J. Wenham*, Library of Hebrew Bible / Old Testament Studies 461 (Edinburgh: T. & T. Clark, 2007), pp. 196–212.

——, 'Royal Expectations in Genesis to Kings: Their Importance for Biblical Theology', *Tyndale Bulletin* 49 (1998), pp. 191–212.

ANONYMOUS, 'Babel, Tower of', in L. Ryken, J. C. Wilhoit and T. Longman III (eds.), *Dictionary of Biblical Imagery* (Downers Grove: IVP; Leicester: IVP, 1998), pp. 66–67.

AVERBECK, R. E., 'Tabernacle', in T. D. Alexander and D. W. Baker (eds.), *Dictionary of the Old Testament: Pentateuch* (Downers Grove: IVP; Leicester: IVP, 2003), pp. 807–827.

BALOIAN, B., '*śāṭān*', in W. A. VanGemeren (ed.), *New International Dictionary of Old Testament Theology and Exegesis*, vol. 3 (Carlisle: Paternoster; Grand Rapids: Zondervan, 1996), pp. 1231–1232.

BANDSTRA, A. J., '"A Kingship and Priests": Inaugurated Eschatology in the Apocalypse', *Calvin Theological Journal* 27 (1992), pp. 10–25.

BARKER, M., *The Gate of Heaven: The History and Symbolism of the Temple in Jerusalem* (London: SPCK, 1991).

——, *The Great High Priest: The Temple Roots of Christian Liturgy* (London: T. & T. Clark, 2003).

——, *On Earth as it Is in Heaven: Temple Symbolism in the New Testament* (Edinburgh: T. & T. Clark, 1995).

BAUCKHAM, R., *The Theology of the Book of Revelation*, New Testament Theology (Cambridge: Cambridge University Press, 1993).

BEALE, G. K., 'The Descent of the Eschatological Temple in the Form of the Spirit at Pentecost: Part 1: The Clearest Evidence', *Tyndale Bulletin* 56.1 (2005), pp. 73–102.

——, 'The Descent of the Eschatological Temple in the Form of the Spirit at Pentecost: Part 2: Corroborating Evidence', *Tyndale Bulletin* 56.2 (2005), pp. 63–90.

——, 'Eden, the Temple, and the Church's Mission in the New Creation', *Journal of the Evangelical Theological Society* 48 (2005), pp. 5–31.

——, 'The Eschatological Conception of New Testament Theology', in K. E. Brower and M. W. Elliott (eds.), *'The Reader Must Understand': Eschatology in Bible and Theology* (Leicester: Apollos, 1997), pp. 11–52.

——, 'The Final Vision of the Apocalypse and its Implications for a Biblical Theology of the Temple', in T. D. Alexander and S. Gathercole (eds.), *Heaven on Earth: The Temple in Biblical Theology* (Carlisle: Paternoster, 2004), pp. 191–209.

——, *The Temple and the Church's Mission: A Biblical Theology of the Dwelling Place of God*, New Studies in Biblical Theology 17 (Leicester: Apollos, 2004).

BEASLEY-MURRAY, G. R., *Jesus and the Kingdom of God* (Grand Rapids: Eerdmans; Exeter: Paternoster, 1986).

BECKWITH, R. T., 'The Temple Restored', in T. D. Alexander and S. Gathercole (eds.), *Heaven on Earth: The Temple in Biblical Theology* (Carlisle: Paternoster, 2004), pp. 71–79.

BLENKINSOPP, J., *Sage, Priest, Prophet: Religious and Intellectual Leadership in Ancient Israel*, Library of Ancient Israel (Louisville: Westminster John Knox, 1995).

BREASTED, J. H., *Ancient Records of Egypt*. Vol. 3: *The Nineteeth Dynasty* (Chicago: University of Chicago Press, 1906).

BROWER, K. E., ' "Let the Reader Understand": Temple and Eschatology in Mark', in K. E. Brower and M. W. Elliott (eds.), *'The Reader Must Understand': Eschatology in Bible and Theology* (Leicester: Apollos, 1997), pp. 191–143.

BRUCE, F. F., *The Epistles of John: Introduction, Exposition and Notes* (London: Pickering & Inglis, 1978).

CAIRD, G. B., *A Commentary on the Revelation of St. John the Divine*, Black's New Testament Commentaries (London: A. & C. Black, 1966).

CAMPBELL, G., 'Antithetical Feminine–Urban Imagery and a Tale of Two Women-Cities in the Book of Revelation', *Tyndale Bulletin* 55 (2004), pp. 81–108.

CASSUTO, U., *Commentary on Exodus* (Jerusalem: Magnes, 1967).

——, *Commentary on Genesis*, vol. 1 (Jerusalem: Magnes, 1964).

CLEMENTS, R. E., 'The Davidic Covenant in the Isaiah Tradition', in A. D. H. Mayes and R. B. Salters (eds.), *Covenant as Context: Essays in Honour of E. W. Nicholson* (New York: Oxford University Press, 2003), pp. 39–69.

——, *God and Temple* (Oxford: Basil Blackwell, 1965).

CLIFFORD, R. J., 'The Temple and the Holy Mountain', in T. G. Madsen (ed.), *Temple in Antiquity: Ancient Records and Modern Perspectives*, The Religious Studies Monograph Series 9 (Provo, Utah: Religious Studies Center, Brigham Young University, 1984), pp. 107–124.

CLOWNEY, E. P., 'The Final Temple', *Westminster Theological Journal* 35 (1973), pp. 156–191.

COLLINS, C. J., 'A Syntactical Note (Genesis 3:15): Is the Woman's Seed Singular or Plural?', *Tyndale Bulletin* 48 (1997), pp. 139–148.

——, 'Galatians 3:16: What Kind of an Exegete Was Paul?', *Tyndale Bulletin* 54 (2003), pp. 75–86.

COMFORT, P. W., 'Temple', in G. F. Hawthorne, R. P. Martin and D. G. Reid (eds.), *Dictionary of Paul and his Letters* (Leicester: IVP; Downers Grove: IVP, 1993), pp. 923–925.

DAVIES, G. I., 'The Presence of God in the Second Temple and Rabbinic Doctrine', in W. Horbury (ed.), *Templum Amicitiae*, Journal for the Study of the New Testament, Supplement Series 48 (Sheffield: JSOT Press, 1991), pp. 32–36.

DAVIES, J. B., S. SANDSTROM, A. SHORROCKS and E. N. WOLFF, 'The World Distribution of Household Wealth' (2006), <http://www.iariw.org/papers/2006/davies.pdf>, accessed 8 Jan. 2008.

DAVIS, E. F., *Proverbs, Ecclesiastes, and the Song of Songs*, Westminster Bible Companion (Louisville: Westminster John Knox, 2000).

DUMBRELL, W. J., *The End of the Beginning: Revelation 21–22 and the Old Testament* (Grand Rapids: Baker, 1985).

——, 'Genesis 2:1–17: A Foreshadowing of the New Creation', in S. J. Hafemann (ed.), *Biblical Theology: Retrospect and Prospect* (Downers Grove: IVP; Leicester: Apollos, 2002), pp. 53–65.

ELLIS, E. E., '2 Corinthians 5:1–10 in Pauline Eschatology', *New Testament Studies* 6 (1960), pp. 211–224.

FRYMER-KENSKY, T., 'The Atrahasis Epic and Its Significance for Our Understanding of Genesis 1–9', *Biblical Archaeologist* 40 (1977), pp. 147–155.

GOMBIS, T. G., 'Being the Fullness of God in Christ by the Spirit: Ephesians 5:18 in its Epistolary Setting', *Tyndale Bulletin* 53 (2002), pp. 259–272.

——, 'Cosmic Lordship and Divine Gift-Giving: Psalm 68 in Ephesians 4:8', *Novum Testamentum* 47 (2005), pp. 367–380.

——, 'Ephesians 2 as a Narrative of Divine Warfare', *Journal for the Study of the New Testament* 26 (2004), pp. 403–418.

——, 'The Triumph of God in Christ: Divine Warfare in the Argument of Ephesians' (PhD thesis, University of St Andrews, St Andrews, 2005).

GORDON, R. P., 'The Week That Made the World: Reflections on the First Pages of the Bible', in J. G. McConville and K. Möller (eds.), *Reading the Law: Studies in Honour of Gordon J. Wenham*, Library of Hebrew Bible / Old Testament Studies 461 (Edinburgh: T. & T. Clark, 2007), pp. 228–241.

GOWAN, D. E., *Eschatology in the Old Testament* (Philadelphia: Fortress, 1986).

HAMILTON, C., and R. DENNISS, *Affluenza: When Too Much Is Never Enough* (Crows Nest, N. S. W.: [Northam: Allen & Unwin; Roundhouse distributor], 2006).

HAMILTON, J. M., *God's Indwelling Presence: The Holy Spirit in the Old and New Testaments*, New American Commentary Studies in Bible and Theology (Nashville: B. & H., 2006).

——, 'The Seed of the Woman and the Blessing of Abraham', *Tyndale Bulletin* 58 (2007), pp. 253–273.

HARAN, M., *Temples and Temple-Service in Ancient Israel* (Oxford: Clarendon, 1978).

HAYWARD, C. T. R., *The Jewish Temple: A Non-Biblical Sourcebook* (London: Routledge, 1996).

HEAD, P. M., 'The Temple in Luke's Gospel', in T. D. Alexander and S. Gathercole (eds.), *Heaven on Earth: The Temple in Biblical Theology* (Carlisle: Paternoster, 2004), pp. 102–119.

HESS, R. S., *Studies in the Personal Names of Genesis 1–11*, Alter Orient und Altes Testament 234 (Kevelaer: Butzon & Bercker, 1993).

HIEBERT, T., 'The Tower of Babel and the Origin of the World's Cultures', *Journal of Biblical Literature* 126 (2007), pp. 29–58.

HILDEBRAND, W., *An Old Testament Theology of the Spirit of God* (Peabody: Hendrickson, 1995).

HOLLAND, T., *Contours of Pauline Theology: A Radical New Survey of the Influences on Paul's Biblical Writings* (Fearn: Mentor, 2004).

HUROWITZ, V., 'YHWH's Exalted House: Aspects of the Design and Symbolism of Solomon's Temple', in J. Day (ed.), *Temple and Worship in Biblical Israel*, Library of Hebrew Bible / Old Testament Studies 422 (London: T. & T. Clark, 2005), pp. 63–110.

JEFFERY, S., M. OVEY and A. SACH, *Pierced for our Transgressions: Rediscovering the Glory of Penal Substitution* (Nottingham: IVP, 2007).

JENSON, P. P., *Graded Holiness: A Key to the Priestly Conception of the World*, Journal for the Study of the Old Testament, Supplement Series 106 (Sheffield: JSOT Press, 1992).

JENSON, R. W., 'Male and Female He Created Them', in C. E. Braaten and C. R. Seitz (eds.), *I Am the Lord Your God: Christian Reflections on the Ten Commandments* (Grand Rapids: Eerdmans, 2005), pp. 175–188.

KAPELRUD, A. S., 'Temple Building, a Task for Gods and Kings', *Orientalia* 32 (1963), pp. 56–62.

KEARNEY, P. J., 'Creation and Liturgy: The P Redaction of Ex 25–40', *Zeitschrift für die alttestamentliche Wissenschaft* 89 (1977), pp. 375–387.

KINGSBURY, J. D., 'The Plot of Matthew's Story', *Interpretation* 46 (1992), pp. 347–356.

KITCHEN, K. A., 'The Desert Tabernacle: Pure Fiction or Plausible Account?', *Biblical Research* 16 (2000), pp. 14–21.

——, *On the Reliability of the Old Testament* (Grand Rapids: Eerdmans, 2003).

——, 'The Tabernacle – a Bronze Age Artefact', *Eretz Israel* 24 (1993), pp. 119–129.

KOESTER, C. R., *The Dwelling of God: The Tabernacle in the Old Testament, Intertestamental Jewish Literature, and the New Testament*, Catholic Biblical Quarterly Monograph Series 22 (Washington: Catholic Biblical Association of America, 1989).

KÖSTENBERGER, A. J., *John*, Baker Exegetical Commentary on the New Testament (Grand Rapids: Baker, 2004).

KÖSTENBERGER, A. J., and P. T. O'BRIEN, *Salvation to the Ends of the Earth: A Biblical Theology of Mission*, New Studies in Biblical Theology 11 (Downers Grove: IVP; Leicester: Apollos, 2001).

KREITZER, L. J., 'The Messianic Man of Peace as Temple Builder: Solomonic Imagery in Ephesians 2:13–22', in J. Day (ed.), *Temple and Worship in Biblical Israel*, Library of Hebrew Bible / Old Testament Studies 422 (London: T. & T. Clark, 2005), pp. 484–512.

KUTSKO, J. F., *Between Heaven and Earth: Divine Presence and Absence in the Book of Ezekiel*, Biblical and Judaic Studies from the University of California, San Diego, 7 (Winona Lake: Eisenbrauns, 2000).

LEVENSON, J. D., *Creation and the Persistence of Evil: The Jewish Drama of Divine Omnipotence* (San Francisco: Harper & Row, 1988).

——, *Sinai and Zion: An Entry into the Jewish Bible* (Minneapolis: Winston, 1985).

——, 'The Temple and the World', *Journal of Religion* 64 (1984), pp. 275–298.

LEWIS, C. S., *Out of the Silent Planet* (London: Pan, 1968).

LONGMAN, T., III, and D. G. REID, *God Is a Warrior*, Studies in Old Testament Biblical Theology (Grand Rapids: Zondervan, 1995).

LUNDQUIST, J. M., 'The Common Temple Ideology of the Ancient Near East', in T. G. Madsen (ed.), *Temple in Antiquity: Ancient Records and Modern Perspectives*, The Religious Studies Monograph Series 9 (Provo, Utah: Religious Studies Center, Brigham Young University, 1984), pp. 53–76.

McCARTNEY, D. G., '*Ecce Homo*: The Coming of the Kingdom as the Restoration of Human Vicegerency', *Westminster Theological Journal* 56 (1994), pp. 1–21.

McCASLAND, S. V., 'Signs and Wonders', *Journal of Biblical Literature* 76 (1957), pp. 149–152.

McCONVILLE, J. G., 'Abraham and Melchizedek: Horizons in Genesis 14', in R. S. Hess, P. E. Satterthwaite and G. J. Wenham (eds.), *He Swore an Oath:*

Biblical Themes from Genesis 20–50, 2nd ed. (Grand Rapids: Baker; Carlisle: Paternoster, 1994), pp. 93–118.

McKelvey, R. J., *The New Temple: The Church in the New Testament*, Oxford Theological Monographs (London: Oxford University Press, 1969).

Martin, R. A., 'The Earliest Messianic Interpretation of Genesis 3:15', *Journal of Biblical Literature* 84 (1965), pp. 425–427.

Meyers, C. L., *The Tabernacle Menorah: A Synthetic Study of a Symbol from the Biblical Cult*, American Schools of Oriental Research Dissertation Series 2 (Missoula: Scholars Press, 1976).

——, 'Temple, Jerusalem', in D. N. Freedman (ed.), *Anchor Bible Dictionary*, vol. 6 (New York: Doubleday, 1992), pp. 350–369.

Middleton, J. R., *The Liberating Image: The Imago Dei in Genesis 1* (Grand Rapids: Brazos, 2005).

Milgrom, J., *Cult and Conscience: The ASHAM and the Priestly Doctrine of Repentance* (Leiden: Brill, 1976).

Nelson, H. H., 'The Significance of the Temple in the Ancient Near East: Part I. The Egyptian Temple', *Biblical Archaeologist* 7 (1944), pp. 44–53.

Nibley, H. W., 'What Is a Temple?', in T. G. Madsen (ed.), *Temple in Antiquity: Ancient Records and Modern Perspectives*, The Religious Studies Monograph Series 9 (Provo, Utah: Religious Studies Center, Brigham Young University, 1984), pp. 19–38.

Niehaus, J. J., *God at Sinai* (Grand Rapids: Zondervan, 1995).

Ninow, F., *Indicators of Typology within the Old Testament: The Exodus Motif*, Friedensauer Schriftenreihe A4 (Frankfurt am Main: Lang, 2001).

O'Brien, P. T., 'The Church as a Heavenly and Eschatological Entity', in D. A. Carson (ed.), *Church in the Bible and the World* (Exeter: Paternoster, 1987), pp. 88–119.

Ortlund, R. C., Jr., *God's Unfaithful Wife: A Biblical Theology of Spiritual Adultery*, New Studies in Biblical Theology 2 (Downers Grove: IVP; Leicester: Apollos, 1996).

Peterson, D., 'The New Temple: Christology and Ecclesiology in Ephesians and 1 Peter', in T. D. Alexander and S. Gathercole (eds.), *Heaven on Earth: The Temple in Biblical Theology* (Carlisle: Paternoster, 2004), pp. 161–176.

——, *Possessed by God: A New Testament Theology of Sanctification and Holiness* (Leicester: Apollos, 1995).

Pitkänen, P., 'From Tent of Meeting to Temple: Presence, Rejection and Renewal of Divine Favour', in T. D. Alexander and S. Gathercole (eds.),

Heaven on Earth: The Temple in Biblical Theology (Carlisle: Paternoster, 2004), pp. 23–34.

RAD, G. VON, *Old Testament Theology*, vol. 1 (Edinburgh: Oliver & Boyd, 1962).

REICHEL, W., *Über vorhellenischen Götterculte* (Vienna: Hölder,1897).

ROSNER, B. S., 'Temple and Holiness in 1 Corinthians 5', *Tyndale Bulletin* 42 (1991), pp. 137–145.

SARNA, N. M., *Exodus*, Jewish Publication Society Torah Commentary (Philadelphia: Jewish Publication Society, 1991).

SATTERTHWAITE, P. E., 'Genealogy in the Old Testament', in W. A. VanGemeren (ed.), *New International Dictionary of Old Testament Theology and Exegesis*, vol. 4 (Carlisle: Paternoster; Grand Rapids: Zondervan, 1996), pp. 654–663.

SEOW, C. L., 'Ark of the Covenant', in D. N. Freedman (ed.), *Anchor Bible Dictionary*, vol. 1 (New York: Doubleday, 1992), pp. 386–393.

SMITH, G. V., 'Structure and Purpose in Genesis 1–11', *Journal of the Evangelical Theological Society* 20 (1977), pp. 307–319.

SMITH, M. S., *The Pilgrimage Pattern in Exodus*, Journal for the Study of the Old Testament, Supplement Series 239 (Sheffield: Sheffield Academic Press, 1997).

STAGER, L. E., 'Jerusalem as Eden', *Biblical Archaeology Review* 26 (2000), pp. 38–47, 66.

SYLVA, D. D., 'The Cryptic Clause *en tois tou patros mou dei einai me* in Lk 2:49b', *Zeitschrift für die neutestamentliche Wissenschaft und die Kunde der älteren Kirche* 78 (1987), pp. 132–140.

TAYLOR, J. B., 'The Temple in Ezekiel', in T. D. Alexander and S. Gathercole (eds.), *Heaven on Earth: The Temple in Biblical Theology* (Carlisle: Paternoster, 2004), pp. 59–70.

TORRANCE, T. F., *The Apocalypse Today* (London: James Clarke, 1960).

TURNER, H. W., *From Temple to Meeting House: The Phenomenology and Theology of Places of Worship* (The Hague: Mouton, 1979).

TURNER, M., 'Ephesians', in D. A. Carson, R. T. France, J. A. Motyer and G. J. Wenham (eds.), *New Bible Commentary (21st Century Edition)* (Leicester: IVP, 1994), pp. 1222–1244.

VAUX, R. DE, *Ancient Israel: Its Life and Institutions*, 2nd ed. (London: Darton, Longman & Todd, 1965).

WALTON, J. H., 'Creation', in T. D. Alexander and D. W. Baker (eds.), *Dictionary of the Old Testament: Pentateuch* (Downers Grove: IVP; Leicester: IVP, 2003), pp. 155–168.

———, 'Eden, Garden of', in T. D. Alexander and D. W. Baker (eds.), *Dictionary of the Old Testament: Pentateuch* (Downers Grove: IVP; Leicester: IVP, 2003), pp. 202–207.

WALTON, S., 'A Tale of Two Perspectives? The Place of the Temple in Acts', in T. D. Alexander and S. Gathercole (eds.), *Heaven on Earth: The Temple in Biblical Theology* (Carlisle: Paternoster, 2004), pp. 135–149.

WATTS, R. E., *Isaiah's New Exodus and Mark*, Biblical Studies Library (Grand Rapids: Baker, 2000).

WEBB, B. G., 'Zion in Transformation: A Literary Approach to Isaiah', in D. J. A. Clines, S. E. Fowl and S. E. Porter (eds.), *The Bible in Three Dimensions*, Journal for the Study of the Old Testament, Supplement Series 87 (Sheffield: JSOT Press, 1990), pp. 65–84.

WEINFELD, M., 'Sabbath, Temple, and the Enthronement of the Lord – the Problem of the "Sitz im Leben" of Genesis 1:1–2:3', in A. Caquot and M. Delcor (eds.), *Mélanges Bibliques et Orientaux en L'honneur de M. Henri Cazelles*, Alter Orient und Altes Testament 212 (Kevelaer: Butzon & Bercker, 1981), pp. 501–512.

WENHAM, G. J., 'Flood', in W. A. VanGemeren (ed.), *New International Dictionary of Old Testament Theology and Exegesis*, vol. 4 (Carlisle: Paternoster; Grand Rapids: Zondervan, 1996), pp. 640–642.

———, *Genesis 1–15*, Word Biblical Commentary 1 (Waco: Word, 1987).

———, 'Sanctuary Symbolism in the Garden of Eden Story', *Proceedings of the World Congress of Jewish Studies* 9 (1986), pp. 19–25.

WILLIAMSON, P. R., *Abraham, Israel and the Nations: The Patriarchal Promise and its Covenantal Development in Genesis*, Journal for the Study of the Old Testament, Supplement Series 315 (Sheffield: Sheffield Academic Press, 2000).

———, *Sealed with an Oath: Covenant in God's Unfolding Purpose*, New Studies in Biblical Theology 23 (Downers Grove: IVP; Leicester: Apollos, 2007).

WRIGHT, G. E., 'The Significance of the Temple in the Ancient Near East: Part III. The Temple in Palestine-Syria', *Biblical Archaeologist* 7 (1944), pp. 65–77.

WRIGHT, N. T., *The New Testament and the People of God*, Christian Origins and the Question of God 1 (London: SPCK, 1993).

INDEX OF BIBLICAL REFERENCES

Old Testament

Genesis
1 *24, 27, 40, 76, 77, 85*
1 – 2 *76*
1:1 – 2:3 *24*
1 – 3 *10, 25*
1 – 11 *27*
1:9–10 *28*
1:14 *24*
1:14–16 *39*
1:14–18 *28*
1:20–21 *28*
1:22 *28*
1:24–25 *28*
1:26 *77*
1:26–27 *28*
1:26–28 *76*
1:28 *28, 31, 77, 83, 190*
1:29–30 *28*
1:31 *40*
2 *25, 26, 27*
2:1 *40*
2:1–3 *24*
2:1–17 *78*
2:2 *40*
2:2–3 *40*
2:3 *40*
2:9 *22*
2:4 – 3:24 *24*
2:9 *22, 155*
2:10 *21, 23*
2:11–12 *23*
2:15 *22, 26*
3 *26, 78, 102, 114, 156, 157*
3:1 *102*
3:8 *23, 107*

3:14–15 *105*
3:15 *105*
3:17–18 *157*
3:17–19 *27*
3:22 *22*
3:22–24 *156*
3:23 *27*
3:24 *22, 26*
4 *107*
4:8 *79*
4:25 *106*
5 *107*
5:22–24 *107*
5:29 *27*
6:9 *28, 107*
6:13 *79*
6:18 *29*
8 *27*
8:1–13 *28*
8:10 *28*
8:12 *28*
8:17 *28*
8:17–19 *28*
8:20 *31*
8:21 *28*
8:22 *28*
9 *27*
9:1 *28, 31, 83*
9:1–7 *29*
9:2 *28*
9:2–6 *83*
9:3 *28*
9:6 *28*
9:7 *28, 31, 83*
11 *48*
11:1–9 *29*
12 – 50 *31, 32*

12:1–3 *31, 32, 83, 164, 189*
12:2–3 *31, 190*
12:7–8 *31, 83*
13:4 *31, 83*
13:10 *42, 45*
13:14–17 *83*
13:18 *31, 83*
14 *80*
14:17–24 *81*
15:1 *83*
15:4–5 *83*
15:5 *83, 164*
15:7 *83*
15:9 *83*
15:9–10 *83*
15:13–16 *80, 83*
15:18–21 *83*
17:1 *107*
17:1–22 *83*
17:2 *31, 190*
17:4–6 *164*
17:6 *31, 83, 190*
17:8 *31, 190*
17:16 *83*
17:20 *31, 83, 190*
18:1–33 *83*
18:18 *164*
20:7 *83*
21:12–13 *83*
21:22–34 *82*
22 *31*
22:1 *83*
22:1–13 *83*
22:9 *31*
22:12 *83*
22:15–18 *83*
22:16–18 *32, 108, 164*

22:17 *83*
22:17–18 *31, 190*
23:6 *82*
24:3 *15*
24:7 *15*
26:3–4 *31, 190*
26:3–5 *32*
26:4 *83*
26:22 *83*
26:24 *31, 190*
26:25 *31*
28:3 *83*
28:3–4 *31, 190*
28:12–17 *15, 32*
28:13–15 *32*
28:19 *32*
32:12 *83*
33:20 *31*
35:1 *31*
35:1–15 *32*
35:3 *31*
35:7 *31*
35:11 *83*
35:11–12 *31, 32, 190*
41:52 *31, 83, 190*
47:27 *31, 83, 190*
48:4 *31, 83, 190*
49:22 *31, 190*

Exodus
1:7 *84*
1:7–11 *85*
3:5 *140*
3:14 *125*
6:6 *124*
12 *127*
12:6 *128*
12:6–11 *127*
12:7 *128*
12:9 *128*
12:10 *128*
12:13 *128*
12:21 *128*
12:21–22 *127*
12:22 *128*
12:23 *128*
12:27 *127*
12:46 *125, 128*
12:47 *128*
13:11–16 *124*
15 *85, 124*
15:11–13 *86*
15:13 *124*
15:17–18 *86*

19 *96*
19:3–6 *84, 85*
19:5–6 *125*
19:6 *29, 129*
19:9–15 *140*
20:2–17 *146*
20:8–11 *145*
22:21 – 23:9 *146*
25 – 31 *34, 87*
25 – 40 *24*
25:7 *23*
25:8 *37*
25:9 *34*
25:17 *23*
25:18–22 *22*
25:22 *34*
25:31 *23*
25:31–35 *22*
26:1 *34*
26:31 *22*
26:33 *38*
27:1–8 *128*
27:21 *35*
27:9 *34*
28:43 *35*
29 *128, 134*
29:4 *35*
29:45 *37*
30:6 *34*
31:2–5 *65, 66*
31:3 *39*
33:7 *35*
35 – 40 *34, 87*
36:35 *22*
38:21 *34*
39 – 40 *40*
39:32 *40*
39:35 *34*
39:43 *40*
40:2 *35*
40:9 *34*
40:20 *34*
40:33 *40*
40:34–35 *17, 35, 43, 68, 169*

Leviticus
1 – 7 *129, 144*
1:1 *35*
3:2 *35*
4:12 *140*
4:2–21 *142*
4:21 *140*
4:22–35 *142*
6:11 *140*

7:19–21 *142*
8 *128, 134*
8:1 – 9:24 *128*
8:10 *34*
10:1–7 *141*
11 *104*
11:1–47 *24, 150*
11:24–25 *143*
11:27–28 *143*
11:39 *143*
11:44 *145*
12 – 15 *142*
14:4 *128*
14:6 *128*
14:49 *128*
14:51 *128*
14:52 *128*
15:24 *143*
16:12–13 *141*
16:16 *142*
16:27 *140*
16:32 *38*
18 *146*
18:20 *142*
18:23–25 *142*
18:27–30 *142*
19 *146*
19:2 *146*
20 *146*
20:2–5 *142*
20:7 *146*
20:8 *145*
21:1–4 *141*
21:8 *145*
21:10–15 *152*
21:15 *145*
21:16–23 *152*
21:17–23 *152*
21:18–20 *152*
21:23 *145*
22:3 *142*
22:9 *142, 145*
22:16 *145*
22:22–24 *152*
22:32 *145*
22:32–33 *146*
23:3 *142*
23:7 *142*
23:21 *142*
23:25 *142*
23:28 *142*
23:35 *142*
26:12 *23*

Numbers
1:1 *35*
1:2–3 *87*
1:45 *87*
1:50–51 *35*
2:2 *35*
3:7–8 *23, 34, 35*
4:1–49 *141*
4:5 *34*
4:5–33 *141*
4:16 *35*
4:18–20 *141*
5:17 *35*
6:1–21 *141*
7:1 *35*
7:89 *34*
8:26 *23, 34*
9:15 *35*
9:15–17 *35*
9:15–22 *35*
9:22 *35*
18:5–6 *23, 34*
19:1–9 *133*
19:6 *128*
19:11 *143*
19:18 *128*
22 *103*
22:21–22 *103*
22:27–31 *103*
22:28 *103*
22:31 *103*
35:16–21 *142*
35:31 *142*

Deuteronomy
5:2–4 *86*
5:12 *26*
6:20–25 *86*
7:8 *124*
10:1–5 *146*
10:5 *34*
14 *104*
14:3–20 *150*
14:3–21 *24*
23:15 *23*
28:15–16 *158*
28:15–45 *158*
28:22 *158*
31:25–26 *147*

Joshua
18:1 *16*
24:6–7 *86*

Judges
18:31 *16*
21:19 *16*

1 Samuel
1:3 *16*
1:9 *16*
1:24 *16*
2:12–17 *42*
4:19–22 *43*
5:1–12 *43*

2 Samuel
5:6–8 *154*
7 *43*
7:2 *43*
7:6–7 *23*

1 Kings
6:20 *20*
6:23–29 *22*
8:9 *34, 147*
8:10–11 *17, 43, 68, 169*
8:30 *34*
8:30–51 *33*
8:31 *34*
8:33 *34*
8:38 *34*
8:39 *34*
8:43 *34*
8:49 *34*

2 Kings
24:10–11 *55*

1 Chronicles
28:2 *33*
28:11–19 *66*

2 Chronicles
1:15 *46*
3:1 *31*
3:14 *22*
6:21 *34*
6:22 *34*
6:22–39 *33*
6:23 *34*
6:24 *34*
6:30 *34*
6:33 *34*
6:38 *34*
6:39 *34*
7:1–2 *17, 43, 68, 169*
9:18 *33*

Ezra
1:2 *15*
5:11–12 *15*
6:9–10 *15*
7:12 *15*
7:21 *15*
7:23 *15*

Nehemiah
1:4–5 *15*
2:4 *15*
2:20 *15*

Job
28:26 *41*
38:4–7 *41*

Psalms
2 *92, 109, 110*
2:4 *15*
2:7 *92*
8 *92, 91, 93*
8:6 *91, 93*
11:4 *15, 34*
14:2 *15, 34*
14:7 *34*
19:4–5 *41*
20:2 *34*
20:6 *34*
24:3–4 *146*
33:7 *41*
33:13 *15*
45 *92*
48:1–3 *46*
48:12–14 *46*
53:2 *15*
72:1–4 *165*
72:7–8 *166*
72:11 *166*
72:17 *165, 166*
72:19 *166*
75:3 *41*
76:2 *34*
76:8 *34*
78 *43*
78:68 *45*
80:1 *34*
80:14 *34*
84 *47*
84:1–5 *48*
87 *46*
87:1–7 *47*
89:3 *43*
93–99 *87*

99:5 *33*
104:2 *41*
104:5 *41*
110 *82*
119:90 *41*
120 – 134 *48*
132:7 *33*
132:13 *45*
132:13–18 *46*
133:1–3 *46*
147:12–14 *46*

Proverbs
3:19 *41*
3:19–20 *39*
7 *178*
7:1–23 *179*
7:4–5 *179*
8:27 *41*

Isaiah
1 *50*
1:4 *50*
1:10–15 *50*
1:10–20 *88*
1:18 *132, 133*
1:21–23 *167*
1:24–26 *59*
2 *166, 168*
2:2–3 *168*
2:2–4 *59*
2:2–5 *51, 167*
4:2–6 *59*
4:4–6 *45*
6 *88*
6:1–5 *56*
6:3 *139*
9:6–7 *92*
11:6–9 *59, 161, 162*
18:7 *59*
24:21–23 *59*
24:23 *53*
25:6–8 *59*
26:1 *59*
27:11 *59*
28:16 *59*
29:8 *59*
30:19–26 *59*
30:23–25 *159*
30:29 *59*
31:4–5 *59*
32:14–20 *59*
32:15 *159*
33:5–6 *59*

33:17–24 *59*
34:8 *59*
35:1–2 *159*
35:4–6 *154*
35:5–6 *154, 156*
35:10 *59*
37:30–32 *59*
40–48 *87*
40:2 *59*
40:9 *59*
40:22 *41*
41:27 *59*
44:3–5 *68*
44:24–28 *59*
45:13 *59*
45:22 *168*
46:13 *59*
48:2 *59*
48:13 *41*
49:14–26 *59*
51:1–3 *59*
51:3 *42, 45*
51:9–11 *59*
51:12–16 *59*
51:13 *41*
51:16 *41*
54:1–17 *59*
54:2–3 *45*
54:11–12 *45*
56:3–8 *59*
57:11–13 *59*
59:20 *59*
60 *54*
60:1–22 *50*
60:2 *54*
60:2–9 *168*
60:10–14 *59*
60:11–22 *168*
60:13 *33*
60:14 *168*
60:15–20 *55*
61:1–11 *59*
62:1–12 *59*
65 *54*
65:17–18 *14, 51, 53, 162*
65:17–25 *52, 53, 59*
65:20 *156*
65:25 *162*
66:1 *33, 59*
66:6 *59*
66:10–14 *59*
66:18–21 *50, 59*
66:20–24 *50*

Jeremiah
3:14–18 *59*
3:16–17 *45*
8:19 *92*
27:22 *59*
29:10–14 *59*
30:18–22 *59*
31 *161*
31:6 *59*
31:10–14 *59*
31:12 *161*
31:23 *59*
31:33 *148*
31:38–40 *59*
32:36–41 *59*
32:44 *59*
33:4–16 *59*
50:4–5; *59*

Lamentations
2:1 *33*

Ezekiel
8:3–16 *56*
8:6 *56*
9:4 *56*
9:9 *56*
10 *56*
11:23 *57*
16:59–63 *59*
17:22–24 *59*
20:40–44 *59*
28:13 *23*
28:13–16 *23*
28:14 *26*
28:16 *26*
34:20–30 *59*
34:8 *103*
36:8–11 *160*
36:17–19 *133*
36:25–28 *148*
36:25–29 *133*
36:27–28 *68*
36:28–35 *160*
36:35 *42, 45*
37:14 *68*
37:24–28 *59*
37:25–28 *45*
40–48 *57, 58, 160*
40:2 *59*
43:12 *59*
45:6–8 *59*
47:1–6 *57*
47:1–12 *23, 59*

47:8–10 57
47:12 156, 161
48:35 57, 59

Daniel
2 110
2:1–49 89
2:18–19 15
2:34–35 45, 111
2:37 15
2:44 15
2:44–45 45, 111
7 93
7:1–28 89
7:18 93
7:27 93
9:2 59
9:24–26 59

Joel
2:3 42, 45
2:24–26 161
2:28–32 68
3 161
3:1–21 110
3:17–21 59
3:18 161

Amos
9:6 41
9:13–15 159

Obadiah
1:15–21 59
1:21 89

Micah
4:1–2 168
4:1–3 167
4:21–13 59
4:11–13 110

Habakkuk
2:5–14 182

Zephaniah
3:14–20 59

Haggai
2:9 59

Zechariah
1:14–17 59
1:16 – 2:11 45

2:1–12 59
3:2 59
8 58
8:1–23 59
8:2 58
8:3 58
8:6 58
8:7–8 58
8:11 58
8:12 161
8:13–15 58
8:20–23 168
9:9–10 59
12:1 41
12:1–9 59
12:2–9 110
13:1 59
14:1–3 110
14:1–21 59
14:9 89, 97
14:12–19 110
14:20 139

Malachi
3:4 59

New Testament

Matthew
3:2 89
3:13 – 4:11 92
4:1–11 112
4:17 89
4:8–10 101
5:2–10 95
5:20 149
5:48 149
6:9–10 97
6:24 185
7:21–23 96
8 – 9 154
8:1–4 154
9:35 153
10:1 153
10:9–11 153
11:4–6 153
12:28 112
13 95
15:17–20 148
21 – 22 115
21:42 70
23:21 17
23:23–28 148
23:37 60

26:61 18
27:51 68
28 168
28:18 91, 115
28:19 168

Mark
1 – 9 114
1:9–13 92
1:13 112, 115
1:23 112
1:23–27 112
1:24 112
1:26 112
1:32 112
1:34 112
1:39 112
3:15 112
3:22 112
3:23–27 113
3:30 112
5:18 112
5:2 112
5:8 112
6:6–12 153
6:13 112
7:20–23 148
7:25 112
8:11 115
8:31 114
8:33 114
9:25 112
9:38 112
10 114
10:2 115
10:45 126
12:10 70
12:15 115
13 115
14:58 18
15:38 68

Luke
1:8–23 67
2:22–38 67
2:41–51 67
2:49 67
3:21–22 92
4:1–13 92, 112
4:9–11 68
9:1–6 153
9:31 68
9:51 68
9:53 68

10:17–20 *113*
10:30–35 *145*
11:20 *112*
11:37–41 *148*
13:34 *60*
19:28 *68*
19:47 *67*
20:1 *67*
20:17 *70*
21:5–6 *68*
21:37–38 *67*
22:3 *114*
22:31 *114*
22:31–34 *114*
22:53 *67*
23:45 *68*
24:53 *67*

John
1:14 *17, 70*
1:29 *132*
1:36 *132*
2:19 *18*
2:19–21 *70*
4:19–21 *18*
8:39–44 *107, 108*
8:44 *118*
12:31 *101*
13:27 *114*
14:30 *101*
15:3 *149*
16:11 *101*
19:36 *125*

Acts
2 *68, 168, 169*
2:5–11 *169*
2:46 *68*
3:1–3 *68*
4:11 *70*
5:20–21 *68*
5:42 *68*
7:49 *33*
8:14–17 *69*
9:13 *135*
9:32 *135*
10:9–16 *151*
10:44–47 *69*
15:9 *149*
26:10 *135*
26:18 *150*

Romans
1:3–4 *90*

1:7 *135*
1:24 *148*
5:17 *94*
6:19 *148, 149*
6:22 *149*
8:15–23 *95*
8:19–22 *163*
8:27 *135*
8:37 *116*
15:16 *149*
15:25 *135*
15:26 *135*
15:31 *135*
16:2 *135*
16:15 *135*
16:20 *105*

1 Corinthians
1:2 *135, 148, 150*
3:10 *65*
3:16 *65*
3:16–17 *63, 64, 116*
5 *65*
5:7 *126*
6:11 *149*
6:19 *64, 150*
11:23–28 *134*
14:25 *65*
15:22–28 *105*
15:24–26 *116*
15:24–28 *90, 91, 116*
15:45 *94*
15:48 *94*
15:50–58 *145*

2 Corinthians
1:12 *149*
11:2 *185*
12:21 *148*
4:16 – 5:5 *65*
4:4 *102*
5 *65*
  6:16 *64, 116*
7:1 *149*

Galatians
3 *165*
3:16 *106, 165*
3:29 *165*
4:4 *115*
4:21–31 *72*
6:14–15 *151*

Ephesians
1:20–22 *116*
2 *61, 63*
2:2 *101*
2:6 *62*
2:13–18 *151*
2:13–22 *62*
2:14–15 *151*
2:15 *151*
2:19–22 *62, 66, 116*
2:20 *70*
2:20–22 *151*
2:21 *71*
2:21–22 *63*
2:22 *61*
3:19 *63*
4:7 *66*
4:12 *71*
4:16 *71*
4:19 *148*
4:24 *149*
5:3 *148*
5:5 *90, 148*
5:18 *63*
5:19–21 *63*
5:21 *62, 90*
5:22 *62*
5:25–33 *185, 186*
6:10–17 *116*
6:12–16 *119*

Philippians
2 *90*
2:7 *116*
2:9 *116*
2:10–11 *116*
3:20 *72*

Colossians
1:12–14 *116*
1:15–20 *90*
1:22 *150*
2 *151*
2:10–14 *151*
2:15 *116*
2:15–17 *151*
2:20–21 *151*
3:1 *116*
3:12 *149*

1 Thessalonians
2:10 *149*
3:13 *149*
4:7 *148*

4:16–17 *116*
5:23 *149*

2 Thessalonians
2:8 *116*
2:13 *149*

1 Timothy
2:12 *95*
2:15 *149*
3:16 *116*
6:10 *185*

2 Timothy
2:8 *148*

Titus
1:8 *149*
2:14 *149*

Hebrews
1:3 *149*
2 *91, 93, 95*
2:5–8 *93*
2:9 *90, 91, 94*
2:11 *150*
2:11–12 *94*
2:14 *105, 116*
5:4–10 *82*
6:19 – 7:1 *82*
7:11–12 *150*
9:16–24 *133*
9:22 *132*
10:4 *132*
10:10 *135, 150*
10:12–13 *132*
10:14 *150*
10:19–22 *134*
10:29 *149*
11:8–10 *72*
11:13–16 *72*
12:10 *149*
12:14 *149*
13:12 *150*
13:14 *73*

James
4:8 *149*

1 Peter
1:2 *149*
1:15–16 *149*
1:18–19 *127*
2:4–6 *66, 67*
2:9 *96*
5:8 *119*

2 Peter
3 *173*
3:1–4 *173*
3:1–13 *174*
3:5–6 *173*
3:7–9 *173*
3:11 *149*

1 John
1:7 *133, 149*
1:9 *149*
2:17 *101*
3:10–12 *108*
5:18–19 *100*

Revelation
1:5–6 *96*
3:12–13 *119*
3:21 *187*
4:1–4 *75*
5 *122, 123, 125, 136*
5:5–6 *123*
5:5–10 *123*
5:9 *163*
5:10 *96*
5:11–12 *137*
11 *67*
12:1 – 13:1 *105*
14:8 *176*
17 *177*
17:1–6 *177*
17:2 *176*
17:3 *176*
17:4 *176, 180*
17:5 *176*
17:6 *176*
17:15 *178*
17:18 *176*
18 *180*
18:3 *176*

18:4 *187*
18:11–13 *180*
18:12–13 *176*
18:12–17 *176*
18:16 *176*
18:23 *176, 180*
18:24 *176*
19:2 *176*
19:6–8 *177*
20 *99, 117*
20 – 22 *10, 11*
20:1–3 *99*
20:2 *99, 104*
20:7–10 *99*
21 *119*
21 – 22 *19, 26, 52, 61, 73, 74,*
   97, 121, 122, 139, 171, 177, 192
21:1 *55*
21:1–3 *13, 53*
21:2 *176*
21:3–4 *170*
21:5–7 *120*
21:6 *176*
21:8 *118*
21:9 *176*
21:9 – 22:9 *175*
21:10 *176*
21:10–14 *172*
21:11–21 *176*
21:14 *122*
21:15–17 *19*
21:15–18 *19*
21:18 *20, 46*
21:22 *20, 122*
21:23 *55, 122*
21:24 *163, 176*
21:26 *163, 176, 180*
21:27 *176*
22 *156*
22:1 *122*
22:1–2 *176*
22:1–3 *75, 155*
22:2 *161, 163*
22:3 *122, 157*
22:3–4 *14*
22:5 *55*
22:14 *176*